LINKING LIFETIMES

*A Global View of
Intergenerational Exchange*

Edited by
Matthew S. Kaplan
Nancy Z. Henkin
Atsuko T. Kusano

University Press of America,® Inc.
Lanham · New York · Oxford

Copyright © 2002 by
University Press of America,® Inc.
4720 Boston Way
Lanham, Maryland 20706
UPA Acquisitions Department (301) 459-3366

12 Hid's Copse Rd.
Cumnor Hill, Oxford OX2 9JJ

Library of Congress Cataloging-in-Publication Data

Linking lifetimes : a global view of intergenerational exchange /
edited by Matthew S. Kaplan, Nancy Z. Henkin, Atsuko T. Kusano.
p.   cm
Includes bibliographical references and index.
1. Intergenerational relations—Cross-cultural studies. I. Kaplan,
Matt. II. Henkin, Nancy Zimmerman. III. Kusano, Atsuko T.

HM726 .L56 2002
305.2—dc21   2002020147 CIP

ISBN 0-7618-2213-5 (paperback : alk. paper)
ISBN 0-7618-2212-7 (clothbound : alk. paper)

Contents

Preface

Section I: Conceptual Issues

(1) A Conceptual Framework for Cross-Cultural Comparisons of Intergenerational Initiatives — Matthew S. Kaplan, Nancy Z. Henkin, & Atsuko T. Kusano   1

(2) Challenging Intergenerational Stereotypes Across Eastern and Western Cultures — Howard Giles, Robert M. McCann, Hiroshi Ota, and Kimberly A. Noels   13

(3) Strengthening Intergenerational Bonds through Volunteerism: A Global Perspective — Anne O'Sullivan   29

(4) Employing Proverbs to Explore Intergenerational Relations Across Cultures — Matthew S. Kaplan   39

Section II: National and Regional Profiles

North America
(5) Advancing an Intergenerational Agenda in the United States — Nancy Z. Henkin and Donna M. Butts   65

(6) Intergenerational Teaching and Learning in Canadian First Nations Partnership Programs — Jessica Ball, Alan Pence, Martina Pierre, & Valerie Kuehne   83

(7) Intergenerational Programs and Possibilities in Hawaii — Matthew S. Kaplan and Joseph W. Lapilio, III   101

Pacific & Asian Region
(8) Intergenerational Initiatives in Singapore: Commitments to Community and Family Building — Leng Leng Thang   119

(9) Intergenerational Initiatives in the Marshall Islands: Implications for Promoting Cultural Continuity — Hilda C. Heine   135

(10) Intergenerational Programs in Japan: Symbolic Extensions of Family Unity — Matthew S. Kaplan and Leng Leng Thang   151

Europe

(11) Intergenerational Community Building in the Netherlands — Kees Penninx
173

(12) Intergenerational Engagement in the UK: A Framework for Creating Inclusive Communities — Gillian Granville and Alan Hatton-Yeo 193

(13) German Pupils and Jewish Seniors: Intergenerational Dialogue as a Framework for Healing History — Toshio Ohsako 209

Latin America

(14) Intergenerational Relationships in Latin America and the Caribbean — Martha Peláez 221

(15) Cuba: Fertile Ground for an Intergenerational Arts Movement — Susan Perlstein 233

South Africa

(16) Intergenerational Initiatives in South Africa: Reflecting and Aiding a Society in Transition — Cathy Gush 237

Section III: Time to Organize

(17) Organizing at the National Level: Lessons Learned from the U.S. and Japan — Donna M. Butts and Atsuko T. Kusano 253

(18) Creating an "International Consortium for Intergenerational Programs" — Sally Newman 263

About the Contributors

Jessica Ball, M.P.H., Ph.D., is Co-Coordinator of First Nations Partnership Programs, principal investigator of the research study on the partnerships, and associate professor in the School of Child and Youth Care at the University of Victoria.

Donna Butts is the executive director of Generations United, the only U.S.-based membership organization focused solely on promoting intergenerational programs, public policies and strategies. She has almost 30 years of experience working with non-profit organizations in the United States. In 1999 she was selected to serve on the United Nations Inter-Regional Expert Group to develop a framework for policies for a society for all ages. She is a graduate of Marylhurst College in Oregon.

Alan Hatton-Yeo is Chief Executive Officer of The Beth Johnson Foundation and Head of the newly-formed UK Centre for Intergenerational Practice.

Howard Giles, Ph.D., D.Sc. (University of Bristol), is a professor of Communication at the University of California, Santa Barbara. He is a Fellow of the Gerontological Society of America, Vice-Chair of the National Communication Association's Commission on Communication and Aging, and past president of the International Communication Association.

Gillian Granville, Ph.D. (University of Keele, U.K.), is Head of Research and Policy at The Beth Johnson Foundation and has published widely on a range of issues concerning aging and older people.

Cathy Gush holds an Honors degree in Sociology from the University of Stellenbosch (South Africa) and an Advanced Diploma for Educators of Adults from the University of Cape Town. She has been extensively involved in educational research, evaluation and project coordination, with a special focus on adult education and family literacy.

Hilda Heine, a former Education Commissioner of the Marshall Islands, is currently Director of the Pacific Resources for Education and Learning (PREL) Comprehensive Center.

Nancy Henkin, Ph.D., is the founder and Executive Director of the Temple University Center for Intergenerational Learning in Philadelphia, Pennsylvania. Since 1979, Dr. Henkin has overseen the development of a wide range of intergenerational programs and has created audio-visual and written materials to facilitate the replication of successful models. As a national leader in the field, she provides consultation services to organizations serving youth and older adults and is a frequent presenter at national conferences. She received her B.A. from Simmons College and her Ph.D. from Temple University.

Matthew S. Kaplan, Ph.D. (Environmental Psychology, City University of New York), is an associate professor of Intergenerational Programs and Aging in the Department of Agricultural and Extension Education at Pennsylvania State University. He has developed intergenerational programs that promote civic involvement, has been active in the creation of statewide networks in New York and Hawaii, and, more recently, has focused on exploring the international dimension of intergenerational work.

Valerie Kuehne, Ph.D., is a specialist in the role of intergenerational relationships across the life span and is an associate professor in the School of Child and Youth Care at the University of Victoria.

Atsuko T. Kusano, Ph.D. (in Medicine from the Tohoku University School of Medicine) is an associate professor in the Department of Education at Shinshu University and chief representative of the Japan Intergenerational Network. She is also one of the authors of *Intergenerational Programs: Support for Children, Youth, and Elders in Japan* published by State University of New York Press in 1998.

Joseph W. Lapilio, III, master's degree in public administration (University of Hawaii), is President and Chief Executive Officer of the Hawaii Community Services Council.

Robert M. McCann, a visiting instructor of communication at the Thai Chamber of Commerce University in Bangkok, Thailand, is currently investigating aging and cross-cultural organizational communication in several countries across the Pacific Rim.

Sally Newman, Ph.D., former Executive Director of Generations Together: Intergenerational Studies program of the University of Pittsburgh, is a University Senior Researcher, member of the School of Education faculty, and pioneer in the intergenerational field as a program developer, trainer, researcher, and author.

Kimberly A. Noels, Ph.D. (University of Ottawa), is an assistant professor at the University of Alberta, Edmonton, Canada. Her research interests concern the social psychology of language and communication processes, with a focus on intercultural intergenerational communication.

Toshio Ohsako, Ed.D. (in educational psychology from Michigan State University), is currently a Senior Research Specialist and Coordinator for Lifelong Learning Programs at the UNESCO Institute for Education in Hamburg, Germany.

Anne O'Sullivan, Master's degree in Public Health (Columbia University), was Executive Director of RSVP International from 1996 to 2000, during which time she conducted presentations and provided consultation on senior volunteering and worldwide aging issues in South Africa, Colombia, Japan, Korea, Argentina, Bolivia, Canada, and several other countries. She is currently working on her Ph.D. in Gerontology at the Graduate School of Social Sciences of Fordham University.

Hiroshi Ota, Ph.D. (University of California Santa Barbara), is an associate professor on the faculty of Studies on Contemporary Society at Aichi Shukutoku University, Nagoya, Japan. His major research interests are communication between people in different generations, communication between Japanese and people from other countries, and second language learning.

Martha Peláez, Ph.D. (Tulane University, New Orleans, Louisiana, U.S.A.), is the Regional Advisor on Aging and Health at the Family Health and Population Program of the Pan American Health Organization/World Health Organization. Prior to her appointment at PAHO/WHO, she was for 13 years the Associate Director of the Southeast Florida Center on Aging, Florida International University.

Alan Pence, Ph.D., is Co-Coordinator of First Nations Partnership Programs, co-principal investigator of the research study, and a professor in the School of Child and Youth Care at the University of Victoria.

Kees Penninx is a sociologist who specializes in management of change in community building and adult education. He is currently coordinator of an innovative national program for the promotion of intergenerational approaches in human services and local community building in the Netherlands.

Martina Pierre, M.Ed., is the Cultural Director of the Mount Currie First Nation and was an instructor and Intergenerational Facilitator in a partnership program with the University of Victoria.

Susan Perlstein is the founding director of Elders Share The Arts (ESTA), an internationally recognized community arts organization founded in 1979 that dedicates itself to honoring diverse traditions and connecting generations and cultures through "living history arts" –theater, dance, music, writing, and visual arts.

Leng Leng Thang, Ph.D. (in anthropology, from the University of Illinois at Urbana-Champaign) is assistant professor of Japanese Studies and assistant director of the Centre for Advanced Studies at the National University of Singapore.

Acknowledgments

The editors are grateful for a Hawaii Pacific University Trustees Scholarly Endeavors Award provided for the first editor, and a publishing award from the "UNIVERS Foundation" provided for the third editor. We are grateful to all of the contributing authors for sharing their insights and experience and shaping this book into a mosaic of intergenerational engagement perspectives and intervention approaches. We would also like to thank Dr. Larry LeDoux of Hawaii Pacific University for copy editing and typesetting the entire manuscript, Dr. Liz Larkin of the University of South Florida for her insightful comments on an earlier draft, and Brenda Holcomb and Jane Auhl for their invaluable editorial assistance.

PREFACE

Kizuna — a network of people connected by mutual understanding and norms of interdependence. This Japanese word, which originally referred to a rope that binds animals, has come to mean the inseparable bond between humans. We see this as an ideal metaphor to help introduce the concept of intergenerational exchange – the full range of ways in which young people and older adults interact, support, and provide care for one another.

A Global View of Intergenerational Exchange

Throughout the world an increasing number of accounts suggest that the *kizuna* knot of human bonds is unraveling. These stories tell of changes in the cultural values and institutional settings that tie people together. At the same time, there are changes in population composition that have profound implications for how we relate to one another. In 1998, a United Nations Population Fund report notes that current growth in the young and elderly segments of the populations of most countries is leading to new challenges in providing these groups with health care, education, financial assistance, and social support systems. In order to meet these challenges, effective strategies for restoring and maintaining bonds across generations are needed. To that end, we present multiple perspectives on intergenerational programs and some implications of looking at the knot of human connection through a cultural lens.

Longevity is one of the great achievements of the twentieth century. Between 1950 and 2000, the combined decline in fertility and mortality rates added 20 years to the average life span, worldwide. We rightly think of this as very good news. But along with the benefits, this change brings challenges that we have never before, in the history of the world, had to face. By the year 2050, one third of the world's population will be over 60 years of age. Population figures show that throughout the world, one million people turn 60 every month. In the developed world, one of every four people will be over the age of 60 in just 25 years. In 30 years time

(2030), that figure becomes one in three. In developing countries this proportion is predicted to be one in five. While the demographic shift in both the proportion and absolute numbers of older persons was slower to take hold in developing countries, 80 percent of the people turning 60 every month are now in the developing world and those countries have begun aging at a rate faster than in the developed world. By the year 2025, 72 percent of the world's older persons, about 858 million people, will be living in developing countries (UN, 1999).

The global aging phenomenon is experienced differently in various parts of the world, due in large part to variability in fertility and mortality rates and in social and economic consequences. However, there is a common realization that an adequate response to this aging trend, which Julia Alvarez, Dominican Republic Ambassador to the United Nations, has termed "AgeQuake," will require new policies, programs and priorities.

Coupled with this aging phenomenon is a trend toward urbanization. The shift in some developing countries from subsistence economies to wage economies has resulted in an increase in the number of working adults migrating to urban areas for employment opportunities. In some small Caribbean nations, for example, working adults are moving to North America and Europe. In Brazil and India, the migration has been from rural areas to larger cities. Often, elderly people are left with few resources in depopulated rural communities, often caring for young grandchildren (Tout, 1989).

Segregation of age groups in terms of living arrangements and social activity also occurs in industrialized nations. Senior housing developments, long term care facilities, and institutions designed to serve the needs of specific age groups all contribute to a breakdown in intergenerational connections. When intergenerational relations are impaired, there are socio-cultural implications as well as psychological ones. As Margaret Mead wrote in 1970: "The continuity of all cultures depends on the living presence of at least three generations." In other words, without intergenerational continuity it is hard to have cultural continuity.

In recent years, increased attention has been focused on finding ways to provide growing aged populations with adequate opportunities for meaningful, productive activity. Various "catch words" and phrases have been used to invoke positive visions and actions for aging societies. One such phrase, "productive aging," first coined by the American Pulitzer Prize winner Robert Butler, M.D., captures a vision of aging that is compelling from various cultural and national frameworks. "Productive aging" refers to:

> ... the capacity of an individual or a population to serve in the paid work force, to serve in volunteer activities, to assist in the family, and to maintain himself or herself as independently as possible (*Productive Aging News*, 1994, Supplement).

In some ways, the integration of productive work with family life that characterizes life in many developing countries is a model for the industrialized world. The majority of older adults in these countries live in multi-generational households and continue to contribute to their families and communities through the provision of child care, agricultural work, and the transmission of culture to younger generations. However, many elderly are living in poverty, with no financial security. It is common in countries such as the Dominican Republic for older adults to continue working in physically demanding jobs just to survive. Illiteracy rates are high and health services minimal in far too many places. Promoting policies that provide income security for the elderly in all nations represents an investment in human resources that will benefit all generations and foster lifelong productivity.

From various cultural and national frameworks, the factors that threaten the *social compact* between the generations bear closer examination, as do the bold efforts to restore or revitalize intergenerational interdependence and solidarity. The challenge facing both developing and developed nations is to find culturally, politically and economically appropriate strategies for promoting lifelong productivity, supporting family caregiving, and ensuring cultural continuity.

Intergenerational programs and policies, the focus of this book, represent effective strategies for supplementing familial support systems and maintaining social cohesion in the face of significant societal changes and evolving conceptions of family and kinship.

Intergenerational programs, as defined by the newly established International Consortium of Intergenerational Programs (based in The Netherlands), are "social vehicles that create purposeful and ongoing exchange of resources and learning among older and younger generations." Intergenerational policies include investment in the education of the young, financial security for older adults, and support for families as they care for their members.

Whereas the literature on intergenerational programs in the United States is quite extensive, having evolved to the extent that such initiatives are increasingly integrated into human service structures and social life,[1] the literature on intergenerational initiatives in other countries is relatively limited. The material presented in this book clearly illustrates that there is a groundswell of intergenerational activity occurring on an international scale. We hope that by drawing more attention to the diversity and prevalence of intergenerational programming models as they are implemented across geographic regions and cultural contexts, we are reinforcing a view of this strategy as one that has international dimensions, going well beyond initiatives of Western genesis.

Hatton-Yeo et al. (2000) articulate this international perspective by emphasizing how intergenerational programs and practices tap into common dimensions of human need:

The relevance of intergenerational programs is evidenced by the universal history of shared and reciprocal needs demonstrated by young and old. In nations across the world, we recognize that the generations need to nurture and be nurtured, to teach and to be taught, to have a successful life review, and to learn from and about the past, to share cultural mores and to have a cultural identity, to communicate positive values, to have positive role models, to leave a legacy and to be connected to a contiguous generation (p. 10).

Overview

In total, this volume consists of 18 articles, written by professionals across the globe with varied experiences in the intergenerational arena. A common thread that runs through most of the articles is the characterization of intergenerational practices as a vital force for promoting cultural continuity, strengthening communities, and supporting and enriching individuals as they navigate their life course.

Articles are placed into three major sections: (1) Conceptual Issues, (2) National and Regional Profiles, and (3) Time to Organize. The articles in the first section help to lay out a conceptual foundation for international comparison of intergenerational initiatives. They outline some of the cultural, linguistic, and conceptual parameters of intergenerational activity and analysis.

In the second section of this book, contributing authors provide profiles of intergenerational program models found in different parts of the world. They draw particular attention to the distinctive ways in which people attribute meaning and socio-cultural significance to intergenerational interaction.

The third section highlights the importance of inter-organizational networking at the national and international levels.

Conceptual issues

In the first article, the three editors of this book discuss the importance of attending to the domain of culture when examining variability in the intergenerational programs and practices found across nations. In the next article, Howard Giles, Robert McCann, Hiroshi Ota, and Kimberly Noels review research which indicates that intergenerational communication patterns and preferences found in different cultural frameworks often run counter to traditional stereotypes of Eastern and Western communication dynamics.

In the third article, Anne O'Sullivan explores volunteerism from an international perspective. She describes some of the ways in which volunteerism is conceptualized and actualized as a force for individual and societal development. The last article, written by Matthew Kaplan, explores the use of language, proverbs in particular, as a tool for drawing inferences about the normative frameworks (popular conceptions) associated with age, aging, and intergenerational discourse.

National and regional profiles

The second section opens with three articles on intergenerational intervention modalities taking root in North America. In the first article, Nancy Henkin and Donna Butts note the underlying rationale, program approaches, policies, and organizational strategies that have driven extensive efforts in the United States over a 30-year period. The next article, written by Jessica Ball, Alan Pence, Martina Pierre, and Valerie Kuehne, describes an innovative intergenerational approach developed in Canada which provides childcare services and early childhood education in a manner which reflects and honors indigenous people's perspectives on education, community, and aging. The third article in this section explores the configuration of intergenerational activity emerging in Hawaii, a land where "East meets West." Matthew Kaplan and Joseph Lapilio, III, describe the diverse efforts to reconnect the young and old generations in the context of Hawaii's unique multicultural landscape, its people, traditions, institutions, and quality of life concerns.

For the next series of articles, the focus shifts to intergenerational programs and practices found in the Asian/Pacific region. Leng Leng Thang describes how the intergenerational programming concept is taking root in Singapore, a country with a very strong sense of national pride and identity and a high regard for intergenerational understanding and respect. The following article by Hilda Heine provides some examples of programs that draw on the expertise of community elders in the Marshall Islands to sustain local cultural heritage, traditions, and language in the midst of sweeping forces for social and cultural change. The third article in the section focuses on Japan; Matthew Kaplan and Leng Leng Thang indicate how intergenerational programs in Japan are often viewed in part as symbolic extensions of family support or even reconstructions of the extended family care concept.[2]

The next few articles highlight intergenerational program approaches taking root in European countries. Kees Penninx describes how the extensive intergenerational work now taking place in the Netherlands is emerging as a function of that nation's social policies, institutions, and priorities. He also provides a strategic framework for the further development of intergenerational programs and policies in the Netherlands. Gillian Granville and Alan Hatton-Yeo describe several intergenerational community action programs and other models in the United Kingdom that have significance in the context of that nation's commitment to reducing "social exclusion." Next Toshio Ohsako describes an intergenerational program in Germany which fits into a "healing history" paradigm; mutual learning experiences are set up for German pupils and Jewish seniors who were born in Hamburg and immigrated to different countries during the Nazi-regime.

The next region considered is Latin America. The first article, written by Martha Palaez, reviews some of the intergenerational initiatives and perspectives found in Central and South American countries. She discusses the multiple layers of significance of these initiatives in the context of indigenous societal values and changing demographics. In the following article, Susan Perlstein, a long-time U.S. intergenerational specialist, discusses cultural practices in Cuba that promote intergenerational relationships and lead to formal and informal partnerships.

In the last of the articles examining intergenerational strategies in geographically distinct areas, Cathy Gush focuses on South Africa. She notes how programs and policies implemented in that country serve as a countermeasure to the fragmentation of family relationships and support systems occurring amidst patterns and pressures of rapid economic development, migration to urban centers, and the AIDS crisis.

Time to organize

The final section of the book consists of two articles which describe organizing and coalition-building efforts that provide vital support for intergenerational programs and policies. Donna Butts and Atsuko Kusano discuss national-level organizing – challenges and successes – in the United States and in Japan. The final chapter, written by Sally Newman, provides an account of recent organizational activity aimed at building international lines of collaboration. She describes the process and outcomes from the "Generations Together: Dortmund International Working Conference" (April, 1999) and the subsequent international conference on intergenerational issues held in the Netherlands (October, 1999) as an event of the U.N. International Year of Older Persons.

In presenting this collection of articles we attempt to examine how the common goal of promoting intergenerational interaction and understanding unfolds into different programmatic strategies as a function of a variety of factors, including the general level of the economy, the culture and organization of society, prevailing social values, demographic trends, and the availability of services. Being explicit about the various contextual factors which influence how intergenerational models are conceived and perceived will move us closer to the point of being able to effectively exchange needed information across national borders. Hopefully, in an effort to get a handle on the relevant issues, the observations and insights shared in this volume will help to set the stage for further discussion and exploration.

Matthew S. Kaplan, Ph.D.
Associate Professor, Intergenerational Programs and Aging
Department of Agricultural and Extension Education
Pennsylvania State University

Nancy Z. Henkin, Ph.D.
Executive Director,
Center for Intergenerational Learning
Temple University

Atsuko T. Kusano, Ph.D.
Associate Professor of Education
Shinshu University

References

Brabazon, K., & Disch, R. (1997). *Intergenerational approaches in aging: Implications for education, policy and practice.* N.Y.: Haworth Press.

Hatton-Yeo, A., Klerq, J., Ohsako, T., & Newman, S. (2000). Public policy and research recommendations: An international perspective. In A. Hatton-Yeo and T. Ohsako (Eds.). *Intergenerational programs: Public Policy and research implications, An international perspective*, pp. 9-17. Hamburg, Germany: UNESCO Institute for Education.

Hawkins, M.O., Backman, K.F., & McGuire, F.A. (1998). *Preparing participants for intergenerational interaction: Training for success.* N.Y.: Haworth Press.

Kaplan, M. Kusano, A., Tsuji, I., & Hisamichi, S. (1998). *Intergenerational programs: Support for children, youth, and elders in Japan,* Albany, NY: SUNY Press.

Kuehne, V.S. (1999). *Intergenerational programs: Understanding what we have created.* Binghamton: The Haworth Press.

Mead, M. (1970). *Culture and commitment.* New York: Natural History Museum.

Newman, S., Ward, C.R., Smith, T.B., & Wilson, J. (1997). *Intergenerational programs: Past, present and future.* Bristol, PA: Taylor & Francis.

UNPF (1998). *The state of world population 1998: The new generations.* N.Y.: United Nations Population Fund.

Tout, K. (1989). *Ageing in developing countries.* N.Y.: Oxford University Press.

UN (1999). *Global life expectancy increases by twenty years*, U.N. Publications.

Winston, L. with Kaplan, M., Perlstein, S., & Tietze, R. (2001). *Grandpartners: Intergenerational learning and civic renewal, K-6.* Portsmouth, NH: Heinemann.

Notes

1 Hundreds of intergenerational program guidebooks and manuals have been published over the past 15 years and, in the past few years in particular, authors in the intergenerational field are finding mainstream venues for their publications (e.g., Brabazon & Disch, 1997; Hawkins et al. 1998; Henkin and Kingson (1998/99); Kaplan et al., 1998; Kuehne (1999), Newman et al., 1997; and Winston, 2001). Intergenerational exchange is a theme gaining increased attention at the

conferences of professional societies from a broad range of fields, including volunteerism, child development, service learning, and gerontology. In all of these venues, there is a growing recognition of the potential of intergenerational methodologies for enhancing people's lives and strengthening communities.

2 This article first appeared in the *Journal of Aging and Identity* special issue on "Intergenerational Programs" (Dec. 1997, Vol. 2, Number 4). Reprinted with publisher's permission.

A Conceptual Framework for Cross-Cultural Comparisons of Intergenerational Initiatives

By Matthew S. Kaplan, Nancy Z. Henkin, and Atsuko T. Kusano

Introduction

The concept of culture, a construct for exploring diversity in human experience and perception, is particularly useful with regard to intergenerational engagement phenomena. Geertz (1979) defines culture in the following way:

> A historically transmitted pattern of meanings embodied in symbols, a system of inherited conceptions expressed in symbolic forms by means of which people communicate, perpetuate, and develop their knowledge about and attitudes toward life (p. 89).

Without entering into the longstanding debate about how to define culture (e.g., see Wolf, 1994), culture is used here in its broadest sense, touching upon the variables of ethnicity, religion, and sense of tradition. As noted throughout this volume, there is significant cross-cultural variation in conceptions of "aging," "family," "community," "volunteerism," and "meaningful" intergenerational interaction. Other factors including history, religion, economic factors, and indigenous patterns of social organization also impact on the nature of intergenerational exchange and the appropriateness of programmatic interventions. This article will explore issues related to cultural distinctiveness and the transmission of cultural values.

Cultural Distinctiveness

A host of variables help define cultural distinctiveness and have an integral role in the development of intergenerational programs and practices, thus suggesting that comparison of programs from one national context to another is an extremely delicate enterprise.

The concept of "family"

When venturing into the international arena and asking questions about how to translate the significance and success of a program model from one country to another, it is important to consider indigenous conceptions of "family." Some questions to be considered: How strong is the pattern of reliance on family ties for resolving individual crisis and stress? What is the culturally defined role of the elder of the family in coordinating family support systems? Is there any sense of "shame" associated with families that receive assistance or participate in government-sponsored programs? What expectations do family members have of each other?

Whereas in the West, access to resources over the life course often requires going outside the family unit, in many other countries kinship ties remain the foundation for lifelong support. Societal norms of reciprocity have a great influence on how people give and receive assistance. In many developing countries reciprocity is seen as a long term process. A recent article in *Global Aging Report* (1999a) reports that the !Kung! in Botswana view caregiving as a quality of human nature. !Kung! elders don't see themselves as burdens; they give to others and expect to receive. They often play a prominent role in their community as healers. When they can no longer care for themselves, they expect others to care for them.

In China, a country with 120 million people over 60, the aging population is increasing at an astounding rate and questions about how to best care for the elderly have arisen. An examination of the Confucian teaching of "*xiao,*" or filial piety, reveals how this core cultural value can be moderated by demographic, social, political and economic factors as well as human service policy directions. *Xiao* is a hallmark component of the Chinese cultural framework for structuring intergenerational relations within the family. The younger generations are obligated to revere, obey, and care for elderly family members, while the elders are reciprocally expected to provide guidance and support for the young and to bind the household together. Coming first among all Confucian virtues, filial piety is central to the social organization of Chinese society.[1]

Though they share the same cultural heritage, Chinese families living in Mainland China, Hong Kong, Taiwan, Indonesia, New Zealand, the

United States and in other countries face different social, economic, and political realities. A question of considerable interest and debate is the extent to which the core value of *xiao* evolves as a function of different national acculturation experiences. To explore the manifestation of *xiao* in Chinese communities in different countries, it is important to consider consider differential demographic configurations and trends as well as differential policies for installing "safety nets" to help meet the financial, health care and social welfare needs of the elderly.

In China and in Singapore, this safety net is propped up with a political mechanism; generational contracts are inscribed into laws which make it possible for parents to sue their children for financial support. Although the abandonment of elderly parents doesn't happen much in China, there is an increasing amount of strain on the child. The government's one child policy enforced on couples for decades by the Communist government has reduced the population and contributed to the phenomenon of "4-2-1": four grandparents, supported by two parents, who are in turn supported by just one child.

Neglect of elderly parents is also rare in Singapore. Walter Woon, a law professor who sponsored the parent-support bill in Singapore's Parliament, notes that his bill is designed to protect the five percent of elderly people who do not receive financial support from their children. Woon states:

> The idea is not to have litigation. If you don't support your parents in a society like this, you're at the highest level of shame. The prospect of going to court would only increase the shame (Wallace, 1994, p. 17).

In Hong Kong, filial piety has evolved to the extent that the binding responsibility to care for elderly relatives is more readily being interpreted in terms of contributions in financial arrangements. Chen (1998) notes that this trend is due to many factors, some of which are tied to the vestiges of industrialization and urbanization, including changing patterns of childcare, migration of working age adults to urban centers, and the prevalence of smaller housing units built for nuclear families.[2]

Ng, Weatherall, Liu, & Loong (1998), in their study of intergenerational relationships in the Chinese community in New Zealand, note that as the Chinese immigrants to New Zealand adapted to the host culture, even in the midst of a decline in the usage of the Chinese language, there was no corresponding loss of filial piety. The presence of values of filial piety was found most readily in those Chinese immigrant respondents who, despite their age group, gender, or English/Chinese level language proficiency, identified with both their Chinese ethnic identity and their New Zealand identity. The authors explain this finding in part by noting the consistency between the Chinese and New Zealand cultures in reference to filial values and pointing out how this congruity helps to facilitate consistency in attitudes toward filial obligation.

Although this finding suggests that Chinese conceptions of filial piety can readily transcend emigration outside of an Asian cultural framework, the process of acculturation to Westernized societies poses an added challenge to the continuity of traditional family values. Ng, Weatherall, Liu, & Loong, (1998) state:

> *Xiao* functioned well in traditional Chinese society. It was supported by the high social status and economic power of elders. The impacts of 'Westernization,' industrialization and urbanization, however, have undermined many of the social conditions that were the foundations of *xiao*. The spread of public education, the displacement of traditional knowledge and practice by science, and the ever-increasing pace of technological development have transferred the power of knowledge from elders to the younger generation (p. 98).

Understanding the primacy of the family as the central social unit in many cultures is critical in planning any programmatic interventions that involve extra-familial intergenerational exchange. For example, as Kaplan and Thang discovered in Japan (see Chapter 10), several cases were found in which public acceptance of intergenerational programs was tied to the effectiveness of nostalgic appeals to traditions and symbols that reflected cultural ideals of family stability and unity. For successful programs such as "Rent-A-Family," initiated in 1990 by the Japan Efficiency Headquarters as a surrogate family service for senior adults in the Tokyo Metropolitan Region, intergenerational re-engagement is cast in the context of the family.

In the United States there are hundreds of "Intergenerational Shared Site" initiatives, defined by Goyer and Zuses (1997) as programs in which "multiple generations receive ongoing services and/or programming at the same site, and generally interact through planned and/or informal intergenerational activities" (p.v). In Singapore, as Thang notes in her review of intergenerational initiatives there (Chapter 8), recently there has been some major movement in terms of developing this type of model. Singapore's "3-in-1" centers combine day care for children and the elderly with other facilities for residents under one roof. Despite the success of these centers, some concerns have been raised by Singapore's Prime Minister, Goh Chok Tong, that intergenerational shared sites and the services they provide can weaken family ties ("Good Leaders Deliver Hardware," March 8, 1999). Although the Prime Minister stated that "these centers make good use of space in land-scarce Singapore" (p. 2), he also emphasized the importance of the moral obligation of families to look after their young and elderly members. He stated, "We have got to find ways to bring in the family to help look after the young children and the elderly, even though they are taken care of by the centers" (p. 2). He suggested holding one-day sessions (offered by the Community Development Ministry) for people who send their family members to the centers; these sessions would not only train them to care for their elderly family members, but also "remind them of their obligations."

Values related to "aging"

It is important to understand societal views about aging and the role of older adults in order to create culturally appropriate intergenerational programs and policies. If we look at views of aging within the Maori community (New Zealand), for example, there appears to be a very different conception of "retirement" than in Western cultures. Higgins states:

> As one ages, cultural responsibilities increase and the experience and wisdom of the older people are acknowledged and treasured. They are often in so much demand there is no thought of retirement (1998, p. 135).

Recognition of this concept would certainly be an important starting point for intergenerational programming in New Zealand. If working in a country in which older people are cast in the role of service recipients (as "needy persons"), then the challenge may be greater to implement intergenerational programs in which older adults are seen as resources for other generations.

We can learn a lot about public perceptions of aging and the aged from the media. For example, in a study comparing Japanese and American television programs for children, Holtzman and Akiyama (1985) noted that in both nations, older adults are rarely portrayed, and when they are portrayed, it is often in a negative or stereotypical manner. There is also value in examining how media representations of the elderly change over time. Ehrlich (1992), who conducted a longitudinal study of how elderly people are characterized in Japanese films, notes that immediately following World War II, films typically depicted the elderly as revered, respected, and exhibiting a steadfast quality. Though faced with harsh realities, they transcended their difficulties (at least in a spiritual sense). In contrast, when elderly people are portrayed in modern Japanese films, they are often presented as being "isolated and disenfranchised." With a backdrop of illness and disease, such films typically convey a tone of hopelessness and bleak pessimism. Ehrlich states:

> In Japanese cinema, the image of the elderly tends to either symbolize an ideal past, now lost or rapidly on the verge of extinction, or else it serves as a mirror of the illnesses of the present (p. 272).

Such findings indicate that Western stereotypes of Japanese society (i.e., expectations for a kind of universal reverence toward older people) are off the mark. Hence, we are reminded to critically question cultural as well as age-related stereotypes. In "Challenging Intergenerational Stereo-types Across Eastern and Western Cultures" (next chapter), Giles et al. provide an in-depth discussion about how people's actual views about aging do not readily fit into cultural stereotypes.

Nature of intergenerational communication

Different cultural frameworks yield different ideas about intergenera-tional communication dynamics. In most United States intergenerational programs, for example, participants generally interact in a manner which reflects "equal status." All participants are generally seen as possessing important knowledge and experiences and they are typically given the opportunity to share their lives and perspectives. In contrast, in some other cultural frameworks such as from a Japanese perspective, verbal and non-verbal interaction reflects the respective status level of the communi-cators. Insofar as age is a major determinant of status, there is a built-in notion of inequality between the generations. Youth are expected to do more listening than speaking when communicating with their elders. This is also the case in intergenerational exchange in venues which reflect Pacific Island cultural values.

The notion of "volunteerism"

Whereas in many Western cultures there is a strong commitment to volunteering in one's community, this is not the case worldwide. In coun-tries such as Finland, the idea of providing support services to one's neighbor has met some resistance due to the long history of state funding for the provision of all social services. The expectation that the govern-ment will care for all of the country's residents is strongly embedded in Finnish consciousness. Many do not feel it is their responsibility to supple-ment the government with volunteer services.

In some developing countries, volunteerism outside the family and church is limited due to economic conditions. The elderly, in particular, may find it difficult to volunteer if they have no pension plan and need to work well into their later years. Offering stipends to retirees, such as those offered in the Dominican Republic to retired teachers who are willing to work in rural areas, is one strategy for promoting the continued contribu-tion of older adults to their communities. Creating income-generating op-portunities for youth and elders might be more appropriate in some situa-tions than promoting volunteer activities.

National Sentiment

For a nationwide intergenerational program to succeed, it must facili-tate relationships in a manner which is consistent with national sentiment. This principle can help explain the success of Help Age Korea, a national program established in Korea in 1982 to help senior adults who were struggling financially. One of the most successful projects for Help Age Korea was its Adopt-A-Granny program. The public (and government) enthusiastically supported this system for allowing wealthier Koreans to provide financial support to less fortunate elders; the program has grown from 23 to 1,500 "grannies receiving help" (Global Aging Report, 1999b). The success of Help Age Korea programs can be understood in the context of popular concerns related to the massive disruption of Korean families occurring as a result of its history of war, conflict, and, more recently, rapid economic expansion.

On the surface, there are components of the Help Age Korea initiative which seem identical to programs found in other countries (e.g., the Friendly Visitor program in the United States). Yet, considering the unique cultural and historical factors that contributed to the growth of this program, and employing a more penetrating analysis of the program's psychological and social significance, will yield additional insight into the program's replicability.

Transmission of Cultural Values

Intergenerational programs can play a significant role in transmitting values from generation to generation within a culture and in promoting understanding and tolerance across cultures. Intergenerational programs can also provide a tool for addressing cycles of intolerance that historically have been passed down through the generations.

The cultural regeneration function

The search for self-identity encompasses the recognition and placement of one's individual and family history into a larger historical experience. Haraven (1978) invokes the phrase "generational memory," to refer to "... the memories which individuals have of their own families' history, as well as more general collective memories about the past" (p. 137). The transmission of collective histories, often an intergenerational enterprise, has implications for strengthening the bond between generations, promoting a sense of cultural continuity, and exposing individuals to a process of learning which promotes cultural awareness, identity, and group consciousness.

In this sense, intergenerational endeavors have a cultural regeneration component. Many programs use storytelling, dance, cultural crafts, healing arts, language, and other modalities to provide participants with a sense of cultural pride and connectedness to a cultural timeline. In this light, intergenerational work presents a powerful approach for promoting cultural values and perspectives and addressing problems associated with cultural discontinuity.

Perhaps nowhere is cultural discontinuity more apparent than in the plight of indigenous peoples who have experienced cultural dislocation, fragmentation, and/or relocation.

In addressing the quest for identity, and even survival, on the part of indigenous peoples, modalities of intergenerational re-connection have been found to help restore cultural knowledge (including indigenous languages), perspectives, and pride. "Na Pua No'eau" (The Center for Gifted and Talented Native Hawaiian Children), a cultural immersion program in Hawaii, involves elders in all aspects of the educational process. They are cast in the role of "conveyers of culture" and, in line with the Native Hawaiian perspective, they are viewed as the ones with the greatest amount of "expertise" on important matters related to personal development, community, and spirituality. In the context of First Nations communities across western Canada, where similar views are held about the value of elders, Ball et al. report on an intergenerational program model for training early childhood educators in a manner which similarly revitalizes indigenous values about the importance of elders in the educational process (see Chapter 6).

Insofar as culture is not a static concept, it is also important to note that the transmission of cultural values and knowledge goes both ways. Through direct contact with young people, adults learn about what is culturally significant and vital for younger generations whose tastes and sensibilities are influenced by a mass-media driven, highly commercialized society that generates a constant flow of technological advancements that seem in many ways alien to older adults.

Cross-cultural understanding

Intergenerational programs and policies can also be used to facilitate tolerance and understanding between cultures. Consistent with prevailing attitudes toward cultural diversity in the United States, some intergenerational models have been created to promote multicultural awareness and acceptance (e.g., Perlstein, 1997; Skilton-Sylvester and Henkin, 1997; and McGowan, 1997). As McGowan notes, weaving cross-cultural experience into intergenerational experience compounds the rich, reflexive insights gained by the participants and stimulates their rejection of ageist and racist/culture-based stereotypes. Project SHINE (Students Helping in the Naturalization of Elders), a national program in the United States which pairs college students with immigrant elders, is an example of intercultural cross-age programming. As students teach English, they hear the stories of older learners and gain an appreciation for their resourcefulness and strengths.

In Chapter 13, Toshio Ohsako, Senior Research Specialist at the UNESCO Institute for Education (Hamburg, Germany) describes a very exciting program in Germany which illustrates how an intergenerational program can function to heal the wounds left from war, ethnic hatred, and discrimination. Based in a school in Hamburg, Germany, this program aims to generate an intergenerational dialogue and mutual learning experience between German pupils and Jewish seniors who were born in Hamburg and immigrated to different countries during the Nazi-regime.

At one level, it would seem obvious that such a "healing history" model has applications in other countries with remaining wounds from past conflicts. However, this is not a simple matter. For example, due to the contention that exists to this day between Japan and its neighbors in terms of perceptions and interpretations of World War II era international relations, events, and policy, it would be difficult to establish similar dialogues of healing between the Japanese, Chinese, and Korean residents of Japan.

The program which succeeded in Germany was a culturally appropriate indigenous initiative. It addressed an "official" priority in the teaching of history in Germany, and it was consistent with Hamburg's multicultural, intergenerational vision of civic life. (The city of Hamburg issues invitations for Jewish seniors every year to participate in this project and in other school projects in Hamburg.) Our main point here is that although there is much to be learned from intergenerational models developed in other countries, this does not imply that replication of successful initiatives is simple or always appropriate.

Conclusion

So, what does all this mean for organizations interested in promoting intergenerational exchange through programmatic interventions?

By looking at the world with an intergenerational lense and examining various patterns of connectivity between old and young, we gain valuable insights into the intersection between culture, social life and social policy. Clearly there are significant opportunities (at the program and policy levels) for working to strengthen intergenerational relationships in families and in communities.

As the domain of intergenerational strategies takes on international parameters, we must remember to develop and conduct intergenerational activities in culturally appropriate ways and take care not to violate culturally relevant conceptions of human growth and development and intergenerational relationships. It is a simple thing to say that intergenerational programs and practices facilitate fulfilling, meaningful, culturally significant, direct contact between the generations. However, it gets complicated when we realize that there is great diversity in what people consider to be "fulfilling," "meaningful," "culturally significant," and "direct contact."

Throughout this book, many examples are presented about how cultural variation underscores fundamental differences in regard to perceptions about intergenerational interaction and preferences for programmatic intervention. Attention paid to the cultural distinctiveness found in any one country can help provide a deeper understanding of the nature (form and function) of indigenous intergenerational initiatives and the viability of replication across cultures.

References

Chen, Z.M. (1998). The making of an update filial piety scale for research with Chinese elderly samples. In *Collected Treatises from the International Conference on the 21st Century Aging Problem*, pp. 163-184, Shanghai: Shanghai Science and Technology Literature Publisher.

Ehrlich, L.C. (1992). The undesired ones: Images of the elderly in Japanese cinema. In S. Formanek & S. Linhart (Eds.) *Japanese biographies: Life histories, life cycles, life stages* (pp. 271-281). Vienna: Austrian Academy of Science.

"Good Leaders Deliver 'Hardware.'" (March 8, 1999). *The Straits Times Interactive* (http://straitstimes.asia1.com.sg).

Geertz, C. (1979*). Meaning and order in Moroccan society: Three essays in cultural analysis.* Cambridge: Cambridge University Press.

Global Aging Report (1999a). Article on the !Kung! of Botswana. Washington, D.C.: AARP.

Global Aging Report (Jan./Feb., 1999b) Using home help and self help to stay independent: "Adopt-a-Granny" in Korea, 4:1, 5.

Goyer, A. and Zuses, R.T. (1997). *Intergenerational shared site project: A study of co-located programs and services for children, youth and older adults.* Washington, D.C.: AARP.

Hareven, T.K. (1978). The search for generational memory: Tribal rites in industrial society. In *Proceedings of the American Academy of Arts and Sciences*, 107:4, 137-149.

Henkin, N. and Kingson, E. (Eds.) (1998/99). Keeping the promise: Intergenerational strategies for strengthening the social compact. Special issue of *Generations* (Journal of the American Society on Aging), 22:4.

Higgins, T.R. (1998). Reflections and prospects. In Ng, S.H., Weatherall, A., Liu, J.H., & Loong, C.S.F. *Ages ahead: Promoting inter-generational relationships.* Wellington, NZ: Victoria University Press, (pp. 134-139).

Holtzman, J.M., & Akiyama, H. (1985). What children see: The aged on television in Japan and the United States. *The Gerontologist, 25* (1), 62-68.

McGowan, T. (1997). Cultural foregrounding and the problem of representation: Combating ageism through reflexive, intergenerational experience. *Journal of Aging and Identity*, 2:4, pp. 229-249.

Ng, S.H., Liu, J.H., Weatherall, A., & Loong, C.S.F. (1998). Intergenerational relationships in the Chinese community. In Ng, S.H., Weatherall, A., Liu, J.H., & Loong, C.S.F. *Ages ahead: Promoting inter-generational relationships.* Wellington, NZ: Victoria University Press, (pp. 85-104).

Perlstein, S. (1997). Intergenerational arts: Cultural continuity and community cohesion. *Journal of Aging and Identity*, 2:4, pp. 273-284.

Productive Aging News (1994, February). *Supplement to issue No. 78.* NY: The International Leadership Center on Longevity and Society (United States), Mount Sinai Medical Center.

Skilton-Sylvester, E. & Henkin, N. (1997). Intergenerational programs for promoting language learning and cultural continuity among elderly immigrants and refugees. *Journal of Aging and Identity*, 2:4, pp. 251-271.

United Nations. (1999). Global life expectancy increases by twenty years. U.N. Document.

Wallace, Charles P. (1994, August 24). Asia's graying population: Demographic time bomb keeps ticking. *The Japan Times*, p. 17.

Wolf, E.R. (1994). Perilous ideas: Race, culture and people. *Current Anthropology*, 35:1, 1-7.

Yuen, F. (1987). Chinese elderly and family care (in Chinese). *Social Research*, 3, 36-43.

Notes

1 Chen (1998), in his historical review of filial piety, notes that this fundamental value actually predates Confucius. He refers to Yuen's (1987) work which illustrates how poems and poetic proverbs of earlier eras, dating back to the Zi Chou period (about 800 B.C.), suggest an atmosphere conducive to norms for filial practices.

2 Chen (1998) presents Yang's (1981) analysis of how industrialization converts family structures in a manner which brings about the dissolution of the extended family. When family life centers around farming, the extended family is kept together and elderly family members fulfill many valued roles. Along with industrialization process in Hong Kong, there was a pattern of nuclearization of the family, with less of a reliance on the skills and knowledge of senior adults.

Challenging Intergenerational Stereotypes Across Eastern and Western Cultures

By Howard Giles, Robert M. McCann, Hiroshi Ota, and Kimberly A. Noels

Introduction

Changes in infant mortality, epidemiology, and life expectancy since the 1960s and earlier have led to large-scale demographic shifts in the world's population. One aspect of these developments is that the proportion of elderly people in almost every nation around the globe, particularly in East Asia, is increasing dramatically. This situation has spawned popular and academic interest in the conditions and processes of aging (Madey, 2000). Research on these issues within the discipline of Communication has, likewise, burgeoned in the last decade or so (see, for example, Nussbaum & Coupland, 1995; Williams & Nussbaum, 2001), albeit not at the same pace as other disciplines (Giles, 1999). Even so, virtually all of the research and theory on the relations between communication and aging has been conducted in Western, Anglophone societies (such as in Canada, Britain, and the United States), and there is very little empirical research that examines intergenerational *communication* across different cultures (see, however, Noor Al-Deen, 1997 and Kaplan's chapter on proverbs in this book). This chapter overviews briefly some of the initial findings from a program of research conducted around the Pacific Rim[1] where stereotypical images of aging have been heralded as grossly different (Levy & Langer, 1994). We believe that the emerging findings have significant theoretical and pragmatic implications.

The cross-cultural backdrop

Western communication patterns

Broadly speaking, we can trace contrasting social perspectives on aging in "the West" and "the East" to their philosophical roots. Although we recognize that this gross dichotomy is simplistic (Triandis, Chen, & Chen, 1998) and camouflages much socially important within-region variability, we invoke it – albeit with interpretive caution – as a conceptual convenience that is consonant with much of the traditional literature on this topic. Many intercultural scholars (e.g., Gudykunst & Matsumoto, 1996; Kim, 1994; Yum, 1988) have described an array of so-called "Eastern" cultures as relatively more collectivistic, oriented toward their in-groups, favoring indirectness and thereby relying more than Western cultures upon the context of communication to specify meanings. The latter, in turn (see Triandis, Dunnette, & Hough, 1994), tend to be relatively more individualistic and favor directness through verbally explicit communication. Although these contrasting value and behavioral patterns are themselves regarded in some quarters (e.g., Matsumoto, 1999; Uleman, Rhee, Bardoliwalla, Semin, and Toyama, 2000) as empirically contentious, the philosophical orientation of the West is said to rest on Liberalism where the primary unit of social life is the individual whose rights and autonomy are paramount. Thus, individuals act rationally, pursue their own rights, and search for personal fulfillment independent from their in-group(s).

Empirical research into Western attitudes toward elders, including traits and stereotypes, has been conducted for several decades and has indicated that elders are viewed very negatively (e.g., Kite & Johnson, 1988). These stereotypes include perceptions of older adults as being nagging, irritable, decrepit, cranky, weak, feeble-minded, verbose, cognitively deficient, asexual, useless, ugly, miserable, and unsatisfied with their lives. More recently, American scholars have identified a number of sub-stereotypes of elderly people (e.g., Hummert, Garstka, Shaner, & Strahm, 1994), most of which are again negative (e.g., "Despondent," "Severely Impaired"), but others that are arguably more positive (e.g., "Golden Ager," "Perfect Grandparent"). In line with Western societies being depicted as "youth-oriented," recent comparative data have led to the suggestion that "young American adults enjoy being young much more and maintain higher life satisfaction than do Japanese youths" (Ota, Harwood, Williams, & Takai, 2001, p. 38).

Given that our communicative behaviors can be, at least in part, fueled by social stereotypes (Hewstone & Giles, 1986; Ota, 2001), it is perhaps not surprising to find Western communication studies showing that many young people "over-accommodate" (e.g., are overly polite, warm, and grammatically and/or ideationally simple) to those they categorize as elderly people. This behavior is particularly, but not only, evident when negative sub-stereotypes are activated (Harwood & Williams, 1998).

Over-accommodation often emerges irrespective of the elder's functional autonomy and is not always valued as entirely appropriate for, or by, many socially- and cognitively-active older people. (For a review of this research area, see Ryan, Hummert, & Boich, 1995.) However, Giles and Williams (1994) have shown that younger people also, in turn, feel patronized by their elders, whom they characterize, for example, as non-listening, over-parenting, and disapproving. In addition, other studies (e.g., Williams, 1996) have indicated that older communicators are construed as "under-accommodating" to their younger interlocutors when talking excessively about their own situations (sometimes painful), and in ways that younger participants find difficult to manage conversationally (Coupland, Coupland, & Giles, 1991). In sum, the communication climate between younger and older adults can, in Western contexts, be characterized as problematic (see Edwards & Giles, 1998), at least from the younger perspective (Williams & Giles, 1996).

Eastern communication patterns

In spite of varying traditions (e.g., Taoism, Buddhism, Confucianism), the single most frequently-cited philosophical influence on Eastern communication patterns is Confucianism which spread throughout the region to many Asian cultures in a variety of ways (Chang, 1997). Confucianism views individuals as part of a relational harmony that emphasizes respect for, and attendance to, ordered social relationships, including affection and righteousness between parent and child. The maintenance of ordered and hierarchical relationships are often based on age, familial (e.g., father-son), and social roles, and long-term lifespan outcomes are important. In fact, obligation to parents and familial elders can extend even beyond the grave as is implicit in the ancient tradition of ancestor worship. Filial piety — the Confucian doctrine of "Xiao Shun" — teaches that elderly people should be respected, and it is the children's responsibility to care for parents and grandparents in their old age (Kiefer, 1992). Furthermore, this ethic should not be restricted to familial elders, but should embrace respect for, and obligations to, older people *per se*. The persistence, these days, of the moral norm of filial piety has been well documented (e.g., Ho, 1994; Sung, 1995) across the East Asian Pacific Rim (e.g., in Korea, China, Japan, Taiwan, and Hong Kong) as well as among Chinese immigrants elsewhere (Ng, Loong, Liu, & Weatherall, 2000). Also well documented are some interesting (and some equivocal) data and analyses that promote ambiguity about our understanding of the actual social perception of elderly people in East Asian societies (e.g., Koyano, 1989; Tien-Hyatt, 1987; Tobin, 1987). While there is evidence that, with changes in family structure, modernization, and westernization, filial piety has eroded in some urban quarters (Ingersoll-Dayton & Saengtienchai, 1999), it is still generally accepted that collectivism, hierarchical relational values, and filial piety influence the perceptions of elders and intergenerational communication in this area of the world. Consequently, we would predict that, in stark contrast to prior (Western) findings in this field, older people in East Asian cultures would be viewed more positively and that the communication climate between younger and older adults would be one of mutual accommodation.

The Research Program

Guiding questions and overview of findings

Guided by our theoretical approach, which views intergenerational relations in "intergroup" terms (see Harwood, Giles, & Ryan, 1995; Tajfel & Turner, 1986), some of the main questions posed were:

(a) Do images of elderly people vary between East Asian and Western cultures?
(b) Is there a more positive intergenerational communication climate in many of the former as opposed to the latter cultures? and
(c) What subjective health implications are there for these intercultural profiles?

As we are forging a new line of research across very different languages for the first time, our research is based on self-reports of past conversational experiences; these, we contend, are crucial schemas for guiding actual interactions between older and younger people.

Regarding question (a) above, the answer is largely affirmative in that Eastern respondents consistently espouse a **less** favorable image of older people than their Western counterparts. We studied this in three domains, namely age stereotyping, filial piety, and age vitality.

First, one study showed, perhaps surprisingly, that there were no differences in young adults' stereotypes about the young, middle-aged, and elderly across Canada, South Korea, the Philippines, the United States, and New Zealand (Harwood et al., 1996). Here, in our sample of over 1000 students, ratings of activity, strength, and the like declined with increasing age whereas ratings of wisdom and generosity increased comparably. But our Hong Kong sample (in this same study) displayed far more negative images than did any of the former countries. Indeed, the Hong Kong respondents even associated **declines** in wisdom and generosity with increasing age. (See also Giles, Harwood, Pierson, Clement, & Fox, 1998.) Similarly, in a companion study examining Australian versus Japanese students' stereotypes, we found that the former had more positive images than the latter (Ota, Giles, & Gallois, 2000). Similar results were found with American-Japanese, American-Thai, and American-Indian comparisons, respectively (Arnhoff, Leon, & Lorge, 1964; Sharp, Price-Sharps, & Hanson, 1998; and Williams, Pandey, Best, Morton, & Pande, 1992). Looking at the other side of the intergenerational coin (Harwood et al., in press), we found that elderly informants from Hong Kong and the People's Republic of China (PRC) also endorsed negative views of their own age group; for them, too, wisdom and generosity declined with age.

Second, we turned empirical attention to beliefs about filial piety by comparing four Eastern and four Western contexts around the Pacific Rim (Gallois et al., 1999).[2] We found that while East Asian students claimed they would indeed look after older people more in terms of tangible, instrumental support (e.g., financial, living arrangements) than Westerners (see also, for example, Knodel, Saengtienchai, & Sittitrai, 1995), it was the latter who expressed greater commitment to socially supporting and listening to their elders. Indeed, Westerners claimed that they would even exceed their presumed elders' expectations in these regards. Easterners, in contrast, contended they would not quite match elders' anticipations of them.

Third, we examined how much status and institutional support (our measure of "age group vitality," see Harwood et al., 1994) was accorded younger and older people across 11 cultural contexts (including India). In this study, vitality assessments of elderly adults (e.g., their representation in the media, business, politics) tended to be lower in Eastern than Western societies, and were particularly low in South Korea, the People's Republic of China, and Singapore (Giles et al., 2000).

The above data align with the notion that industrialization and urbanization in recent years have eroded traditional values. An alternative explanation might be that public avowals of filial piety — a cognitive veneer — belie private ascription to a negative view of aging and older adults (see Levy, 1999; McGee & Barker, 1982). With this consistently more positive profile emerging for Westerners, we examined question (b) above concerning individuals' perceptions of the intergenerational **communication** climates evident. A sequence of studies provided a picture complementary to that emerging for question (a).

In the first of these (Williams et al., 1997), we asked students across nine cultures (including a region of the south-east of the People's Republic of China where there was little Western influence)[3] to rate their experiences of encounters they had had with (non-family) older people (mostly over 65-75 years of age). The instrument included scalar items crafted on the basis of open-ended accounts of intergenerational communication satisfaction-dissatisfaction we had garnered previously (Williams & Giles, 1996). Although patterns differed among the East Asian nations, the self-reports indicated a more negative intergenerational communication climate for younger people in this region. Easterners found elderly people far more <u>non</u>-accommodating (i.e., not listening, complaining, being self-centered, and so forth), particularly South Koreans who felt the most obligated to be polite and "bite their tongues." Westerners reported relatively more positively-emotive and satisfying interactions with older people and felt the latter to be more accommodating (i.e., telling interesting stories, being supportive, and so forth). Interestingly, there was little variability among the samples of Western students who rated age as mattering less to them in intergenerational encounters. That said, there was a tendency (among the Western samples) for the most positive ratings to be Canadian, a finding that is explicable in terms of their unique social welfare system (see, however, Best & Williams, 1996).

In three follow-up studies, we contrasted the views of Euro-Americans versus Taiwanese, Anglo-Australian versus Hong Kong, and Euro-Americans versus Japanese young respondents (Giles, Liang, Noels, & McCann, in press; Noels, Giles, Gallois, & Ng, in press). This time, however, we asked them to evaluate their conversations with their **same**-aged peers as well (with the order varying across respondents). Again, the same intercultural pattern emerged. That is, the Eastern samples reported less favorable intergenerational communication experiences, despite the fact that they felt more obligation to be respectful to older than younger people. Although there was some empirical variation across studies, young people found their elderly counterparts to be more non-accommodating than their same-aged peers, and younger adults tended to close off or avoid intergenerational interaction — tendencies that were accentuated by Eastern respondents (see also, Yeh, Williams, & Maruyama, 1998).

In a further cross-cultural study (Giles et al., 2000), this pattern held true even when **family** elders were included in the evaluative frame. Although the conversations with family elderly were more favorably construed than non-family elderly (but less so, again, by Eastern than Western respondents), they were, nonetheless, regarded as more non-accommodating compared to interactions with their peers (see also Ng, Liu, Weatherall, & Loong, 1997). Interestingly, Westerners (i.e., Australians, New Zealanders, and Americans) reported more positive communication experiences with even family elders than Korean, Filipino, and Japanese students.

In some of these (and other) studies, we investigated, in tandem, *elderly* people's (70-80-year-olds') views of their intra- and intergenerational communication experiences (Cai, Giles, & Noels, 1998; Noels, Giles, Cai, & Turay, 1999; Noels et al., in press; Ota, 2001). A number of compelling findings emerged. First, elderly people, too, have some negative intergenerational experiences to report, irrespective of their cultural origins. For them, the communication gap is reciprocally felt to the extent that both age groups perceived their own age peers to be more accommodating to them than the other age group. Second, and somewhat surprisingly, a number of our elderly respondents reported communication problems with people of their same age group. (Of course, whether all older people consider others of their age bracket as being "age peers" is a cogent question; see Paoletti, 1998.) More specifically, they found other older people more non-accommodating than younger people. This tendency was exacerbated amongst our Hong Kong, People's Republic of China, and Japanese informants. For these people, **intra**generational communication was seemingly as dissatisfactory as was intergenerational contact. Interestingly, however, our Australian elderly sample reported few inter- or intragenerational problems and were the least avoidant of either of the groups so far studied.

At a number of our research sites, the data collection exercise also allowed us to include measures of psychological well-being — namely, self-esteem (Rosenberg, 1965), a sense of life coherence and meaning (Antonovsky, 1987), and depression (Brink et al., 1982) — among our elderly respondents. In this way, we could address Question (c) above. Relatedly, one of our theoretical frameworks – the communication predicament model — proposes important relationships between intergenerational communication experiences and subjective health (Ryan, Giles, Bartolucci, & Henwood, 1986; Harwood, Giles, Fox, Ryan, & Williams, 1993). Understanding how communications across generations are more or less positive is not only relevant to promoting harmony in interpersonal interactions, but may also have direct implications for the psychological health of older people. The model relates to how young people's negative stereotypes of older people may induce communication with them in a manner that reflects their negative inclinations. For instance, they may regard older people as feeble and incompetent, and hence speak to them in a patronizing tone. Repeated interactions of this kind may eventually lead some older people to wonder if they truly are as incompetent as the behavior of some younger people toward them would suggest. In response, they may even assume some of the age characteristics implied by the younger person's communication style. Hence they may act more dependent and deferential toward the younger person when, in fact, they are actually quite competent and independent individuals (Bieman-Copland, Ryan, & Cassano, 1998). Over time, self-stereotyping in these terms (cf. Turner, 1987; Levy, Hausdorff, Hencke, & Wei, 2000), may lead older persons to believe that they really are less competent. This poor self-perception may be linked with a lessened sense of self-worth and decreased sense of well-being. In other words, understanding communicative processes may be fundamental to understanding the social construction of aging, and even death.

In order to test this theoretical position, to answer question (c), and to explore the relationship between communication variables and psychological adjustment variables, a series of standard multiple regression equations were calculated. We were interested to know how well the communication variables pertaining to older people and the communication variables pertaining to younger people predicted each adjustment variable (i.e., life satisfaction and self-esteem). The results were supportive of the communication predicament model in some ways. Amongst other predictors, it was found that perceptions of low levels of accommodative communication from young family members predicted depression among People's Republic of China elderly (Cai et al., 1998), and perceptions of higher levels of younger accommodation predicted higher self-esteem and life satisfaction among Australian older people. Nevertheless, intergenerational communication with young, non-family adults did not predict psychological adjustment among Hong Kong Chinese, nor Japanese elders (Noels et al., 1999; Noels et al., in press; Ota, 2001). For them, as well as for the American sample population, being the recipient of lower levels of accommodation from *other older* people predicted lower self-esteem. Interestingly, being polite to, and respectful of, other older adults was related to elders' self-esteem in these three Asian contexts. This highlights anew the significance of in-group relations to psychological well-being in these nations.

Epilogue

We believe that we have shared some interesting information in answer to the questions posed at the outset. Differing social images and communication experiences are associated with older people around the Pacific Rim and in ways that are meaningfully predictive of psychological well-being. Our research program suggests that intergenerational exchanges in Western centers are actually perceived to be *more* favorable than in the many Eastern contexts we have studied. This finding is somewhat dismaying given that prior research has shown ubiquitous stigmatization of the elderly in the West! It is clear that the intergenerational gap is mutually felt to exist by both age groups, albeit more intensely by young people. And, crucially, we have documented that negative communication experiences are associated with subjective ill-being for older people (albeit not, predictably, for younger people, see Noels et al., 1999). Hence, any interventions via intergenerational contact programs — and these are clearly deemed necessary in the light of the data — must take into account the perspectives, needs, motivations of, and likely outcomes for, **both** younger and older participants (Bieman-Copland et al., 1998).

Importantly, we have also found that **intra**generational communication can invoke serious problems too and, again, in ways that have not been central to planning and implementing elderly intervention programs. Put another way, older people's "ingroup" conversations with others of peer age can also be dissatisfying (especially in the East) and are linked to poor subjective well-being in ways that communication theory (such as the predicament model) has as yet neither acknowledged nor appreciated (see Auslander & Litwin, 1991). As Pushkar and Arbuckle (1998, p. 169) commented, "competence in interpersonal or social functioning has received less attention in research with elderly people than among younger populations." The finding that Eastern images of, and talk to and from, aging people are even more deprecatory than Western ones may be surprising to some. We believe this finding may derive, in large part, from the transfer of social power, finance, and influence from older to younger people as well as the strong resistance to such changes by some older people as, in recent times, their cultures have experienced technological change, modernization, and westernization.

Our findings, then, hold out real significance for the world's so-called "undeveloped" societies that will sooner or later undergo radical transformations in industry, commerce, medicine, and the like. Contemporary theoretical models of communication and aging thus need to be revised to take into account cultural and macro-social factors (such as dimensions of filial piety and age vitality, respectively), and we need to map more specifically the potential interrelationships of these and communicative experiences.

Clearly, there are limitations to the generality of our findings and the methodological procedures adopted. First, the empirical origins of our methods are Western; we need to develop culturally-sensitive measures of communicative behaviors and health outcomes (both subjective and objective) for each research site. That said, we are encouraged by Zhang and Hummert's (in press) study of young and older adults' generated accounts of intergenerational communication in the People's Republic of China. These found that although some culturally-specific Chinese themes did emerge, the overriding conclusion was that the kinds of communicative ingredients in between-age encounters similar to those featured in this chapter were clearly evident there too. Nonetheless, it is also necessary to determine how predictive communication variables are of various indices of well-being when other critical social factors — such as economic, health, personality, and lifestyle choices — are introduced. Second, the types of elderly and young samples investigated (as well as social "targets" rated) need to be extended to appeal to other variables and populations (e.g., immigrants, ethnic minorities). Third, we need to conduct replication studies in other (less modernized and rural) Eastern settings as well as (more collectivistic) Latin American settings, and elsewhere (see Williams et al., 1992). Indeed, we have other data currently being analyzed or collected from our ongoing research sites as well as from Thailand, Laos, Cambodia, South Vietnam, Italy, and other West and East European centers.

We are also beginning to study intergenerational communication at a different juncture in the lifespan — namely, between younger and older (middle-aged) workers holding differing social ranks in varying organizational spheres. (See McCann & Giles, in press, for a discussion of communication and agism in the workplace). It is our contention that some of the communication problems we have uncovered herein may have their origins at earlier points in development (see also, Grams & Albee, 1995). In this vein, we have observed that communicative agism (Williams & Giles, 1998) and agist sentiments — perhaps in parallel to the intragenerational communication problems we have documented above — can be harmfully exchanged amongst age peers at midlife, and by impactful means that they had not expected so soon in their lifespans. Finally, we need to better understand not only the dilemmas and predicaments of aging across the lifespan, but also the social conditions — when, how, and where — of "healthy" communication between and within generations (Williams & Coupland, 1998), and the ways in which it may contribute to successful aging (Ng, Weatherall, Liu, & Loong, 1998) and assist us in elaborating communication models of this complex process (Nussbaum, 1985). All this notwithstanding, the cross-cultural patterns of communicative discord, both between and within generations, described above, demands our utmost empirical energies.

Program planners rarely appear cognizant of the actual forms of communication and allied intergroup identities that overlay or emerge from intergenerational relations (Abrams & Giles, 1999; Fox & Giles, 1993). Our data, whether derived from Asian or Western sites, underscore the fact that younger and older adults are not accommodating to each other appropriately (Giles, Coupland, & Coupland, 1991). At one level, it seems evident that we should not ignore such miscommunications, let alone their propensity to do considerable social damage. It might, therefore, be prudent to seek ways of intervening that engender communicative practices from both sides that are perceived to be more mutually accommodative.

In addition, however, we should also explore the potential of existing nonaccommodations (e.g., talking a lot about one's own problems) to accomplish some quite positive social functions for those that regularly enact them (see Coupland et al.,1991). If the causes of such communication behavior could be appreciated (and even tolerated) by both parties, then a healthy, realistic blend of (legitimate) accommodations and (understood) nonaccommodations could be fostered on both sides.

As the communicative predicaments we have documented are transcontinental (see Masataka, 2000), clearly specific contact programs need to take into account the local cultural dynamics operating in cross generational communication (e.g., filial piety). Until recently, much of the literature on intergenerational contact programs implicitly assumes cultural equivalence. One encouraging recent exception is the development of educational programs focusing upon Japan and Taiwan that have acknowledged cultural factors in their aims for developing communication skills (e.g., listening) among middle-aged and older people, particularly as they anticipate the taking on of the socially-critical, new roles of grandparenting in a family setting (Strom & Strom, 1996; Strom et al., 1999). Furthermore, local culture is everywhere changing rapidly. The economic and political situations of people of different age groups are undergoing drastic changes in many Asian countries (and elsewhere) as manifest, for example, in the promulgation of laws relating to elderly people (Koyano, 1999; Martin, 1988). People's perceptions, expectations, and attitudes toward people in other age groups are influenced by such societal transformations and, thus, are expressed in inter-group communication. Therefore, it is essential that contact program planners make themselves aware of the extent of emerging changes in cultural factors as they pertain to intergenerational relationships.

References

Abrams, J., & Giles, H. (1999). Epilogue: Intergenerational contact as intergroup communication. *Child and Youth Services, 20*, 203-217.

Antonovsky, A. (1987). *Unraveling the mystery of health: How people manage stress and stay well.* San Francisco: Jossey Bass.

Arnhoff, F.N., Leon, H., & Lorge, I. (1964). Cross-cultural acceptance of stereotypes toward aging. *Journal of Social Psychology, 63*, 41-58.

Ausland, G.K., & Litwin, H. (1991). Social networks, social support, and self-ratings of health among older persons. *Journal of Aging and Health, 3*, 493-510.

Bengston, V.L., & Smith, D.H. (1968). Social modernity and attitudes toward aging: A cross-cultural survey. *The Gerontologist, 8*, 26.

Best, D.L., & Williams, J.E. (1996). Anticipation of aging: A cross-cultural examination of young adults' views of growing old. In J. Pandey, D. Sinha, D.P.S. Bhawuk (Eds.), *Asian contributions to cross-cultural psychology* (pp. 274-288). New Delhi: Sage.

Bieman-Copland, S., Ryan, E.B., & Cassano, J. (1998). Responding to the challenges of late life. In D. Pushkar, W. Bukowski, A. Schwartzmann, D. Stack, & D. White (Eds.), *Improving competence across the lifespan* (pp. 141-157). New York: Plenum.

Brink, T. L., Yesavage, J. A., Lum, O., Heersema, P. H., Adey, M., & Rose, T. L. (1982). Screening tests for geriatric depression. *Clinical Gerontologist, 1*, 37-43.

Cai, D., Giles, H., & Noels, K. (1998). Elderly perceptions of communication with older and younger adults in China: Implications for mental health. *Journal of Applied Communication Research, 26*, 32-51.

Chang, H.C. (1997). Language and words: Communication and the Analects of Confucius. *Journal of Language and Social Psychology, 16*, 107-131.

Chow, N. (1999). Diminishing filial piety and the changing role and status of the elders in Hong Kong. *Hallym International Journal of Aging, 1*, 67-77.

Coupland, N., Coupland, J., & Giles, H. (1991). *Language, society, and the elderly.* Oxford: Blackwell.

Edwards, H., & Giles, H. (1998). Prologue on two dimensions: The risk and management of intergenerational communication. *Journal of Applied Communication Research, 26*, 1-12.

Fox, S., & Giles, H. (1993). Accommodating intergenerational contact: A critique and theoretical model. *Journal of Aging Studies, 7*, 423-451.

Gallois, C., Giles, H., Ota, H., Pierson, H.D., Ng, S.H., Lim, T-S., Maher, J., Somera, L., Ryan, E.B., & Harwood, J. (1999). Intergenerational communication across the Pacific Rim: The impact of filial piety. In J-C. Lasry, J. Adair, & K. Dion (Eds.), *Latest contributions to cross-cultural psychology* (pp. 192-211). Lisse, The Netherlands: Swets & Zeitlinger.

Giles, H. (1999). Managing dilemmas in the "silent revolution": A call to arms! *Journal of Communication, 49*, 170-182.

Giles, H., Coupland, N., & Coupland, J. (Eds.) (1991). *The contexts of accommodation.* New York: Cambridge University Press.

Giles, H., Harwood, J., Pierson, H.B., Clement, R., & Fox, S. (1998). Stereotypes of the elderly and evaluations of patronizing speech: A cross-cultural foray. In R.K. Agnihotri, A.L. Khanna, & I. Sachdev (Eds.), *Social psychological perspectives on second language learning* (pp. 151-186). (Research in applied linguistics series IV). New Delhi: Sage.

Giles, H., Liang, B., Noels, K.A., & McCann, R.M. (in press). Communicating across and within generations: Taiwanese, Chinese-Americans, and Euro-Americans' perceptions of communication. *Journal of Asian Pacific Communication.*

Giles, H., Noels, K.A., Ota, H., Ng., S.H., Gallois, C., Ryan, E.B., Williams, A., Lim, T-S., Somera, L. Tao, H., Lim, T.-S., & Sachdev, I. (2000). Age vitality across 11 nations. *Journal of Multilingual & Multicultural Development, 21*, 308-323.

Giles, H., Noels, K.A., Williams, A., Lim, T-S., Ng, S.H., Ryan, E.B., Somera, L., & Ota, H. (2000). *Intergenerational communication across cultures: Young people's perceptions of conversations with family elders, non-family elders, and same-age peers.* Manuscript submitted for review.

Giles, H., & Williams, A. (1994). Patronizing the young: Forms and evaluations. *International Journal of Aging and Human Development, 39*, 33-53.

Grams, A., & Albee, G.W. (1995). Primary prevention in the service of aging. In L.A. Bond, S.J. Cutler, & A. Grams (Eds.), *Promoting successful and productive aging* (pp. 5-35). Thousand Oaks, CA: Sage.

Gudykunst, W. B., & Matsumoto, Y. (1996). Cross-cultural variability of communication in personal relationships. In W. B. Gudykunst, S. Ting-Toomey, & T. Nishida (Eds.), *Communication in personal relationships across cultures* (pp. 19-56). Thousand Oaks, CA: Sage.

Harwood, J., Giles, H., Clément, R., Pierson, H., & Fox, S. (1994). Perceived vitality of age categories in California and Hong Kong. *Journal of Multilingual and Multicultural Development, 15*, 311-318.

Harwood, J., Giles, H., Fox, S., Ryan, E.B., & Williams, A. (1993). Patronizing speech and reactive responses. *Journal of Applied Communication Research, 21*, 211-226.

Harwood, J., Giles, H., McCann, R.M., Cai, D., Somera, L, Ng, S-H., Gallois, C., & Noels, K.A. (in press). Older adults' trait ratings of three age groups around the Pacific Rim. *Journal of Cross-Cultural Gerontology.*

Harwood, J., Giles, H., & Ryan, E.B. (1995). Aging, communication, and intergroup theory: Social identity and intergenerational communication. In J.F. Nussbaum & J. Coupland (Eds.), *Handbook of communication and aging research* (pp. 133-160). Mahwah, NJ: Erlbaum.

Harwood, J., Giles, H., Ota, H., Pierson, H.D., Gallois, C., Ng, S.H., Lim, T-S., & Somera, L. (1996). College students' trait ratings of three age groups around the Pacific Rim. *Journal of Cross-Cultural Gerontology, 11*, 307-317.

Harwood, J., & Williams, A. (1998). Expectations for communication with positive and negative subtypes of older adults. *International Journal of Aging and Human Development, 47*, 11-33.

Hewstone, M., & Giles, H. (1986). Social groups and social stereotypes in intergroup communication: Review and model of intergroup communication breakdown. In W.B. Gudykunst (Ed.), *Intergroup communication* (pp. 10-26). London: Edward Arnold.

Ho, D. Y-F. (1994). Filial piety, authoritarian moralism, and cognitive conservatism in Chinese societies. *Genetic, Social, and General Psychology Monographs, 120*, 347-365.

Hummert, M.L., Garstka, T.A., Shaner, J.L., & Strahm, S. (1994). Stereotypes of the elderly held by young, middle-aged and elderly adults. *Journal of Gerontology: Psychological Sciences, 49*, 240-249.

Ingersoll-Dayton, B., & Saengtienchai, C. (1999). Respect for older persons in Asia: Stability and change. *International Journal of Aging and Human Development, 48*, 113-130.

Kiefer, C.W. (1992). Aging in Eastern cultures: A historical overview. In T.R. Cole, D.D. Van Tassel, & R. Kastenbaum (Eds.), *Handbook of the humanities and aging* (pp. 96-123). New York: Springer.

Kim, U. (1994). Individualism and collectivism: Conceptual clarification and elaboration. In U. Kim, H.C. Triandis, C. Kagitcibais, S-C Choi, & G. Yoon (Eds.), *Individualism and collectivism: Theory, method, and application* (pp. 19-40). Thousand Oaks: Sage.

Kite, M.E., & Johnson, B.T. (1988). Attitudes toward older and younger adults: A meta-analysis. *Psychology and Aging, 3*, 233-244.

Knodel, J, Saengtienchai, C., & Sittitrai, W. (1995). Living arrangements of the elderly in Thailand: Views of the populace. *Journal of Cross Cultural Gerontology, 10*, 79-111.

Koyano, W. (1989). Japanese attitudes toward the elderly: A review of research findings. *Journal of Cross-Cultural Gerontology, 4*, 335-345.

Koyano, W. (1999). Population aging, changes in living arrangement, and the new long term care system in Japan. *Journal of Sociology and Social Welfare, 26*, 155-167.

Levy, B.R. (1999). The inner self of the Japanese elderly: A defense against negative stereotypes of aging. *International Journal of Aging and Human Development, 48*, 131-144.

Levy, B.R., Hausdorff, J.M., Hencke, R., & Wei, J.J. (2000). Reducing cardiovascular stress with positive self-stereotypes of aging. *Journal of Gerontology: Psychological Sciences, 55B*, 205-213.

Levy, B.R., & Langer, E. (1994). Aging from negative stereotypes: Successful memory in China and among the American deaf. *Journal of Personality and*

Social Psychology, 66, 989-997.

Madey, S.F. (Ed.) (2000). The social psychology of aging. *Basic and Applied Social Psychology, 22,* 133-261.

Martin, L. G. (1988). The aging of Asia. *Journal of Gerontology: Social Sciences, 43,* 99-113.

Masataka, N. (2000). *Oiwa koushite tsukurareru: Kokorotokaradano kareihenka (People age in this way: Psychological and physical ageing).* Tokyo: Chukoshinsho.

Matsumoto, D. (1999). Culture and self: An empirical assessment of Markus and Kitayama's theory of independent and interdependent self-construal. *Asian Journal of Social Psychology, 2,* 289-310.

McCann, R.M, & Giles, H. (in press). Agism and the workplace: A communication perspective. In T. Nelson (Ed.), *Agism.* Boston: MIT Press.

McGee, J., & Barker, M. (1982). Deference and dominance in old age: An exploration in social theory. *International Journal of Aging and Human Development, 15,* 247-262.

Ng, S.H., Liu, J.H., Weatherall, A., & Loong, C.S.F. (1997). Younger adults' communication experiences and contact with elders and peers. *Human Communication Research, 24,* 82-108.

Ng, S.H., Loong, C.S.F., Liu, J,H., & Weatherall, A. (2000). Will the young support the old? An individual- and family-level study of filial obligations in two New Zealand cultures. *Asian Journal of Social Psychology, 3,* 163-182.

Ng, S.H., Weatherall, A., Liu, J.H., & Loong, S.F.C. (1998). *Ages ahead: Promoting inter-generational relationships.* Wellington, New Zealand: Victoria University Press.

Noels, K., Giles, H., Cai, D., & Turay, L. (1999). Intergenerational communication and health in the United States and the People's Republic of China. *South Pacific Journal of Psychology, 10,* 120-134.

Noels, K., Giles, H., Gallois, C., & Ng, S.H. (in press). Intergenerational communication and health across the Pacific Rim. In M.L. Hummert & J.F. Nussbaum (Eds.), *Communication, aging, and health: Multidisciplinary perspectives.* Mahwah, NJ: Erlbaum.

Noor Al-Deen, H.S. (Ed.) (1997). *Cross-cultural communication and aging in the United States.* Mahwah, NJ: Erlbaum

Nussbaum, J.F. (1985). Successful aging: A communication model. *Communication Quarterly, 33,* 262-269.

Nussbaum, J.F., & Coupland, J. (Eds.) (1995). *Handbook of communication and aging research.* Mahwah, NJ: Erlbaum.

Ota, H. (2001). *Intergenerational communication in Japan and the United States: Debunking the myth of respect for older adults in contemporary Japan.* University of California, Santa Barbara: Ph.D. dissertation.

Ota, H., Giles, H., & Gallois, C. (2001). *Age stereotypes and vitality in Japan and Australia.* Manuscript submitted under review.

Ota, H., Harwood, J., Williams, A., & Takai, J. (2000). A cross-cultural analysis of age identity in Japan and the United States. *Journal of Multilingual and Multicultural Development, 21,* 33-41.

Paoletti, I. (1998). *Being an older woman: A case study in the social production of identity.* Mahwah, NJ: Erlbaum.

Pushkar, D., & Arbuckle, T. (1998). Interventions to improve cognitive, emotional, and social competence in late maturity. In D. Pushkar, W. Bukowski, A. Schwartzmann, D. Stack, & D. White (Eds.), *Improving competence across the lifespan* (pp.159-176). New York: Plenum.

Ryan, E.B., Giles, H., Bartolucci, G., & Henwood, K. (1986). Psycholinguistic and social psychological components of communication by and with the elderly. *Language and Communication, 6*, 1-24.

Ryan, E.B., Hummert, M.L., & Boich, L. (1995). Communication predicaments of aging: Patronizing behavior toward older adults. *Journal of Language and Social Psychology, 13*, 144-166.

Sharps, M. J., Price-Sharps, J. L., & Hanson, J. (1998). Attitudes of young adults toward older adults: Evidence from the United States and Thailand. *Educational Gerontology, 24*, 655-660.

Strom, R.D. & Strom, S.K. (1996). Developing curricula for grandparents in Japan. *Educational Gerontology, 22*, 781-894.

Strom, R.D., Strom, S.K., Wang, C-W., Shen, Y-L., Griswold, D., Chan, H-S., & Yang, C-Y. (1999). Grandparents in the United States and the Republic of China: A comparison of generations and cultures. *International Journal of Aging and Human Development, 49*, 279-317.

Sung, K. (1995). Measures and dimensions of filial piety in Korea. *The Gerontologist, 35*, 240-247.

Tajfel, H., & Turner, J. C. (1986). The social psychology of intergroup behavior. In S. Worchel & W.G. Austin (Eds.), *Psychology of intergroup relations* (pp. 7-24). Chicago: Nelson-Hall.

Tien-Hyatt, J.L. (1987). Self-perceptions of aging across cultures: Myth or reality? *International Journal of Aging and Human Development, 24*, 129-148.

Tobin, J.J. (1987). The American idealization of old age in Japan. *The Gerontologist, 27*, 53-58.

Triandis, H.C., Chen, X.P., & Chan, D. (1998).Scenarios for the measurement of collectivism and individualism. *Journal of Cross-Cultural Psychology, 29*, 275-89.

Triandis, H.C., Dunnette, M.D., & Hough, L.M. (Eds.) (1994). *Handbook of industrial and organizational psychology, Vol. 4* (2nd Ed.). Palo Alto, CA: Consulting Psychologists Press.

Turner, J.C. (1987). *Rediscovering the social group: A self-categorization theory.* Oxford, Blackwell.

Uleman, M.S., Rhee, E., Bardoliwalla, N., Semin, G., & Toyama, M. (2000). The relational self: Closeness to ingroups depends on who they are, culture and type of closeness. *Asian Journal of Social Psychology, 3*, 1-18.

Williams, A. (1996). Young people's evaluations of intergenerational versus peer underaccommodation: Sometimes older is better? *Journal of Language and Social Psychology, 15*, 291-311.

Williams, A., & Coupland, N. (1998). Epilogue: The socio-political framing of communication and aging. *Journal of Applied Communication Research, 26*, 139-154.

Williams, A., & Giles, H. (1996). Intergenerational conversations: Young adults' retrospective accounts. *Human Communication Research, 23*, 220-250.

Williams, A., & Giles, H. (1998). Communication of ageism. In M. Hecht (Ed.),

Communication prejudice (pp. 136-160). Thousand Oaks: Sage.

Williams, A., & Nussbaum, J.F. (2001). *Intergenerational communication across the lifespan.* Mahwah, NJ: Erlbaum.

Williams, A., Ota, H., Giles, H., Pierson, H.D., Gallois, C., Ng, S.H., Lim, T-S., Ryan, E.B., Somera, L., Maher, J., & Harwood, J. (1997). Young peoples' beliefs about intergenerational communication: An initial cross-cultural comparison. *Communication Research, 24,* 370-393.

Williams, J. E., Pandey, J., Best, D. L., Morton, K. R., & Pande, N. (1992). Young adults' view of old adults in India and the United States. In S. Iwawaki, Y. Kashima, & K. Leung (Eds.), *Innovations in cross-cultural psychology* (pp. 227-234). Amsterdam: Swets & Zeitlinger.

Yeh, Y-h., Williams, A., & Maruyama, M. (1998). Approving and disapproving grandmothers and strangers: Young Taiwanese and American comparisons. *Journal of Asian Pacific Communication, 8,* 125-150.

Yum, J.O. (1988). The impact of Confucianism on interpersonal relations and communication patterns in East Asia. *Communication Monographs, 55,* 374-388.

Zhang, Y.B., & Hummert, M.L. (in press). Harmonies and tensions in Chinese intergenerational communication: Younger and older adults' accounts. *Journal of Asian Pacific Communication.*

Acknowledgements

We are grateful to the many scholars around the Pacific Rim who have contributed to our ongoing collaborative efforts, including Beatrice Liang, Deborah Cai, Cynthia Gallois, Jake Harwood, Tae-Seop Lim, John C. Maher, Sik Hung Ng, Herbert Pierson, Ellen B. Ryan, Itesh Sachdev, LilnaBeth Somera, Hongyin Tao, Lisa Turay, and Angie Williams. In addition, we appreciate greatly the University of California Pacific Rim Agency for its continuing support of our research program as well as Matt Kaplan and Nancy Henkin for their comments on earlier drafts of this chapter.

Notes

1 National research sites contributing data referred to in this chapter are: Australia, Canada, New Zealand, U.S.A., Singapore, South Korea, Thailand, The Philippines, Hong Kong, Taiwan, People's Republic of China, and Japan.

2 These contexts were Hong, South Korea, Japan, and The Philippines on the one hand, and the United States of America, Canada, Australia, and New Zealand on the other.

3 For a specification of the other eight research sites, see the previous footnote.

Strengthening Intergenerational Bonds through Volunteerism-- A Global Perspective

By Anne O'Sullivan

Introduction

The world-wide aging phenomenon that Ambassador Julia Alvarez, a member of the Permanent Mission to the United Nations from the Dominican Republic, has termed an "AgeQuake" (Alvarez, 1999), will profoundly affect the way societies of the future function. In every corner of the world the decisions we reach on social, political and economic issues will be — indeed, are currently being — influenced by this unique and dramatic shift in worldwide demographics. The effects of this so-called silent revolution, "...are being felt by every individual, family, neighborhood and nation throughout the world" (U.N., 1999).

One of the most significant outcomes of the combined effects of an increase in the population of older people, a reduced birth rate, a rise in out-migration, and general mobility — particularly among the young — is the loss of opportunities for frequent, casual interaction among generations. As the day-to-day lives of the generations become separated and the social values of one generation conflict with those of another, tensions mount. This is particularly true in countries where generations perceive that they are in competition for scarce resources. This separation leads to stereotyping and other behavior that exacerbates the lack of understanding and tension between generations.

The phenomenon of the AgeQuake can be viewed as a problem for societies attempting to provide adequate health care, assure financial security and address issues of poverty and discrimination against older persons. It can also be looked upon as an opportunity, however. In designating 1999 as the International Year of Older Persons, the United Nations General Assembly resolution declared that the Year was being observed, "...in recognition of humanity's demographic coming of age and the promise it holds for maturing attitudes and capabilities in social, economic, cultural and spiritual undertakings, not least for global peace and development in the next century." The theme for the International Year of Older Persons, "Towards a Society for All Ages," speaks to the potential to utilize the skills and experience of older citizens in resourceful ways that, in combination with the contributions of other generations, enhance the quality of life for everyone.

Intergenerational Volunteerism

The prospects for using volunteer opportunities to build and enhance relationships among the generations is, of course, strongly influenced by the culture in which those relationships arise and by the traditional roles of the generations within that culture. In addition to attitudes toward other generations, cultural attitudes toward socio-economic status, ethnic heritage and the concept of volunteerism itself, must all be taken into account in developing programs and policies related to promoting specific types of relationships among individuals from differing generations.

Volunteerism becomes increasingly important in a world where the role of government in service provision is diminishing. In areas as diverse as Australia, North America and Eastern Europe, governments have begun to back away from providing direct services (de Vaus & Qu, 1997). However, these countries all have strong traditions of volunteerism that may enable NGOs (non-governmental organizations) to take up the slack.

In contrast, in the transitional economies of the former Soviet Union, where government services are also shrinking, the use of the word "volunteer" may be associated with the social policies of the communist regime and, therefore, have a negative connotation. In that part of the world, a wide gulf often exists between the older and younger generations as a result of the rapid social and economic changes which have occurred in recent years. A representative of the Elderly Women's Activities Center (EWAC) in Lithuania states, "Young people often say that older people are simply a drain on the country's resources and complain that the work of the young pays the pensions of the old." The EWAC is changing that perception through promoting and supporting volunteerism among its members (Urban Age, 2000a). Until recently, the older generations spent their lives under an economic system in which the government provided all-inclusive health and welfare services. They were hard hit — both financially and socially — by the change to a market economy. The younger, more entrepreneurial generations have a completely different frame of reference. They see the opportunities inherent in a free market economy and have been generally willing to take on the risks inherent in that system. Furthermore, they see governmental involvement in their lives as a negative. These attitudes clearly impact on the development of intergenerational volunteer programs.

Several approaches at bridging this generational gap are currently under way in Eastern Europe. As reported in a series of articles entitled, *Growing in Numbers, Growing in Strength: Aging, A Special Report* published by *Urban Age* (2000b), "Experts with decades of experience and young people with ideas for changing the world," met in Budapest "to talk about what it means to grow old in today's world." A major focus of this meeting was a competition among architectural students who submitted urban designs which accommodated the needs of older persons. It was reported that, "...the elements of a new paradigm....emerged, where longer life is not a burden but an opportunity, where society as a whole embraces its senior citizens fully, and where the young and the old intermingle and recognize each others needs" (Urban Age, 2000b, 5).

Slovenia has formed the National Network of Intergenerational Groups for Older People to provide opportunities for older persons to interact with younger generations through volunteer activities. In Western Europe the 1:4 Project (named for the proportion of Europeans who will be over 50 in 2025) was created by NGOs and broadcasters from the United Kingdom, Ireland, Denmark and The Netherlands to develop a documentary in which older persons join young environmental activists in lobbying and demonstrating for their cause. In Estonia, where current law mandates that families must take care of their older relatives and relieves the government of any responsibility for providing health, social and economic services to older persons, the Gerontologic and Geriatric Association (EGGA) is working to effect a governmental policy change which impacts on intergenerational relationships (Urban Age, 2000c).

In many countries the tradition of formal volunteerism has arisen within a socially sanctioned classification based on socio-economic class and ethnic/racial heritage. Within that context, volunteerism has generally been motivated by two major forces: (i) a *noblesse oblige* philosophy, and/or (ii) the religious concept of *charity*. In both, an implicit distinction is made between "eligible receivers" and "eligible providers" of volunteer services. Although exceptions abound, the traditional *noblesse oblige* philosophy mandates that those in the higher socio-economic classes are the providers of volunteer services while the poor, and in many cases, indigenous peoples, are the recipients. A strong correlation can be shown between participation in formal volunteering and socio-economic class, with those in the higher socio-economic groups almost twice as likely to participate in formal volunteering (Davis Smith, 1998). The same is true of age distinctions: the very young and the very old are more likely to be seen as recipients while those in the middle generations are usually categorized as providers.

This serves as a reminder that generalizations must always be used with caution. The world comprises a vast array of countries that are both multi-lingual and multi-cultural. While employing generalizations may be reasonable in discussing issues in broad terms, examples can be found to contradict those generalizations in every country. Furthermore, globalization and technological advances are rapidly bringing changes to all parts of the world. Marginalized people in every country are recognizing that their past does not have to be their future, and change is occurring. Older persons are, therefore, more likely to be recruited as volunteers in greater numbers today than ever before.

It is not just that there are more older persons; recent global events and initiatives are reinforcing the trend. The International Year of Older Person (U.N., 1999), the International Year of Volunteers (2001) and initiatives like the Retired and Senior Volunteer Program International highlight the skills, time and talent of older persons and the ways by which they can stay integrated in a developing society. As younger generations recognize the contribution older volunteers are making, more intergenerational and multigenerational volunteer opportunities will be realized.

One of the most powerful mechanisms for breaking down stereotypical and prejudicial thinking is ongoing contact, particularly contact in which persons from differing social groups are able to work together toward a common goal. Volunteering is a powerful mechanism for bringing about that scenario. Volunteerism provides:

(i) a service which is useful to the recipient;
(ii) a way for volunteers to express their desire to "do good"; and
(iii) a way to strengthen the social fabric of the community.

All of these contribute to the building of strong and cohesive communities as well as play a role in the building of social capital and economic regeneration. In addition to the obvious economic and social value of providing needed services, this type of interaction between generations provides emotional support, allays loneliness and isolation, and can improve both the mental and physical health of both the recipient and the volunteer. (Granville, 2000; Davis Smith, 1999).

Relevant Concepts

Intergenerational vs. multigenerational

A distinction is often made between the use of the terms intergenerational and multigenerational. The former is meant to denote the relationship between two groups — e.g. children and older persons — while the latter is reserved for discussions which include all generations. Given the crucial role "middle" generations play in the support and care of both the very young and the very old, it behooves us not to exclude them from discussions of generational relationships. Many specific programs and policies are directed at bringing together children/youth and older persons. These are properly termed intergenerational. When discussing overall relationships between generations, however, the term multigenerational is more appropriate since it is presumed that the overarching objective is to develop and support good relationships among all generations.

Tangible personal and societal benefits accrue from ongoing, meaningful and supportive relationships between generations. These benefits have practical implications, such as when grandparents take on child-caring roles in the absence of parents, when adult children provide home maintenance services or take on driving responsibilities for an elderly parent, or when young adults assist older persons in the use of computers and other modern communication equipment. Other, less tangible benefits can also accrue as a result of any type of generational relationship. Be it the practical types of interaction cited above or more casual social connections, these less tangible benefits can be significant on both a personal and societal level. The most obvious social benefit is providing an opportunity for different generations to gain knowledge and understanding about one another. It is a truism that animosity toward those who are different is nurtured through a lack of familiarity. Ignorance about the "other" fosters stereotypes and prejudicial attitudes. This is as true with relations across generations as it is across ethnic, racial, religious and other types of social characteristics.

Formal vs. informal volunteering

How volunteerism is defined — indeed, whether the word/concept is even recognized — differs from society to society. Informal volunteerism exists in all societies albeit in differing forms and under different names. What the residents of the Marshall Islands call *kumit,* for example, is essentially what those in the United States or Canada would term informal volunteerism — i.e., working together with others in the community toward a specific goal without expectation of compensation. Formal volunteering is less universal. In some parts of the world where a history of forced labor haunts segments of a society, formal volunteerism can be seen as a negative concept which means little more than being asked to work without wages. (Davis Smith, 1999)

When attempting to develop formal volunteer programs in South Africa, for instance, such stereotypes were the immediate cause of a quickly apparent problem. The black population, which had been in a servile position for years and which was still economically disadvantaged, was not willing to enter into a formal volunteering structure which, in effect, asked them once again to work without adequate compensation. Although many white citizens were willing to volunteer their services in the black community, the vast socio-economic differences between them made it difficult and would have perpetuated the *noblesse oblige* mentality of the apartheid era. The black communities did, of course, have a long tradition of informal mutual aid to which they were committed, although, given the mass population shifts in the post-apartheid period, many of those traditions had broken down. The difficulty was the formal commitment.

Every family, clan, community and society survives through some level of implicit mutual support system. When family or community members voluntarily provide support to those within their immediate social structure without any outside stimulus to do so, it is generally categorized as *informal* volunteering. Informal volunteering is thought of as internally motivated by the desire to help those we care about and, presumably, in the hope that others will reciprocate when we need help. Clearly, in addition to any inborn propensity toward social cooperation that might exist, motivation may also be socially constructed though the values and ethos of the community. Informal volunteerism involves only two entities—a provider and a recipient— and is thought of as an informal exchange of services between the two.

Formal volunteerism occurs when a third entity becomes part of the exchange. That third component usually entails some type of organizational structure which recruits, screens and trains volunteers, identifies those who could benefit from the provision of volunteer services, makes appropriate matches between the two and then monitors the exchange on an ongoing basis to assure that the objectives of the volunteer project are being met.

Reciprocity and equity

As part of its welcome to the 1999 "International Year of Older Persons," the United Nations declared that the year's theme, "a society for all ages," is one that enables the generations to invest in one another and share in the fruits of that investment, guided by the twin principles of **reciprocity** and **equity**" [emphasis added].

Reciprocity

The dictionary defines reciprocity as a "mutual exchange." Reciprocity among generations means that a relatively even exchange of support—emotional, physical and practical—takes place. It assumes mutual respect across generations as well as concern by each generation for the personal, social and economic issues that affect other generations. When a grandmother cares for her grandchildren so that her daughter can earn a salary and, in return, is provided with services which she is unable to afford or access on her own, that is a reciprocal relationship.

More generally, volunteerism that involves "mutual aid" such as the tradition of *Confianza* in Mexico, is, by definition reciprocal (Davis Smith, 1999). The reciprocal system known as Service Credits (or Time Dollars in the United States) epitomizes the concept of reciprocity. In this systematized form of mutual aid, individuals provide a specified service for a specific number of hours or offer goods of a specified value to another member of the community. In return, they garner "credits" in the form of an equal number of hours of service or the value of time expended converted into needed goods (Cahn and Rowe, 1992). The reciprocal services/goods may be an equal exchange between two parties or, on a more complex level, it may involve other members of the community in a kind of "round robin" exchange of services. The system is analogous to depositing money in a bank. Although we expect to be able to withdraw the exact amount of money we have deposited, the actual dollars we receive are not the same bills we deposited. So an elderly man might provide house-painting services for a young couple in return for someone fixing his roof or plowing his fields. This is usually a formal type of volunteering in that some third entity keeps track of hours banked, owed, and utilized.

Equity

Equity, on the other hand, is defined as "fairness." It implies that all generations within a society are treated fairly and given equal access to opportunities to fulfil their potential, irrespective of age or generational affiliation. The *United Nations Principles for Older Persons* (1991), for example, encourage governments to develop policies and programs which enhance older persons' dignity, independence, participation and integration in society, access to care and protection, and opportunities for self-fulfillment—characteristics which persons of all generations want their governments to make available to them. Similarly, the *Four Dimensions of the Conceptual Framework* developed by the United Nations for the International Year of Older Persons in 1999 are categorized as:

(i)   The social, economic, physical and emotional situation of older persons;
(ii) Opportunities for life-long development;
(iii) Enhancement of multi-generational relationships (and reduction of

circumstances which promote tensions between generations); and
(iv) Consideration of older persons' needs and abilities within the context of socio-economic development.

These United Nations documents are meant to provide guidance and a firm basis for the development of programs and policies that support equity across generations and to assure that older persons are not left behind as countries move toward modernization and economic independence.

Types of Intergenerational Volunteerism

Intergenerational volunteering falls into three categories:

Seniors providing volunteer services for young people

Examples of this type of intergenerational volunteering abound. In Colombia, as in other countries, older volunteers work in hospitals with newborn infants and other children, in schools as teachers' assistants, in homes as baby sitters for working parents, and they conduct special classes or tours related to their past work experiences.

Young people providing volunteer services for seniors

This type of intergenerational volunteering is also quite common. Younger volunteers often visit hospitals, nursing homes and senior housing facilities to provide company for homebound older persons, assist professional staff and/or engage in ancillary activities such as circulating books, showing videos and teaching computer skills, for example.

Young and old working together on volunteer projects

This type of intergenerational volunteering, though less common, is perhaps the most powerful way of cementing relationships between generations. Working toward successfully completing a common goal builds strong relationships among everyone involved and, unlike the two previous types of intergenerational volunteering, old and young come together as equals rather than as provider and receiver of services. Each then has the opportunity to experience the strengths and competence of other generations, thus building respect and understanding.

Environmental projects or other volunteer opportunities which require a combination of experience, knowledge and physical stamina work well using this type of volunteer relationship. For instance, older engineers or science teachers can provide the know-how for an environmental project, but they may no longer have the physical stamina which allows them to spend long hours in the field collecting data. That task is ideally suited to younger volunteers, and the project provides an opportunity for the young to learn from the old, thereby utilizing their knowledge and skill which, in turn, lets older volunteers know that they are valued and useful.

Home construction such as that done by Habitat for Humanity is another good example. Older volunteers can contribute experience and knowledge and/or provide support services to the construction workers while the younger volunteers can do the more strenuous construction jobs that require strength and stamina. Older persons might do the painting, landscaping or help to clean up, for instance. Or they may do administrative or coordination jobs or provide lunch for the construction workers. The combination makes use of the strengths of both groups in a cooperative effort that benefits society.

Conclusion

The development of intergenerational volunteer programs can be a valuable component in strengthening relationships between and among generations. The legitimacy of the interchange of volunteer services is very useful in overcoming the awkwardness of "forced" social interactions by providing opportunities for casual contact between the generations, the ability to work together toward a common goal, and the wherewithal to reach that goal. This is true whether the provider of services is a young person, an older person or whether the generations are volunteering together on a project. In addition, all parties participate in developing social capital and thus bettering their communities. Government policies can encourage this process by providing financial and other resources, by developing and enforcing anti-discrimination policies, and by providing incentives for persons of all ages to become involved in volunteering. The media can assist by avoiding stereotyping and projecting positive images of all generations as well as by educating the public about opportunities for intergenerational volunteering.

Intergenerational volunteering is a win-win situation in which everyone benefits.

References

Alvarez, J. T. (1999) Reflections on an AgeQuake: Selected quotes from the writings of Ambassador Julia T. Alvarez.

Cahn, E. S., and Rowe, J. (1992*). Time dollars: The new currency that enables Americans to turn their hidden resource-time into personal security and community renewal.* Emmaus, Pa.: Rodale.

Davis Smith, J. (1998). The 1997 National Survey of Volunteering. Institute of Volunteering Research (UK).

Davis Smith, J. (1999) Discussion paper for International Year of Volunteers. United Nations.

de Vaus, D. & Qu (1997) Intergenerational exchange: Bulletin on ageing Nos. 2, 3. Department of Economic and Social Affairs, United Nations Secretariat.

Granville, G. (2000) The experience of older volunteers in school-based projects. *Voluntary Action, 2, 3.*

United Nations. (1999). *Ageless thinking in the next millennium.* U.N. document.

United Nations. (1991). *The United Nations principles for older persons.* U.N. document.

Urban Age. (2000a). *The aging world as a community.* Soros Supported Projects, p. 2.

Urban Age. (2000b*). Growing in numbers, growing in strength: The elderly women's activity center.* Soros Supported Projects, p. 5.

Urban Age. (2000c). *National networks of intergenerational groups for older people.* Soros Supported Projects, p. 7.

Employing Proverbs to Explore Intergenerational Relations Across Cultures[1]

Matthew S. Kaplan, Ph.D.

Introduction

There is an old Lebanese saying, "A proverb never tells a lie" (Freyha, 1974, p. 642). Drawing upon the compelling nature of proverbs and the intrinsic truths they imply, this chapter aims to explore culturally diverse conceptions about aging and intergenerational exchange.

According to the standard dictionary definition, a "proverb" is "a short saying in common use that strikingly expresses some obvious truth or familiar experience" (Guralnik & Solomon, 1980, p. 1144). The condensed nature of proverbs allows them to be interpreted again and again, across time and in different situations. They are interesting because they not only tap into universal themes in the human condition, such as the physiological rhythms of the human life cycle, but they also vary in ways that appear to reflect the specific cultural contexts in which they arise.

An examination of proverbs and popular sayings, particularly in societies that have a strong oral tradition, can yield valuable insights into how people think and live. In the Latino community, popular sayings are known as "dichos." Burciaga (1997) refers to:

> The popularity of dichos (popular sayings), with their wonderful style and manner of teaching: they offer a way to make pronouncements, edicts, and judgments, to affirm the culture's self-evident truths,

fundamental principles, and rules of conduct. Dichos represent the popular mainstream wisdom of the common people in their daily lives. They seek to form a common bond of mutual understanding and respect in society.... Dichos remind us that long before schools were invented, children were taught at home with proverbs (p. xiii).

Farghal (1995) points out that, "As the mirror of a culture, proverbs are efficient linguistic means to express national convictions, ideals, and values" (p. 19). The idea of drawing connections between language (in this case, proverbs and common phrases) and people's sensibilities about intergenerational exchange finds support from an existing tradition that explores culturally diverse meanings and associations through linguistic analysis. Anna Wierzbicka, in her book, *Understanding Cultures Through Their Key Words* (1997), demonstrates how the insights gained from comparative linguistic analyses can be beneficial for cultural analysis. To make her point, she invokes the words of noted linguist Edward Sapir: "Language (is) a symbolic guide to culture (Sapir, 1949, p. 162)." She further notes that language provides a window through which to view "historically transmitted patterns of meaning" (Wierzbicka, 1997, p. 21).

Cultural geographers Terry Jordan-Bychov and Mona Domosh (1999) provide further discourse about the relationship between language and culture:

Language contains the very essence of culture and provides the single most common variable by which different cultural groups are identified. A mutually agreed-upon system of symbolic communication, language offers the main means by which learned customs and skills pass from one generation to the next (p. 181).

If we accept the above propositions, then a comparative investigation of words and phrases in different languages could be quite useful as a tool for drawing inferences about how, from different cultural contexts, the aging process is viewed, and how people of different generations perceive and relate to each other.

Before launching this investigation of proverbs and common phrases, however, several words of caution are in order. Despite the power of proverbs, which lies in their widespread appeal and perceived accuracy, it is problematic to assume that proverbs necessarily reflect underlying "truths" about people and societies. For one thing, some proverbs are objectionable on the grounds that they convey stereotypical and defamatory notions about groups of people, whether distinguished as a function of ethnicity, age, or some other characteristic (Nuessel, 2000). Like all stereotypes, because they are so condensed and pithy, they erroneously obscure individual differences. Another problem with proverbs is raised by

Epstein (1997) who notes that many proverbs coexist with their exact opposites or with proverbs that give different advice. He thereby suggests that there are limits to the degree to which a review of proverbs can yield reliable, consistent insights about people's values and actions. Various other issues in the study of proverbs have yet to be fully considered and thus bear further investigation. For example, there are unanswered questions in regard to the extent to which people actually adhere to proverbs, and when and how they invoke them and why.

Notwithstanding the complexities and risks associated with an analysis of proverbs, the current study ventures to employ proverbs (and common phrases) to explore perceptions of intergenerational relations across cultures. Most of the proverbs and phrases noted in this study were obtained through a survey conducted with native speakers of 26 languages. Survey findings are supplemented with examples of proverbs in different languages found through a review of the literature. Based on these two streams of investigation, several themes are presented for how attitudes toward intergenerational phenomena are reflected in language. Insofar as neither of these methods constitutes an intensive or exhaustive linguistic analysis, the examples provided in this chapter are intended merely to be suggestive of culturally diverse ways of viewing intergenerational relations.

Methods

The primary method of investigation was the "Vocabularies of Intergenerational Exchange" survey (see Appendix A). This survey tool was distributed widely to the student and faculty body of Hawaii Pacific University, a university with a distinctively international student body.[2] Respondents obtained copies of the surveys from information tables in public areas, from their professors (particularly in English Foundation Program classes which consist exclusively of international students), and, for faculty, staff, and club members, through university mailboxes. Those who responded represent a self-selected (non-random) sample.

Those who did respond listed as many popular sayings, proverbs, or phrases they could think of in their native languages (other than English) that relate to the following topics:

- Views about the elderly and the aging process
- Views about young people
- Patterns of communication between different generations[3]

In addition to writing out the sayings and phrases they could recall in their native languages, respondents were asked to provide English translations and write comments about the cultural, philosophical, and historical significance of the proverbs they shared. In a few cases, when contact information was provided, telephone calls were placed to respondents to gain clarification about the sayings they provided and the cultural/national significance of these sayings.

The results were analyzed for content using the following procedure. As a group, the research team (consisting of the author and three undergraduate research assistants) reviewed 20 surveys and jointly endeavored to create categories that were reflective of the basic content of the proverbs and phrases. To determine inter-rater reliability, two research team members independently reviewed another 10 surveys and categorized responses. After comparing categorization decisions, it was determined that the raters were in agreement 77 percent of the time, and disagreements between the independent judges were reconciled. In analyzing the content of the remaining surveys, the entire research team discussed and jointly made categorization decisions for those responses that were vague or which did not clearly fit into one category.[4]

Research team members also searched for proverbs in languages other than English in books, articles, and web sites. Once these resources were obtained, the search for proverbs centered on the topics of the aging process, views about elderly people, views about young people, and patterns of communication between different generations.

Results

Characteristics of survey sample

Surveys were returned by 117 respondents, each of whom was fluent in a language other than English. Of the surveys that were completed, 26 different languages were represented (see Appendix B). Since the number of responses in each language was too small to enable meaningful statistical analyses to be conducted, the languages were re-categorized into five main language groups: Asian (N=80, 67.8 percent), Pacific Island (N=13, 11 percent), Western European (N=20, 16.9 percent), and Eastern European (N=5, 4.2 percent).

Languages that were categorized as Asian include: Cantonese (3), Tegalo and Ilicano (Phillipines, 7), Indonesian (3), Japanese (27), Korean (5), Mandarin (30), Thai (2), Vietnamese (2), Indian (1), and Malay (1). Pacific Island languages included Hawaiian (4), Tongan (4), and Chamuro (indigenous language of Guam, 3). Western European languages included: German (3), Italian (1), French (1), Swedish (6), Spanish (3), Portuguese (4), Finnish (1) and Icelandic (1). Eastern European languages included: Hungarian (1), Romanian (1), Slovak (1), Croatian (1), and Serbian (1).[5]

The asymmetrical nature of this data set, in terms of the high proportion of respondents speaking Asian and Pacific Island languages, is in part an artifact of the location in which the survey was distributed (an international university in Hawaii).

The age of the respondents ranged from 17 to 73, with 84.1 percent fitting into the age range of 17 to 30. In terms of gender, 42 (35.9 percent) of the respondents were male and 70 (59.8 percent) were female; gender information was not provided by five respondents (4.2 percent).

Views about the elderly and the aging process

In investigating how older adults and the aging process were characterized in the proverbs and phrases found in different languages, several basic themes were identified.

- There appear to be more positive than negative characterizations.
- For many of the languages that were considered, there is a juxtaposition of sayings which reflect strikingly positive views toward the elderly and sayings which reflect strikingly negative views.
- ·Characterizations of the elderly and the aging process are rich and varied and draw upon a wide range of metaphors including those tied to the natural environment, animals, and food.

When conducting a content analysis (chi-square analysis) to compare survey responses of a combined Asian and Pacific Island languages group to those of a combined European languages group, no significant differences were found. Furthermore, the themes noted above appear to cut across many of the languages that were considered.

As a group, survey respondents provided over twice as many sayings which convey positive views about elderly people than sayings which convey negative views; 83 of the 117 sayings provided about the elderly (70.9 percent) were positive and 37 (31.6 percent) were negative. Survey responses that indicated positive conceptions about elderly people tended to emphasize the themes of "deserved enjoyment" (N=36), "wisdom/experience" (N=26), "respect" (N=11), "elevated status" (N=6), and "empowerment" (N=4). Sayings conveying negative conceptions about the elderly tended to emphasize themes of "increased dependency" (N=8), "closed mindedness" (N=8), "diminished prestige" (N=7), "social awkwardness" (N=4), and "inevitable death" (N=4). Several of the negative sayings (N=5) consisted of generally derisive statements about the elderly.

Similarly, in terms of the 83 proverbs which respondents provided to characterize the "aging process," most emphasized positive aspects such as the "improvement of skills" (N=41) and the "natural process" of aging (N=23). Sayings which provide more pessimistic appraisals of the aging process tended to emphasize "deterioration and decline" (N=16), and the "unflattering nature of physical change" (N=3).

Some examples of proverbs fitting into these response categories are presented below.

Many of the proverbs reflect views about elderly people that are strikingly positive and hopeful. One theme is the characterization of old age as a time of enjoyment.

Italian [survey]:
> "*La pensione e la seconda giovinezza.*" — "Retirement is like a second childhood."

Japanese [survey]:
> "*Dai ni no jinsei.*" — "The second life." (Respondent's comments: "They (can now) have fun for themselves.")

The following sayings convey the notion that along with old age comes a greater level of wisdom and life experience:

Romanian [survey]:
> "*Batrineùea aduce multa iscusinùa*" — "The older you get the more knowledgeable you are."

Spanish [survey]:
> "*Mas sabe el diablo por viejo que por diablo.*" "The devil knows more because he's old than because he's the devil." (Respondent's comments: "It makes you remember that old people have a lot of knowledge.")

Chinese [survey]:
> "*Wo chi guo de yian bi ni chi guo de fuan hai duo.*" — "I have eaten more salt than you have eaten rice." (Respondent's comments: It's like saying, "I am old enough to have more knowledge and experience than you.")

Sayings and phrases were also found which reflect negative experiences often associated with aging and old age, though these sayings were not as prevalent as those reflecting positive views. The following sayings cast images of loneliness, vulnerability, and struggle.

Swedish:
> "*Unga lever sina liv i flock, vuxna i par, och gamla ensamma.*" — "Youth goes in a flock, manhood in pairs, and old age alone" (Mieder, 1986, p. 558).

Hawaiian [survey]:
> "*Elemakule kama 'ole moe I ke ala.*" — "An oldster who has never reared children sleeps by the roadside."

Hebrew:
> "Youth is a garland of roses, age is a crown of thorns." (Christy, 1888, p. 20).

The following sayings expound the "deterioration and decline" theme:

German [survey]:
"Wer rastet der rostet." — "The person who rests will rust."
French:
"Un homme est aussi vieux que ses arteres." "A man is as old as his arteries." (Davidoff, 1946, p. 8).
Chinese (Mandarin) [Survey]:
"Sheng lau bing si." — "Born, old, sick, die."

A duality of perceptions

There appears to be a pattern of substantial within-language variance in terms of how elderly people are categorized; very positive and very negative statements about aging and the aged were found within each of several of the target languages. Pairs of proverbs are presented below in Italian, Spanish, Lebanese, Swedish, and Korean which reflect this juxtaposition:

Italian:
(pos.) *"Onorate il senno antico."* — "Age commands respect." (Jones, 1963, p. 445).
(neg.) [survey:] *"L'invecchiamento e come ferro alla pioggia-arrugginisce."* — "The aging process is like a piece of iron in the rain. It gets rusty."
Spanish:
(pos.) *"Dichos de los viejitos son evangelios chiquitos."* — "The sayings of our elders should be taken as gospel." (Burciaga, 1997, p. ix).
(neg.) [survey] *"Eres un Carroza"* — You are such a carriage." (Respondent's comments: "Carriage" in this saying refers to the old vehicles used in the past.)
Arabic (Lebanese):
(pos.) "He who has not any old man (in his household), let him buy one." — "An old man in a family is a fount of wisdom and right counsel" (Freyha, 1974, p. 117).
(neg.) "A man of sixty is only good for slaughtering." — Slaughtering is translated literally as "for the knife" (Also in Freyha, 1974, p. 9).

Swedish [surveys]:
(pos.) *"Gammal ar vis."* — "Old is wise." (Respondent's comments: "You gain wisdom with the years.")
(neg.) *"Den gra maffian."* — "The grey mafia." (Respondent's comments: "There is a perception that many old people only care about getting their pension and saving money on rebates.")
Korean [surveys]:

(pos.) "*Yaeshun sal yi dueltae insaeng yi shijhak duep ni da.*" — "Life begins when you are sixty." (Respondent's comments: "We have a special way to count years. The same year comes back after every 60 years....")

(neg.) "*Nhulghumyun jook au yah hahnda.*" — "If I get old, I have to die!"

Consistent with this theme of duality, there appears to be a broad range of conceptions in the literature that examines how age and aging are portrayed in other languages as well. In the English language, for example, there are popular sayings in praise of the virtues of senior adults, such as "The older the wiser," as well as those which degrade the elderly, such as "Out to pasture." (By presenting a metaphor of racehorses that no longer race, this last saying associates retirement with idleness.)

In the United States, such a juxtaposition of perspectives is supported by studies into the nature and range of the stereotypes held about older adults. These indicate that there are mixed perceptions or, as described by Hummert et al. (1994), "multiple stereotypes." In his study of the history of terms used in the English language to represent old people, aging, and the effects of aging, Covey (1988) states: "Terms applied to old age range the full gamut of positive to negative connotations. The negative and positive terminology that has coexisted throughout history represents a duality of perception of the old" (p. 292).

Covey (1988) further contends that the words used to characterize the elderly change over time as a function of socioeconomic changes, changing ideology, and changes in the power and status held by elderly people.

A cursory review of Japanese words and phrases associated with old age similarly indicates multi-dimensional perceptions of aging. In Japanese, the word "*kanreki*," which refers to reaching one's 60th year of age,[6] has positive connotations. Ishii (1991), in referring to the longevity revolution in Japan, states the following:

> In Japan a 60th birthday, '*kanreki*,' is especially celebrated because once it was rare to achieve that age.... Not only do people live well past *kanreki*, they remain active and fulfilled into their 70's and beyond (p. 11).

In contrast to images of senior adults as active and happy, there are certain phrases which paint a different picture of the experience of being a senior adult in Japan. Seo (1991) writes:

> Life after retirement for a *sarariman* ("salaryman" or white collar worker) is relatively unfortunate. Having dedicated heart and soul to work, after retirement they are at a loss for purpose. Some of these men are called "*nureochiba*," "wet dead leaves," since they stick to their wives when they go out (p. 12).

From *"kanreki"* to *"nureochiba,"* such diverse characterizations of elderly people illustrate that there is no singular, unidimensional view about how well the elderly are faring in modern Japan.

Many of the proverbs that were encountered in this study utilize poignant metaphors to generate striking images of the elderly. Examples are provided below of proverbs that allude to certain characteristics of the natural environment, food, animals, industry and body parts to invoke positive as well as negative characterizations of old age and the process of aging, many of which underscore the themes noted above.

Metaphors related to the natural environment
Chinese [survey]:
> *"Lao yuen shian qua bau."* — "Older people are valuable like precious stones."

Spanish (from Mexico) [survey]:
> *"Viejos los cerros y reverrecen."* — "Even though mountains are old, every year they will have the seasons of good weather." (Respondent's comments: "This saying is common in rural towns.")

Tongan [survey]:
> *"Tukutukulaumea"* — "'*Tukutuku*' means the controlled release or distribution of something, the measured and deliberate act of letting something go. '*Laumea*' refers to the changing in the color of leaves from green (young) to brown (old) and all the shades in between."

Tongan [survey]:
> *"Tauhifonua"* — (Literally) "Keeper of the land." (Respondent's comments: "They (people 60 years of age and older, who have worked hard throughout their lives to sustain a family or a community) are the guardians and custodians of community norms, history, wisdom and protocols. They (males and females) are well respected and revered.")

Swedish [survey]:
> *"Alderdomen ar som ett trad om hosten, loven faller av, men stammen ar fortfarande stark."* — "The aging process is like a tree in the fall, the leaves fall off, but the trunk is still strong." (Respondent's comments: "The elderly might be less flexible and weaker than people of other generations, but their wisdom is strong.")

Indonesian [survey]:
> *"Cita-cita memeluk gunung, apa daya tangan tak sampai."* — "Desire to hug a mountain, however hands can't reach around it." (Respondent's comments: "The older generation can be a burden to the nation, and they do not have much respect for the younger generation.")

Metaphors related to food (and drink)
Portuguese: [survey]:

"Panela velha e' que faz comida boa." — "The old pan is the one that makes good food."

Chinese (Mandarin) [survey]:
"Jiang hai shi lao de la." — "Old ginger tastes spiciest."

Lebanese:
"Like a gourd, the older it gets, the lighter it gets." — "Said of an old man who is not serious" (Freyha, 1974, p. 639).

Spanish:
"Cuendo un viejo no puede beber prepara su tumba." — "When an old man cannot drink, prepare his grave" (Davidoff, 1946, p. 8).

Metaphors related to animals

Chinese (Mandarin) [survey]:
"Lao ma shi tu." — "An old horse will never get lost." (Respondent's comments: Young people must respect elderly people because elderly people have more knowledge and experience.)

Chinese (Cantonese) [survey]:
"... *Lie ngow seong su."* — (Teaching an old person to learn is like) "asking a cow to climb a tree."

Irish:
"The old man hasn't the place of the cat in the ashes" (Gaffney & Cashman, 1974, p. 16).

Other metaphors

Sayings about the elderly draw upon many other aspects of life for metaphorical content, including, as the following proverbs indicate, industry and body parts.

Chinese (Mandarin):
"Fa hui yu re." — "Contributing the left over heat." This saying utilizes a metaphor drawn from metal work to describe senior adults after retirement. It refers to what some people consider the ideal for retirement, whereby elderly persons still have something of value to contribute. However, some senior adults who are still working in professional roles have negative perceptions of this saying, particularly the part about being "heat" that is "left over." The sentiment is that they still have knowledge to contribute (J. Qicheng, personal communication, 1999).

Spanish:
"El corazon no envejece, el cuero es lo que se arruga." "The heart doesn't age; it's only the skin that shrivels" (Burciaga, 1997, p. 29).

Views about young people

As in the previous section, in the proverbs noted by respondents to describe "views about young people" no distinction could be drawn between the different language groupings (i.e., a combined Asian and Pacific Island languages group was compared to a combined European languages group). Many of the general themes noted below appear to cut across languages.

The proverbs and phrases provided by survey respondents were slightly more likely to portray young people in negative than positive terms. (This runs counter to the positive emphasis found in respondents' characterizations of the elderly and the aging process). Of the identified 107 proverbs which describe young people, 61 (57percent) had negative connotations as opposed to 46 (43percent) which conveyed positive connotations.

Survey respondents who provided proverbs noting negative conceptions about young people most readily emphasized their "naivete and inexperience" (N=43), "undisciplined" nature (N=8), and tendency to be "lazy and inactive" (N=3). Proverbs conveying positive conceptions about young people tended to emphasize how youth represent "the future" (N=18), are "strong and energetic" (N=14), exude a sense of "hopefulness" (N=5), and have a "natural" way about them (N=5).

Some negative themes

The most common proverbs which characterize young people emphasize their naivete and inexperience. Here are some examples.
Hungarian [survey]:
   "*It tojashe'j a seggeden van*" — "The eggshell is still on your butt." (Respondent's comments: "Youth are inexperienced.")
Korean [survey]:
   "*Namooae kajika maneulsuruk toe maneun paramyi bunda.*" — "There is blood on your head and it is not dried off yet." — (Respondent's comments: The blood on the head refers to when somebody is born.)
Chinese:
   "*Zui shang mei mao, shuo hua bu lao.*" — "He who has no hair on his lip can't be trusted to do anything well" (Cordry, 1997, p. 295).
Spanish:
   "*La juventud es un mal que cura el tiempo.*" — "Youth is an illness that time cures." (Burciaga, 1997, p. 26).
Hawaiian [survey]:
   "*He 'opu'u 'oe, he kakala kela.*" — "You are a bud, he is spurred." (Respondent's comments: "Said as a warning for a youngster not to challenge one stronger than he.")

As indicated in the following examples, young people are also charac-

terized as being impulsive, undisciplined, and lazy.
Portuguese [survey]:
> *"Nunca ponha a corroca na frente dos bois."* — "The hurry is the number one enemy of perfection." (Respondent's comment: "Old people say that young people are always in a hurry.")

Chinese (Mandarin) [survey]:
> *"San si er xing."* — "Think things three times before you do it." (Respondent's comments: "Do not do things hurriedly.")

Portuguese [survey]:
> *"Boi lerdo bebe agua suja."* — "The sluggish ox drinks dirty water. (Respondent's comments: "This is what old people often say to young people who are lazy.")

Positive Themes
As the following sayings indicate, childhood and youth are also portrayed as times of hopefulness and celebration.
Spanish:
> *"La juventud vive de la esperanza y la vejez de recuerdos."*— "Youth lives on hope and old age on memories." (Burciaga, 1997, p. 21).

Japanese [survey]:
> *"Seishun jidai."*— "The flower of youth." (Respondent's comments: This phrase suggests that youth is a time to be celebrated because it is fleeting and temporary.)

Kannada (India) [survey]:
> *"Ewattina yuwaka yuwakeeyara shikshanika palana mattu poshana nalina jageittina karyakarta."* — "The upbringing of today's youth determines tomorrow's world."

Chinese (Mandarin) [survey]:
> *"Qin nian yen yu chu sheng de tai yang."* — "Young people are like the rising sun." (Respondent's comments: Young people represent energy and hope for the future.)

Patterns of intergenerational communication
Of the 79 responses that were obtained which allude to patterns of intergenerational communication, the most common theme was a reference to difficulties of communication (N=30). Other response categories were "youth respect elders" (N=20), "seniors contribute" (N=11), "hierarchical (unequal) power relationships" (N=11), and "youth lack respect" (N=5). Two responses fit into an "other" category.

When comparing responses from the combined Asian and Pacific Island languages group of respondents to those provided by the combined European language group, again, no major distinctions were found.

Difficulties associated with intergenerational relations

A popular phrase in American society that emphasizes tension or mis-understanding between the generations is "generation gap." Several sayings and phrases were found in other languages that convey a similar sentiment about the challenges of intergenerational communication.

Chinese (Cantonese) [survey:]

> "*Dui niao tan qin.*" — "(Intergenerational communication is like) playing music to a cow."

Chinese (Mandarin) [survey]:

> "*Ji tong ya jiang.*" — "(A young person talking to an older adult is like) a chicken talking to a duck." (Respondent's comments: "Chickens and ducks are both birds, but of different species." When old and young talk to each other, they express different opinions.)

Indonesia:

> "... *Bogain pihany dibelah dua.*" — "(Intergenerational communication is like) areca nut divided into two." (Respondent's comments: "There is a big gap in views and communication among the young and the old due to lack of respect and understanding of each other.")

Japanese [survey]:

> "Tsujinai." — "communication difficulty between two parties." (Respondent's comments: "'Tsujinai' refers to how people of different generations have difficulties communicating [with] and understanding each other.") More specifically, "tsujinai" refers to the "sheer failure of communication between the two parties involved in a certain dialogue despite all the intents and efforts of the sender so as to let the receiver get it right. It implies the existence of some sort of impediment such as a language barrier, a cultural difference, or even a generation gap" (S. Nishizawa, personal communication, 2000).

Positive aspects of intergenerational communication:
Notions of interdependence

In contrast to the negative imagery noted above, the research group also found several prevalent statements in other languages that convey profound concepts of intergenerational interdependence. For example, in China there is the well-known phrase:

Chinese [survey]:

> "*Chang jiang hou lang tui qian lang, yi dai gen bi yi dai qiang.*" — "As in the Yangtse River the waves behind drive on those ahead, so each young generation should excel the last one" (Heng & Zhang, 1988, 444). (Respondent's comments: There is a lot to this saying. In one sense, it is used to describe the relations between the young and the old; young people are represented by the waves in the back, pushing forward with a lot of energy and adding to the momentum of the river.)

Also in Chinese:

"*Qian ren zai shu, hou ren cheng liang.*" "One generation plants the trees under whose shade future generations rest" (Heng & Zhang, 1988, 469).

Hawaiian:

"*Amakua*" (ancestral spirits) are sometimes symbolically used to convey positive intergenerational relations within the family unit. In the theological tradition of pre-Western-contact Hawai'i, the *amakua* referred to family or personal gods deeded by ancestors to their descendants. There is a popular story, once displayed as part of an exhibit in the Kauai Museum, of a family whose *amakua* was a "*mo'o*" (literally a lizard, in this case a six-legged Chinese dragon). This lizard is a representation of unity and interdependence among family members. The front feet of the lizard represent the young, always changing in position. The middle feet represent the parents, the providers of food and security. The hind feet represents the elders who make an invaluable contribution to the stability of the family (LeDoux, 1992).

Youth respect for elders

Several sayings and commonly used phrases were found which allude to youth respect for elders.

India [survey]:

"*Doddawara Helikegalige sada kretagnatawagiro.*" — "Always be grateful for the advice you receive from elders." (Respondent's comments: "Elders are frequently approached for advice.")

Tongan [survey]:

"*Te leleva', te ai e Polumei.*" — "When the young want to hang out with the old." (Respondent's comments: "The child wants a lot of attention.... It's an honor to be able to spend time with the elders.")

Chinese (Mandarin) [survey]:

"*Jin lao ai you.*" — "Respect the elders and love the young." (Respondent's comments: "(The saying) shows how in Asian cultures we value our elders.")

Hawaiian [survey]:

"*Na hulu kupuna.*" — "Our precious elders." (Respondent's comments: This is a common phrase in Hawaiian that is a declaration of respect for the elderly. It reflects a tradition of respecting the power and prestige of elders.)[7]

Emphasis on family
Family ties and responsibilities

Hawaiian [survey]:

"*Ola na 'iwi.*" — "The bones live." (Respondent's comments: "Said of a respected oldster who is well cared for by his family.")

Hawaiian:
> *"He keika mea kupuna."* — "(It shows that) the child has a grandparent." This saying is said in admiration of a child whose grandparents show affection by making beautiful things for his use or composing songs and chants in his honor (Pukui, 1983).

Chuuk:[8]
> *"Aramas chok money, aramas chok angang, aramas chok mongo."* — "When one has many relatives, he is like a chief. He can accomplish anything. He has money, work goes well, and food is provided."

Similarly, in Korean, there is the well known saying:
> *"Namuae Gajiga Maneulsuruk, Duh Maneun Baramyi Bubnida."* — "The more branches a tree has, the more winds it attracts." (Yong-Chol, 1991, p. 192).

Ilocano (Phillipines) [survey]:
> *"Taripatuen daguiti ubbing. Isu dan to ti nangtaripato kenca no lumakay ca."*— "Take care of the young and they will take care of you in your old age."

Several sayings were found which convey a "like father, like son" theme.
Spanish [survey]:
> *"De tal palo, tal astilla."* — "From such a stick, such a splinter."

Japanese [survey]:
> *"Kaeru no ko wa kaeru."* — "Children of frogs are frogs." (Respondent's comments: Like father , like son.")

Korean:
> *"Pu chon cha chon."* — "Father hands down, son hands down" (Grant, 1982, p. 19).[9]

Reference to ancestors

Hawaiian [survey]:
> *"Nana i ke kumu."* — "Look to the source." (Respondent's comments: "Seek knowledge from the ancestors.)

Korean:
> *"An twe myon cho sang ui t'at."* — "Blame the ancestors for failure" (Grant, 1982). This saying highlights a concept of family in which "ancestors" play an integral part.[10]

Zulu:
> *"Ubuntu."* — "We are who we are today because of you who came before us." This sub-Saharan intergenerational concept was one of the driving themes of the Third Global Conference of the International Federation of Aging held in Durban, South Africa in October of 1997 (Newman, 1998).

Relations with mothers-in-law

The only sayings found about mothers-in-law were negative in content. Here are two of the more striking examples.

Japanese:

> *"Yome to shutome, inu to saru"* — "Daughters-in-law and mothers-in-law are like dogs and monkeys" (Cherry, 1987, p. 134).

Lebanese:

> "I would rather be drowned or burned to death than have my mother-in-law live with me at home." (Freyha, 1974, p. 693).[11]

Distribution of power in intergenerational relationships
Hierarchical relations

Tongan [Survey]:

> *"Lauvale"* — "Uttering of fools." (Respondent's comments: "When you are of a younger generation, you are often referred to as the *'lauvale.'* That you are from a generation that has not mastered language yet. You don't give speeches, or become master/mistress of ceremonies.")

Swedish [survey]:

> *"Den ar som en flod. Den flyter nedstroms."* — "It is like a river. It flows downstream." (Respondent's comments: "The older people pass down knowledge rather than having a dialogue.")

Chinese [survey]:

> *"Bu ting lao ren yen, chi kui zai yan qian."*— "If you don't listen to older people's suggestions, you will get into trouble." (Respondent's comments: Pay attention to elders.)

Indian (Tamil):

> *"An unsubmissive youth is useless."* (Mieder, 1986, p. 558).

Spanish:

> *"Dichos de los viejitos son evangelios chiquitos."* — "The sayings of our elders should be taken as gospel." (Burciaga, 1997, p. ix).

Youthful rebellion

Several sayings and phrases were found which reject the notion that intergenerational relationships should be hierarchical in nature.

Swedish [survey]:

> *"Om Stenalderns barn hade lytt sina foraldrar hade vi fortfarande levat i Stenaldern."* — "If the Stone Age children had obeyed their parents, we would still be living in the Stone Age." (Respondent's comments: Young people disobey/are rebellious.)

Swedish [survey]:

> *"I en familj ar kvinnan regeringen, mannen folket och barnen oppositionen."* — "In a family, the mother is the government, the father is the people, and the kid is the opposition." (Respondent's comments: Kids disobey.)

Icelandic [survey]:

"*Unglingaveiki.*" — "Teen illness." (Respondent's comments: This word is used to describe a rebellious youth who does not respond to authority.)

Japanese [survey]:

"*Oite wa ko ni shitagae.*" — "When you become old, you should obey your child." (Respondent's comments: When you become old, don't be a hardheaded man. You should try to accept new ideas.)

Discussion

Countering stereotypes

Members of the research team assumed that for languages derived from traditional cultures, including cultures found in Asia and the Pacific Islands, proverbs and phrases would highlight views of aging that reflect reverence and perceived wisdom. A corollary assumption was also being tested: that for relatively modern societies such as the United States, terminology used to describe aging would convey primarily negative stereotypical views. On both counts, we were wrong. Proverbs were found in Asian languages that reflected negative views as well as positive views toward the elderly. Furthermore, the results of our research and the literature we consulted indicate that in the English language, terminology used to characterize the elderly neither emphasizes nor reflects unidimensionally negative stereotypes.

In a sense, the realization that there is great diversity within as well as between cultures, in conceptions about age and aging, is quite obvious. It would be absurd to expect there to be only one "type" of elderly people in any country.

Stereotypical notions of Western and Eastern concepts of aging are challenged in other places as well. Preliminary results of a new Harris Interactive poll, sponsored by the International Longevity Center and the Jewish Home and Hospital (both in New York City), indicates that Americans are currently quite positive about aging. Survey respondents, consisting of 3,000 people age 18 and older, expressed views about people 65 years and older which indicate that this group leads active, healthy, sexual, and financially secure lives (Kleyman, 2000). Conversely, recent research on aging and intergenerational relationships in many Asian countries is challenging stereotypical notions of unidimensionally positive portrayals of senior adults and harmonious patterns of intergenerational communication (see Giles et al. in this book).

Another unexpected result was that the proverbs provided by survey respondents to describe young people were weighted (slightly) on the negative side whereas those provided for older adults were skewed (sharply) on the positive side. Considering that in recent years there has been so much attention on the challenges faced by senior adults around the world, challenges such as age discrimination, elder abuse, and ageism, survey findings that indicate a pattern of comparative negativity in terms of how young people are portrayed serve as a reminder that young people too are engaged in struggles to receive adequate levels of respect and social standing.

Views about aging:

In considering people's attitudes toward aging, an important variable to consider is that of gender. Perhaps the negativity aimed at mothers-in-law, as displayed in the proverbs presented above, can be understood in part as a function of the pervasiveness of gender inequalities across cultures. In the English language, for example, terminology used to represent elderly people clearly reflects a gender bias. The words used for older women have more negative connotations than those used for older men. As Covey (1988) notes:

> The English language has a long history of separating old men from old women.... Terms for old women are focused on mysticism, bad temper, disagreeableness, spinsterhood, bossiness, unattractiveness, spitefulness, and repulsiveness. Terms for old men are sometimes defined in positive tones connoting wisdom and respect. Old women have not been so fortunate in the biased, male-oriented cultural tradition. If old women possessed wisdom, it was interpreted as mystical wisdom (p. 291).

Gender also appears to be a critical factor in the selection of terminology used in some other languages to represent the old. Cherry (1987) notes that gender inequalities in Japanese society extend into older adulthood, and this extension is reflected in the language. When a woman's husband dies, for example, she begins to be called a "*mibojin*" (a "not-yet-dead person"), a phrase that is thought to have originated among widows. The original implication is that "once a woman's husband is dead, she has outlived her purpose and has nothing left to do but await death herself" (p. 127).

Intergenerational communication:

The findings reported in this paper are supportive of some of the assumptions made by advocates of the intergenerational field. The portrayals of the old and the young conveyed via popular sayings suggest complementary characteristics. Of the proverbs that were obtained via the survey, older adults were most readily portrayed as experienced and in possession of wisdom, whereas young people were often depicted as inexperienced and in need of that wisdom. Those proverbs that associate childhood and youth with hope and energy, and characterize old age as a time of status devaluation and deterioration, also suggest a foundation for an inverse dynamic of meaningful intergenerational exchange, one that is based on the realization that young people have something of value to offer to older adults.

Study results also suggest that there is no singular orientation for understanding the benefits of intergenerational engagement. In the United States, for example, the sense of imperative for developing intergenerational initiatives is commonly tied to concerns about patterns of age segregation and negative stereotypes associated with aging. Popular colloquialisms such as "generation gap" and "ageism" denote such perceptions. Although some of the popular phrases and sayings found in non-English-speaking countries convey similar sentiment (in regard to the difficulties associated with intergenerational communication), others were found that convey quite different notions, where the emphasis is on intergenerational interdependence and harmony.

From a Western perspective, in the context of efforts to strengthen communities and social support systems, the use of metaphors such as the waves of the Yangtze River and the coordinated movements of a lizard's body to convey norms of intergenerational relations marked by interdependency is quite illuminating. The powerful images invoked by these metaphors stand in contrast to the images of generational conflict that occasionally creep into American public policy debate.

It is also useful to note how in non-Western languages, proverbs and phrases related to intergenerational communication commonly emphasize family relationships. This finding suggests that, in multicultural contexts, it would be prudent for intergenerational program developers to conceive intergenerational intervention proposals that are consistent with the accentuation of family life and supportive of family ties and responsibilities.

Research Considerations

There are several limitations and challenges inherent in this particular study and language analysis in general. First, this study lacked a mechanism for corroborating the respondents' words/phrases/ sayings and the meanings ascribed to them. One such procedure would involve hiring outside "informants," native speakers of each language, to comment upon their perceptions of cultural salience in regard to each of the proverbs provided by the respondents. Such a reexamination would be useful for filtering out idiosyncratic responses that are not reflective of socially recognized proverbs.

Another limitation of this study is the lack of age diversity in the pool of respondents. This is likely an artifact of the university setting; most respondents were of college age. With more age diversity, it would be possible to explore interesting questions such as how people's attitudes toward the aging process vary as a function of their age. For this reason, in structuring follow-up studies, it may be prudent to establish data collection procedures involving a variety of community institutions.

There are also some larger conceptual issues tied to the research approach which require attention. First, it should be noted that there is an energetic debate surrounding the principle of cultural elaboration based on linguistic analysis. Countering the points made by linguists such as Wierzbicka, as noted in the Introduction section, above, there are those who argue that there is universality in human perception and thinking processes and that the concept of culture, in itself, is an abstraction, a "speculative venture" (e.g., Pinker, 1994).

Even among those who advocate using linguistic inquiry as a tool for exploring culture, there is an acknowledgement of the subjective nature of much of this work. As noted by Wierzbicka (1997), there is no "objective discovery procedure" (established methodology). "To show that a particular word is of special importance in a given culture, one has to make a case for it" (p. 16).

Another front of criticism is tied to the idea of trying to study "culture" as though each society has a distinct set of cultural preoccupations. One challenge is on the grounds that cultures are interconnected (they exchange ideas and materials) and they evolve; they are not static monolithic entities or "essences" (Wolf, 1994). In considering the type of study presented in this chapter, it is necessary to remember that words and phrases are often transported between languages; they don't necessarily represent distinctive cultural phenomenon. For example, an African proverb, "It takes a Village to Raise a Child," has arguably become integrated into the unfolding American heritage of childcare.

In considering the preliminary nature of this study and the methodological and conceptual issues noted in this section, any conclusions drawn from the material presented in this chapter should be viewed as tentative. A far more ambitious study (or set of studies), with larger pools of respondents and varied data collection strategies and procedures, would be required to conduct definitive statistical analysis and reach the point of being able to make stronger conclusive statements in regard to cultural variations in perceptions and behaviors in regard to intergenerational communication.

Last Word

This survey of proverbs and phrases is based on the assumptions that such common collocations can help to reveal core cultural values and that the medium of language can be utilized to explore and analyze these values. Despite the limitations of the survey data set (i.e., the small sample and unbalanced regional representation) and the preliminary nature of this undertaking, this study may still have value in terms of stimulating new discussion and deeper investigation into the diverse ways in which intergenerational relations are construed.

The power of words is undeniable. Words not only provide insights into what we think, they also inspire us to new modes of thought. In the words of Aristotle, "The most powerful force on earth is the use of metaphors in the form of imagery." Researchers in Germany have demonstrated how journalists, advertisers and caricaturists use proverbs and sayings to capture the public's attention, enhance memory of advertising messages, and provoke a sense of familiarity with target products (Mieder, 1999; Forgacs, 1997). In the home and in other community settings alike, proverbs are used to pass on rich cultural traditions, for transmitting folklore and communicating expected codes of behavior across generations. Alternatively, proverbs have also played prominent roles in oral traditions of resistance to dominant cultural values (Soares, 1997) and political ideals (Birnbaum, 1987).

Proverbs also serve as effective educational tools in the classroom. For example, Cruz & Duff (1996) discuss how selectively chosen proverbs can be used to facilitate literacy skills development and help to bridge school- and home-based learning. Schnurer (1995) notes how proverbs can be included in secondary-school curricula to promote greater intercultural tolerance and understanding.

The proverbs and phrases presented in this chapter can certainly be used to enliven formal and non-formal educational programs. They contain "lessons" related to age and aging, cultural differences and similarities, family dynamics, societal stereotypes, and intergenerational relationships. Considering the richness and breadth of the proverbs and phrases, it is feasible that they may be productively drawn upon to embellish themes presented throughout an entire course of gerontology or intergenerational programs and policy study. Moreover, many of these proverbs and phrases can also serve as fun "warm-up" or "getting-to-know-you" activities for participants of intergenerational groups; facilitators can simply read selected ones aloud, one-by-one, and elicit discussion centered on participants' interpretations.

It is hoped that the array of proverbs presented in this chapter will be used in ways to heighten our sensitivity to how other people view the world and will stimulate critical thinking of our own normative frameworks and value assumptions about intergenerational relationships.

60   *Linking Lifetimes: A Global View of Intergenerational Exchange*

References

Birnbaum, L. C. (1987). Oral Tradition of Italian-Americans. Paper presented at the Annual Conference of the Society for the Study of the Multi-Ethnic Literature of the United States (1st, Irvine, CA, April 24-30, 1987).

Blair, J. (1997, Sept. 30). College recruiters cast a global net. *Christian Science Monitor.*

Burciaga, J.A. (1997). *In few words [En pocas palabras]: A compendium of Latino Folk wit and wisdom.* Mercury House: San Francisco.

Cherry, K. (1987). *Womansword: What Japanese words say about women.* Tokyo: Kodansha International Ltd.

Christy, R. (1888). *Proverbs, maxims and phrases of all ages.* N.Y.: The Knickerbocker Press.

Cordry, H.Y. (1997). *The multicultural dictionary of proverbs.* Jefferson, NC: McFarland & Co.

Covey, H.C. (1988). Historical terminology used to represent older people. *The Gerontologist, 28* (3), 291-297.

Cruz, M.C. & Duff, O.B. (1996, Nov.). Rainbow teachers/rainbow students: New worlds, old wisdom. *Urbana,* pp. 116-118.

Davidoff, H. (1946). *A world treasury of proverbs from twenty-five languages.* N.Y.: Random House.

Epstein, R. (1997, Nov./Dec.). Folk wisdom: Was your grandmother right? *Psychology Today, 30,* 46-50.

Farghal, M. (1995). Jordanian proverbs: An ethnographic and translational perspective, *Sendebar (Spain), 6,* 197-208.

Forgacs, E. (1997). In proverbs resides truth [?]: On playful use of proverbs and expressions. [In German: Im Sprichwort Liegt die Wahrheit (?): Zur spielerischen Verwendung von Sprichwortern und geflugelten Worten]. *Beitrage zur Fremdsprachenvermittlung aus dem Konstanzer SLI, 31,* 78-88.

Freyha, A. (1974). *A dictionary of modern Lebanese proverbs.* Beirut: Librairie Du Liban.

Gaffney, S. & Cashman, S. (Eds.). (1974). *Proverbs and sayings of Ireland.* Dublin: Wolfhound Press.

Giles et. al. (2001). Challenging intergenerational stereotypes across Eastern and Western cultures. (Chapter in this book.)

Grant, B.K. (1982). *Korean proverbs.* Salt Lake City, Utah: Moth House Publications.

Guralnik, D.B. & Solomon, S. (Eds.) (1980). *Websters new world dictionary* (2nd ed.). Cleveland: William Collins Publishers, 1144.

Heng, X.J. & Zhang X.Z. (1988). *A Chinese-English dictionary of idioms and proverbs.* Tubingen: M. Niemeyer.

Hummert, M.S., Garstka, T.A., Shaner, J.L. & Strahm, S. (1994). Stereotypes of the elderly held by young, middle-aged, and elderly adults. *Journal of Gerontology Psychological Sciences:, 49* (5), 240-249.

Ishii, Takemochi (1991, April). Generations: Aging in Japan. *Look Japan,* 10-11.

Jones, H.P. (1963). *Dictionary of foreign phrases and classical quotations.* Edinburgh: John Grant Booksellers.

Jordan-Bychov, T. & Domosh, M. (1999). *The human mosaic: A thematic introduction to cultural geography* (8th ed.). N.Y.: Addison-Wesley Educational Publishers, Inc.

Kleyman, P. (2000, May/June). Survey exposes myths of aging. *Aging Today*, pp. 1-2.

LeDoux, L.V. (1992, June). Old Hawaii: Part three: Life, religion, art. *Hawaii Magazine*, pp.39-43.

Levy, B. R. (1999). The inner self of the Japanese elderly: A defense against negative stereotypes of aging. *International Journal of Aging & Human Development, 48* (2), 131-144.

Mieder, W. (1999). A proverb says more than a thousand words: On the Proverbial Language of the Mass Media. [In German: *Ein Sprichwort sagt mehr als tausend Worte: Zur sprichwortlichen Sprache der Massenmedien.*] *Sprachdienst, 43* (4), 137-153.

Mieder, W. (1986). *The Prentice-Hall encyclopedia of world proverbs: a treasury of wit and wisdom through the ages.* Prentice Hall: Englewood Cliffs, N.J.

Newman, S. (1998, Winter). "Ubantu": Its role in the future of South Africa. *Exchange* (Pittsburgh: Generations Together newsletter on intergenerational issues, programs, and research), 13, p. 6.

Nuessel, F. (2000). The depiction of older adults and aging in Italian proverbs. *Proverbium, 17*, 299-314.

Pinker, S. (1994). *The language instinct.* N.Y.: William Morrow.

Pukui, M.K. (1983). *Hawaiian proverbs and poetical sayings.* Bernice P. Bishop Museum Special Publication No. 71. Honolulu: Bishop Museum Press.

Sapir, E. (1949). *Selected writings of Edward Sapir in language, culture and personality.* (D. Mandelbaum, ed.) Berkeley: University of California Press.

Schnurer, J. (1995, Nov.). Proverbs as the way to understanding African cultures. [In German: *Sprichworter als Zugang zum Verstandnis von afrikanischen Kulturen.*] *Lernen, 15* (2), 140-149.

Seo, Akwi (1991, April). Generations: Retired people. *Look Japan*, p. 12.

Soares, V. L. (1997). Oral tradition and literary writing: The case of African francophone literature. [In Portuguese: *Tradicao oral e escrita literaria: o exemplo das literaturas africanas de lingua francesa.*] *Revista Letras, 47*, pp. 123-130.

Wierzbicka, A. (1997). *Understanding cultures through their key words.* N.Y.: Oxford University Press.

Wolf, E.R. (1994). Perilous ideas: Race, culture and people. *Current Anthropology, 35* (1), 1-7.

Yong-Chol, K. (1991). *Proverbs, East and West: An anthology of Chinese, Korean, and Japanese sayings with Western equivalents.* Elizabeth, NJ: Hollym International Corp.

Notes

1 The author would like to acknowledge the research assistance provided by Brett Gordon, Mark Olival, Astrid Robinson, Xiaorong Shao, Sookyoung Cho, and Thomas Strandberg and express appreciation to Howard Giles and Linda Winston for their comments on an earlier draft of this chapter.

2 According to a recent Christian Science Monitor article entitled "College Recruiters Cast a Global Net," it is noted that with 26.8 percent of the Hawaii

Pacific University student body being foreign students, this university is ranked as number one in the country in terms of percentage of foreign students (Blair, September 30, 1997).

3 A "community/volunteerism" category was originally considered in an effort to gain insight into the values which influence extra-familial relationships, such as the norm of reciprocity. Response for this category was minimal and is therefore not reported here.

4 Responses which were still unclear or which indicated a lack of understanding of the directions on the part of respondents (e.g., several respondents provided straight translations of the category titles) were recorded as "missing cases."

5 Language grouping decisions are not meant to imply uniformity in terms of religion, language characteristics, or social norms. As an example of the great diversity existing within groupings, for Japan and China, both categorized as fitting into the "Asian" languages group, research shows there are substantial differences in terms of how aging is viewed and experienced (Levy, 1999).

6 "Kan" means "to go back to the beginning," and "reki" means "calendar." "Kanreki" literally means to go back to one's year of the 12 signs of the Chinese zodiac; 12 times 5 equals 60, which is the kanreki year.

7 Although "kupuna" is typically translated as "elder," its literal translation, "standing at the headwaters," denotes status and significance.

8 Chuuk, with 49,000 people, is the most populous of the Federated States of Micronesia. The following proverb was shared by a participant in one of the sessions of the 15th Annual Pacific Educational Conference, sponsored by Pacific Resources for Education and Learning, and held August 4-6, 1998 in Kauai, Hawaii.

9 Although this is a universal maxim, it has an implication that is strictly Confucian. Grant (1982) notes, "Not only does a son inherit certain traits, he passes them on to future generations. This multi-generational concept is typical of the long view of life in Korean society" (p. 19).

10 Grant (1982) provides further discussion of this saying: "This proverb means to blame others for one's own errors. In old Korea, it was thought that the relative tranquility of one's ancestors directly influenced the fortunes of descendants. Even today, disturbing a tomb is a very serious matter, one which can have repercussions for living family members. Hence, it is easy to blame ancestors for, say, a business failure... It is considered by some to be bad form to use this saying except in a joking manner, perhaps in the style of a famous American comedian who laments how 'the devil made me do it!'" (p. 6)

11 Freyha (1974) presents another striking Lebanese saying about mothers-in-law: "If my stepmother loves me she sends me to the oven; if my mother-in-law hates me she sends me to the oven" (p. 129).

Appendix A:
The Language of Intergenerational Exchange Survey

Appendix A: The Language of Intergenerational Exchange Survey

Introduction:
This survey is part of a larger study on how people from different countries think about issues related to aging and how people of different generations view each other. Our strategy is to explore cultural values and beliefs by looking at the words and phrases used in different languages to describe the aging process and patterns of intergenerational relations. If you speak any languages other than English, your participation would be much appreciated. Your responses will be kept confidential.

Instructions:
For each language you speak (other than English), please fill out this brief questionnaire. For each topic presented below, write down and provide the translation for as many words, phrases, or sayings (idioms) that come to your mind. Try to list those words that most readily reflect culturally significant values and beliefs. Use the back of this form if necessary.

About you: Language (this form): _____   Age: ____   Gender: ____   Name and contact information (optional): _____

Topic	Sayings that reflect cultural values and beliefs	Translation into English	Comments about how this saying reflects cultural/national philosophy, history, concerns, etc.
1. The aging process:			
2. Views about elderly people (and what it means to "retire"):			
3. Views about young people:			
4. Patterns of communication between different generations:			
5. Sense of community/Spirit of volunteerism:			

Appendix B:
Languages Represented in Survey Sample

Appendix B: Languages Represented in Survey Sample

Language	Cantonese	Chamoru	Croatian	Filipino/Ilicano/Tagalog	German	Hawaiian	Indonesian	Italian	Japanese
Frequency	3	3	1	7	3	4	3	1	27

Language	Korean	Mandarin	Spanish	Swedish	Thai	Tongan	Vienamese	Finish	Hungarian
Frequency	5	30	3	6	2	4	23	1	1

Language	Icelandic	Romanian	Slovak	Indian	French	Malay	Portuguese	Serbian
Frequency	1	1	1	1	1	1	4	1

Advancing an Intergenerational Agenda in the United States

By Nancy Henkin, Ph.D., and Donna Butts

Introduction

Over the past 30 years, the concept of bringing generations together to foster interdependence, meet societal needs, and promote cultural continuity has grown increasingly popular in the United States. Intergenerational strategies are not only sources of mutual support, they also represent effective vehicles for building a more civil and caring society. There is now a body of knowledge and experience that can move this approach from a collection of model projects to a more coordinated strategy for strengthening communities and improving the lives of individuals and families throughout the course of their lives (Kingson, Cornman, and Leavitt, 1997). Yet the potential of this approach is still far greater than the current practice. The following discussion will explore the rationale for promoting an intergenerational agenda at this point in American history, provide an overview of the field, examine some of the factors that are inhibiting and facilitating the growth of this approach, and delineate strategies for moving this concept forward.

Promoting an intergenerational agenda now

The demographic revolution, the fraying of the social compact, and the unmet needs of individuals, families, and communities are all forces currently driving the pursuit of an intergenerational agenda.

The demographic revolution

Major demographic trends are having a dramatic impact on the composition of American communities and the nature of relationships across age, race, ethnic, and socio-economic groups. The increase in the size of the older population in the last century, from three million people age 65 or older in 1900 (4 percent of the population) to 35 million in 2000 (nearly 13 percent of the population) is one of the most significant trends. By 2030, one in five people will be over age 65 (more than 70 million), with the 85+ population growing faster than any other age group (Federal Interagency Forum, 2000). This increase is due primarily to increases in life expectancy. Males born in 1996 in the United States can be expected to live 72.5 years, and females to live 79 years (Hooyman and Kiyak, 1999).

The older population of the United States is diverse in terms of gender, race, and ethnicity. Approximately 58 percent of the older population are women, and more than half of them live alone. In 2000, 83.5 percent of the older adult population were non-Hispanic white, 8.1 percent were non-Hispanic black, 5.6 percent were Hispanic, 2.4 percent were non-Hispanic Asian and Pacific Islander, and 0.4 percent were American Indian and Alaska Native (Federal Interagency Forum, 2000). The proportion of older persons is expected to increase at a higher rate for the nonwhite population than for the white population due to the large proportion of children in these groups who are expected to reach old age (Hooyman and Kiyak, 1999).

In addition to an increase in the size of the older adult population, there have been changes in age distribution. In 1995 there were five working people per older person; by the year 2020 it is anticipated that there will be fewer than four working people per retiree (U.S. Administration on Aging, 1996). The gap between the percentage of older adults and children in the population has narrowed; by 2030 each group will constitute approximately 22 percent of the total population (U.S. Department of Human Services, 1991, p.8-9; in Newman p. 22).

The longevity revolution, combined with other demographic trends, will continue to have a dramatic impact on the nature of age relations and the ability of families and communities to support individuals throughout the life course. Longer life span means more older adults will be seeking an array of volunteer, employment and educational opportunities to enhance the quality of this later stage of life. There will also be an increased demand for culturally appropriate support services to help older people remain in their homes as long as possible. Young people and families, too, will need additional support as they face the challenges of a more complex and diverse society.

For some, like Pete Peterson, former Nixon Commerce secretary, the aging of America is "a demographic time bomb" and a source of impending strife. In his book *Gray Dawn* (1999), he portrays older adults as a "callous leisure class," disinterested in younger generations and concerned only about their own entitlements. He and some other economists suggest that generational warfare is inevitable, with seniors voting down school bonds and engaging in self-indulgent behaviors.

Others, like Marc Freedman in his book *Prime Time: How Baby Boomers Will Revolutionize Retirement and Transform America,* see the aging of America as an "opportunity to be seized—provided we can learn to capture the time, talent, and experience of the older population and apply this largely untapped resource to some of the most urgent unmet needs of society," (1999). Freedman refers to this population group as our only *increasing* natural resource. America's challenge is to redefine the roles and responsibilities of this resource—the largest, healthiest, and best-educated group of older adults in its history.

The fraying of the social compact

The "social compact" refers to the age-old set of obligations of persons of different generations to nurture and support each other. Alexis de Tocqueville, in his 1840 masterpiece *Democracy in America,* saw the need for American leaders to develop new forms of social compacts, and he envisioned the role of government as supplementing not supplanting family connections (Achenbaum, 1998-99). Though the United States has periodically asserted the public's interest over private interests, particularly in the areas of health care for the elderly, social security, public education, child labor, and progressive taxes (Reich, 1998-99), the social compact has become weakened over the past 50 years. Expectations and obligations across generations are not clear, and there have been few public policies that support caregiving families. The number of children being raised by single parents and grandparents has risen dramatically, more and more generations are living apart, civic engagement has declined, and violence has become commonplace in far too many neighborhoods (Cornman and Kingson, 1996). Significant gains in life expectancy and changes in marriage and divorce patterns will place even more stress on individuals and families, thus necessitating the creation of new strategies for fostering interdependence across generations.

Addressing unmet needs

As a result of our changing demographics and the deterioration of the social compact, children, youth, older adults, families, and communities experience many challenges.

Issues facing children and youth

According to the Children's Defense Fund's Yearbook 2000, one in five children or 13.5 million children are living in poverty in America. Half of these children live in stressful family environments and are four times more likely to have serious behavioral and emotional problems, low engagement in school, and feelings of worthlessness than those in less stressful situations (CDF Yearbook 2000). The CDF yearbook reports that:

- Only 31 percent of fourth graders in America read at or above proficiency; only 1 percent of fourth graders write at an advanced level.
- An estimated 2.8 million children were reported as suspected child abuse or neglect cases in 1998; more than 900,000 were confirmed as victims.
- Ten children die each day from gunfire, approximately one every 2.5 hours.

Data from the National Longitudinal Study of Adolescent Health (2000) indicates that problems facing adolescents of all socio-economic levels include violence, drinking/drugs, suicide, and early sexual activity. According to this study, a quarter of U.S. teens have been involved with weapons and 10 percent say they drink weekly. School failure and unsupervised time spent with friends are reported to be far more predictive of unhealthy behaviors than race, income, or family structure. The study confirms the importance of caring relationships with adults, structured after school and community service programs, and supports to ensure academic success.

Issues facing older adults

Although improvements in the financial and health conditions of many older people have resulted in better life circumstances, there are still many needs that have not been met. The percentage of older adults living in poverty has actually decreased from 35 percent in 1959 to 11 percent in 1998 due to the expansion of social security and other pension protection. However, the poverty rate for older minorities and women is higher than for the rest of the older population. Although older Americans are healthier today than ever before, more than 8.5 million older people need some kind of assistance to remain in the community (Federal Interagency Forum, 2000). Approximately 4 percent of older adults live in nursing homes; 25 percent of them have symptoms of Alzheimer's disease. Loneliness and depression are feelings experienced by many older adults, particularly those who are homebound or who are geographically separated from their families.

One of the greatest challenges for many retirees is determining how to spend the 18 to 25 hours per week that retirement frees for both women and men. Though some psychologists stress the importance of passing life's lessons on to the next generation, a recent study indicates that less than one third of all older people work as volunteers, and those who do spend an average of just two hours per week volunteering (Rowe and

Kahn, 1998). A survey by the Administration on Aging puts the number of potential volunteers at 14 million (Freedman, 1999). Creating opportunities for older adults to remain contributing members of their communities is one of the challenges that can be met through an intentional intergenerational agenda.

Issues facing families

Although families have always been the major providers of support for individuals over the life course, increased involvement of women in the workforce, high rates of divorce, the longevity revolution, and geographic mobility have made it more difficult to meet all the needs of members. Today in the United States nearly 30 percent of all working adults have caregiving responsibility for older dependent adults (Dychwald, 1998). It is anticipated that adults will spend more time caring for parents than for children (Roszak, 1998).

The challenge of childcare for American families is as great as elder care. With more than 72 percent of mothers in the work force, the need for quality child care and after school care is critical. More than five million children are home alone after school, and the cost of day care for young children is prohibitive, particularly for low-wage families (CDF, 2000). Another major concern for children is lack of quality time with family members due to the demanding jobs and long commutes so many parents face. A recent Kaiser Family Foundation survey (1999) found that American children spend an average of five hours and 29 minutes per day unsupervised, using some type of media rather than social interaction to entertain themselves.

Another growing area of concern is the dramatic increase in the number of children being raised by grandparents and other relatives. In 1998, the U.S. Census Bureau estimated that there were 2.13 million children living in households headed by a relative with no parent present; of these, 1.4 million are being raised solely by their grandparents (Lugaila, 1998). This number had increased 51.1 percent between 1990 and 1998 (CDF, 2000). The challenges faced by these families are many, ranging from physical and emotional problems experienced by children who have been affected by their parents' alcohol and drug abuse, illness, or incarceration to difficulty obtaining benefits and services because caregivers may lack legal guardianship or custody.

Issues facing communities

There is a great deal of concern about the quality of life in communities across the country. Violence, hate crimes, and racial/ethnic tension cause many children and older adults to feel like prisoners in their own homes. There is also growing evidence of a social disconnection in American communities. Robert Putnam, in his book entitled *Bowling Alone*, speaks about the erosion of "social capital"—the connections among individuals that are characterized by reciprocity and mutual support. He suggests that Americans have become increasingly disconnected from friends, neighbors, family, and social structures such as religious institutions, civic associations, political parties, and recreational clubs (Putnam, 2000). Putnam and a group of other researchers and community leaders who participated in the Saguaro Seminar helped design the Social Capital Community Benchmark Survey (2001) that was administered to 30,000 people in 40 communities. The survey revealed that levels of civic engagement—the degree to which community residents trust, socialize and join others—predicted the quality of community life and residents' happiness more than educational or income levels. Improved civic education in schools, well-designed service projects, community and family-oriented workplace practices, and new forms of electronic entertainment and communication that promote rather than impede community engagement are among the strategies suggested to stem the tide of disconnectedness (Putnam, 2000). Integrating intergenerational approaches into these initiatives would further strengthen the connection between individuals and their communities.

Overview of the Intergenerational Field in the United States

Now that the reasons driving the need for an intergenerational agenda have been examined, it is important to look at the development of intergenerational programs over the years and survey the range of programs that are currently in operation.

History

For more than 30 years, programs have been developed across the United States that intentionally bring together people of different generations. During the 1960s and 1970s, most of these programs focused on dispelling age-related stereotypes and fostering understanding between youth and older adults as well as providing financial support for low-income elders. The largest of these were the Foster Grandparent and Retired and Senior Volunteer programs. For more than 30 years, Foster Grandparents has matched low-income elderly with children who have special needs, and the Retired and Senior Volunteer Program has placed millions of older adults in a variety of institutions and organizations. During the 1980s and 1990s, the focus of programs shifted from reducing generational separation to addressing community problems (Newman, 1999). Intergenerational programs have been developed to address issues such as literacy/education, family support, elder/child care, health, and cross-cultural understanding. In 1986 Generations United, a national coalition of children, youth and aging organizations, was formed to foster intergenerational collaboration on public policy and programs. Over the last decade, Generations United has helped create state and local intergenerational networks and has served as a central information and referral resource.

Range of programs

Currently, millions of older adults and youth in the United States are engaged in cross-age activities that address critical community needs. These programs take place in schools, senior centers, long term care facilities, childcare centers, libraries, recreation centers, and other community-based organizations. They involve children and older adults with a range of skills, needs, and experiences. Successful programs address specific community needs; represent partnerships between organizations serving different age groups; foster reciprocity between individuals; provide opportunities for personal growth and learning; and have solid infra-structures to recruit, train and support volunteers. Profiles of some of these programs, organized by social issue, follows. This list is by no means exhaustive, but rather is intended to raise awareness of the diversity of programs that are currently operating across the United States. Additional information on these and other programs can be found in Generations United's program profile database (www.gu.org).

Literacy/Education

In communities across America, intergenerational programs are addressing the literacy and academic needs of youth and older adults.

It is estimated that more than two million **older adults** are serving as reading tutors, mentors, after school volunteers, parent outreach coordinators, and oral historians (Newman, 1999). Although most programs are developed locally and involve volunteers 2-4 hours/week, a new national initiative called the **Experience Corps** has taken this idea to another level. Coordinated by Civic Ventures in San Francisco and operating in 17 cities, the Experience Corps mobilizes older adults to devote 15 hours/week to enhancing the reading and writing skills of students in elementary schools. Participants work in teams and receive stipends based on the number of hours served.

Programs in which **students** help older adults improve their literacy/language and/or technology skills are less prevalent, but growing. These activities are often built into academic courses or are part of structured after-school programs. An example is **Project SHINE** (Students Helping in the Naturalization of Elders), a national program coordinated by the Center for Intergenerational Learning at Temple University that mobilizes college students to help elderly immigrants and refugees learn English and prepare to become U.S. citizens.

Intergenerational *education* programs that bring diverse age groups together for learning and enrichment have also been created across the country. Examples include:

- **Elderhostel**, a network of short-term residential programs held on university campuses that offers a myriad of intergenerational experiences for grandparents and grandchildren.
- The **North Carolina Center for Creative Retirement**, a university-based program that brings college students and retirees together for shared learning experiences.

Family support

Intergenerational initiatives are also successful strategies for addressing the needs of families trying to care for their members. Examples of national programs that focus on family support are:

- **Family Friends**, a network of 35 programs coordinated by the National Council for the Aging that involves older adults as mentors to parents who are raising children with special needs, teen mothers, and families who have been reported for child abuse and neglect.
- **Kin Net** (Kin Nurturing, Educating, and Teaching), spearheaded by Generations United, is establishing a national network of support groups and online assistance for grandparents and other relatives raising kin in the formal foster care system.

In addition, several new intergenerational housing initiatives have been designed to support children in foster care and kinship caregivers:

- In Illinois, **Generations of Hope** oversees Hope Meadows, a community in which foster children are placed in the care of families who live rent-free in exchange for parenting three to four children. These families are supported by older adults who receive reduced rent for providing a range of volunteer services.
- In Massachusetts, **Grandfamilies** is a specially designed housing development for grandparent-headed families. It includes 26 apartments, an on-site pre-school, an after-school and computer learning center, and on-site support for caregivers.

Child care

An increasing number of older people are being recruited and trained as childcare workers. They serve as paid and volunteer caregivers for young children in both preschool and after school programs. In some communities, older adults who are homebound or reside in a nursing home provide telephone reassurance to children who are alone in the after school hours. **Grandma Please** in Chicago is one such program in which a centralized service matches homebound elders with children who are home alone after school.

Elder care

Many opportunities now exist for students to provide a variety of support services for older adults who live at home or reside in long term care facilities.

- In New York City, **DOROT** recruits, trains and matches young volunteers with homebound elders for weekly visits that enhance the lives of both groups.
- In Philadelphia, Temple University's **Time Out** program recruits college students to provide low-cost respite care to families caring for elderly members.
- Elsewhere young people perform chore services, visit residents of long term care facilities, and conduct oral histories.

The emergence of **shared sites**, which offer services to both children and older adults, is an exciting new development in the intergenerational landscape. Nursing homes with on-site child care centers, adult and child day care services co-located in the same building, senior centers offering after school programs, and senior centers within schools are all examples of this growing phenomenon. **Project SHARE** (Sharing Helps All Resources Expand), one of the new initiatives of Generations United, has begun to promote the expansion of these program models as well as encourage supportive public policies.

Youth development

In recognition of the importance of caring adults in the lives of children, there has been a major growth in mentoring programs throughout the country. A number of these programs utilize older adults in the mentoring role.

- **Across Ages**, a drug prevention program developed at the Center for Intergenerational Learning at Temple University, matches older adult mentors with middle school children, teaches life skills, and engages children in community service activities. It is now being replicated nationally.
- **Big Brothers/Big Sisters of America** and **Save the Children** are currently engaged in major campaigns to recruit older adults as mentors and volunteers in their programs.
- In Maryland, the **Bridges** program matches English speaking older adults with immigrant children to ease their transition to American society.

Other youth development efforts engage students in service activities that support older adults who need assistance.

Health care/legal services

Over the past few years, several intergenerational program models focused on specific groups of retired professionals have emerged. In California, Florida, and South Carolina, retired physicians are providing free medical care to the working poor in their communities:

- At **Samaritan House** in San Jose, California, a group of volunteer physicians, nurses, and social workers provide care to more than 500 patients a month.
- In New York, **Legal Services for Children** mobilizes retired lawyers, as well as women who have returned to work after raising families, to serve young, low-income clients free of charge.

Community building

Initiatives that involve youth and elders working together to build healthy, inclusive communities have also gained increased popularity.

- In Florida, the **Miami-Dade County Public Schools** have developed a wide range of intergenerational initiatives including Intergenerational Citizens Action Forums that are organized jointly by youth and older adults and focus on issues such as social security reform, the impact of violence on youth, health care reform, and environmental protection.
- **Elders Share the Arts** in New York City has conducted a wide range of projects that engage intergenerational groups in theater, music, and the visual arts to build connections in communities. Projects include mapping a neighborhood's history and using theater to highlight social and political issues.
- Through **Neighborhoods 2000**, a program developed at City University of New York Graduate School, older adults and students in grades four through six examine their neighborhood and present their ideas on community building to those responsible for making local development decisions.
- In Arkansas, older volunteers are paired with at risk youth in a program called **Mentor Link**. In addition to mentoring and tutoring, youth and older adults participate in service projects that address community needs and teach youth about teamwork and social responsibility.

Factors Inhibiting and Facilitating an Intergenerational Agenda

In order to move forward, it is important to examine the barriers that impede the expansion of intergenerational strategies as well as the factors that promote their growth.

Factors inhibiting the growth of intergenerational strategies

Despite the number of highly successful program models and the evidence that intergenerational strategies strengthen communities, families, and individuals, there is a major gap between the **promise** and the **practice** of this approach. Following are some of the challenges to moving from a collection of disparate programs to a coordinated intergenerational agenda.

Ageism

Negative attitudes toward both older adults and youth constitute a major barrier to moving forward. Many people view these two population groups as problems to be solved rather than resources to be tapped. Youth and older adults themselves often believe these stereotypes and are consequently reluctant to become involved in ongoing intergenerational initiatives.

Lack of program institutionalization

Most current intergenerational programs are relatively small and not fully integrated into existing service systems or large scale initiatives that focus on issues such as educational reform, long-term care, or violence prevention. Too many of these programs are totally dependent on the enthusiasm of a coordinator or a short-term grant. Increasing the size and intensity of programs and working toward their institutionalization are strategies needed to close the gap between what currently exists and what is possible.

Limited mechanisms for identifying and sharing best practices

Currently there are no vehicles for systematically replicating successful program models, evaluating programs, or enhancing the capacity of organizations to integrate the intergenerational approach into their programmatic structure. Although several university-based intergenerational centers and regional intergenerational networks offer periodic training workshops, and Generations United conducts a bi-annual conference, a coordinated effort to identify and document best practices that can be adapted by diverse communities does not exist. Program evaluation efforts, too, are fragmented and don't always focus on behavioral as well as attitudinal outcomes.

Age-segregated funding streams

Age-segregated funding streams as well as a lack of collaboration among funding sources have made it difficult to create initiatives that address issues from a life span perspective. For example, the education of children and older adults are seen as separate enterprises rather than as integral parts of a lifelong learning agenda. Private and public funding agencies could promote the development of intergenerational initiatives by encouraging organizations representing different age groups to collaborate in holistic community building efforts.

Factors facilitating growth of intergenerational strategies
Baby boomers redefining retirement

The more than 70 million baby boomers coming of age within the next two to three decades will greatly impact the nature of retirement and America's vision of old age. A 1999 survey by Peter D. Hart Research Associates of persons aged 50 to 75 revealed that 65 percent of those interviewed see retirement as "a time to begin a new chapter in life by being active and involved" rather than "a time to take it easy, enjoy leisure activities, and take a rest from work and daily responsibilities" (Hart, 1999). Other surveys indicate that many baby boomers are seeking socially redeeming educational opportunities and part-time employment in addition to volunteer activities (Freedman, 1999).

Increased interest in lifelong service

Although America has always promoted the notion of volunteerism, over the past decade the federal government has taken an increasingly pro-active role in fostering service opportunities for persons of all ages:

- The Corporation for National Service was created in 1993 through the National and Community Service Trust Act to serve as the umbrella for a number of national service programs, including *Americorps* (a stipended, full-time service corps), *Learn and Serve America* (a grant program that connects service and academic learning in grades K-12 and in institutions of higher education), and the *National Senior Service Corps* (oversees the Foster Grandparent, Senior Companion, and Retired and Senior Volunteer Programs).
- The Points of Light Foundation in Washington, D.C. promotes service opportunities through a network of more than 500 Volunteer Centers.
- America's Promise, the outgrowth of the Presidential Summit of 1997, mobilizes individuals and organizations to build the competence of youth.
- AARP (formerly known as the American Association of Retired Persons), the nation's largest organization of older adults, has begun a major initiative to involve its members in community service.

Research on healthy development and social connectedness

A strength-based model of development is gradually replacing the traditional deficit model in both the aging and youth fields. Recent work in the areas of positive youth development and successful aging suggest a convergence in strategies that promote healthy development across the life course. Researchers in youth development have moved away from a focus on individually-oriented prevention and treatment to a more community-oriented approach that emphasizes positive youth outcomes (Zeldin, 2000). This requires that we pay more attention to the elements of a healthy community, particularly the active participation of all age groups (including youth) in community-building efforts. Several studies indicate that involvement of youth in positive social relationships and meaningful activities is associated with a reduction in risky behavior and an increase in resiliency (Camino, 2000). In the National Longitudinal Study of Adolescent Health (2000), the largest survey of adolescence ever completed in America, connection to a caring adult other than a parent was found to be one of the highest rated protective factors for youth.

"Successful aging" has been defined as a combination of physical and functional health, high cognitive functioning, and active involvement with society (Rowe and Kahn, 1998). A longitudinal study of older adults by the MacArthur Foundation found that social ties and productive activities were essential components of successful aging (Rowe and Kahn, 1998). Other researchers add that a sense of purpose or contribution to society is also a critical element in this process (Fisher, 1996).

Additional research by Harvard University's Center for Society and Health points to the importance of social connectedness. Researchers there indicate that social isolation is a chronically stressful condition that has a direct biological effect on the body (Berkman, 1995). Creating strong networks, promoting partnerships between youth and adults, and developing social institutions that support the creation of fulfilling experiences at each stage of life can improve the social health of individuals and communities.

The Future

Moving the intergenerational agenda forward in the United States will require four major strategies: changing attitudes, transforming social institutions, building the capacity of communities to more effectively utilize the resources of youth and elders, and reforming public policy.

Changing attitudes

We must change the way Americans view retirement and the roles and responsibilities of individuals at each stage of life. This change will require a major public relations/social marketing campaign that will expand our vision of the "third stage of life," promote the importance of contributing to one's community, and emphasize the value of intergenerational connections. Publicizing the contributions of high-profile role models like former president Jimmy Carter and astronaut John Glenn has been an effective first step. We now need a national "Call to Action" campaign that sends a strong message to retirees that they have an essential contribution to make to communities (Freedman, 1999). Likewise, we need to promote examples of young people taking responsibility by doing such things as serving on boards of directors, reporting on public radio, and mentoring their peers. Educators and health/human service practitioners must begin to think differently about youth and elders, focusing on creative ways to promote "productive aging" and "positive youth development."

Transforming social institutions

Current social structures that define expectations and opportunities throughout the life cycle have not kept pace with changes in longevity, health, and lifestyle (Riley, Kahn, and Foner, 1994). Closing this "structural lag" between the capacities of older Americans and the kinds of opportunities available to them will require a retooling of existing social institutions as well as the creation of new ones. Transforming age-differentiated structures such as schools, nursing homes, retirement communities, and youth recreation facilities into age-integrated structures in which different ages can interact on a continuous basis and individuals can intersperse periods of education, work and leisure over their lives is one strategy that holds great promise. Educational institutions are already exploring ways to become sites for lifelong learning/service, and a growing number of housing developments are intentionally mixing ages in order to foster cross-age support systems.

In the work arena, some corporations are developing policies that permit reduced work time (e.g., sabbaticals, flex time, job sharing) and phased retirement plans that include opportunities for older adults to serve as mentors to new employees.

The social service delivery system also has to move from its current fragmented state to a coordinated continuum of services. This will require that community agencies create a common vision, share information, and "collaborate in a new turf-less, comprehensive structure that recognizes the interdependence of generations" (Newman,1997, p.178).

In addition to changing existing institutions, we need to create new kinds of infrastructures for engaging people in productive roles at different life stages. The service learning movement has grown at a rapid pace over the past decade. Schools partner with community agencies to recruit, train, and support students in meaningful experiences. In order to mobilize large numbers of older adults to become engaged in their communities, we need to develop institutions that offer a continuum of opportunities for service, learning, and personal growth.

Building capacity to implement intergenerational strategies

A more systematic and intentional effort must be made to build the capacity of organizations to successfully integrate intergenerational strategies into their missions and services and to enhance the skills of practitioners responsible for implementing intergenerational initiatives. The Center for Intergenerational Learning at Temple University currently offers a range of training and technical assistance services to educators and human service practitioners and is developing practical materials to help organizations implement successful initiatives. Increasing numbers of institutions of higher education are offering intergenerational courses, modules, research projects and service-learning options. Generations Together at the University of Pittsburgh offers a Certificate in Intergenerational Studies, and the University of Findlay is working with the University of South Florida to establish academically-based national standards for intergenerational professionals.

Much more needs to be done. We need new funding streams that support capacity-building efforts in addition to the development of demonstration programs. Integrating information about intergenerational community building strategies into teacher education, social work, allied health and other pre-professional programs and promoting the inclusion of this approach into major national youth, aging, or community development initiatives are other avenues to explore for advancing the intergenerational agenda.

Reframing public policy

There is a need to take an intergenerational perspective on many current social issues in order to create policies that respond to the needs of all generations. Young and old are bound together by issues such as access to age-appropriate health care, safe neighborhoods, quality public education, lifelong learning, and the maintenance of a strong social security program.

Public policy should be used to unite and not separate the generations. For example, the Older Americans Act has several provisions that provide opportunities for seniors to actively participate in intergenerational programs offered in schools. It also includes the National Family Caregiver Support Act that not only supports families caring for frail elderly, but also provides resources to grandparents raising grandchildren. As youth advocates work on the development of a Younger Americans Act, intergenerational advocates are working on language that would explicitly encourage the involvement of seniors in advisory groups and programs created through this Act. Efforts are also underway to alter language in proposed legislation supporting after school programs to specifically include older volunteers as providers of service in these programs.

A template is needed to ensure that proposed policies support reciprocity across the lifespan and reinforce intergenerational connection and cooperation. Questions that address these issues include but are not limited to:

1) Is one generation unfairly being used to help another?
2) Does the policy encourage intergenerational transfers through shared care or services?
3) Are people of all ages being viewed as resources?
4) Is the policy sensitive to intergenerational family structures such as grandparents who are raising grandchildren?

Through Generations United, advocates for young and old are learning to work together to create a mutually supportive public policy agenda. However, while the opportunities for intergenerational activism are growing at the federal level, there has been limited progress at the state and local government levels. Given the current trend toward decentralization of funding and services, we need to pay increased attention to the development of local policies that foster intergenerational support and exchange.

Conclusion

All factors indicate that the early 21st Century will be an optimum time for the expansion of intergenerational programs and public policies in the United States. The ongoing work of national centers/organizations created to support the field and the commitment of a growing number of opinion leaders to this approach provide an unparalleled opportunity to inject the intergenerational philosophy into new arenas. But much more needs to be done to move the intergenerational agenda forward:

• We need to identify new champions to add further credence to the movement.
• Leading organizations need to work more closely together to develop clear messages about the effectiveness of intergenerational approaches and to support the growing number of intergenerational programs and professionals.
• The growing national dialogue about civic engagement and social connectedness needs to include intergenerational strategies.

Although progress has been made towards moving the image of intergenerational work from superficial to essential, it will take a much more concerted effort to fully integrate this concept into the fabric of American society.

References

Achenbaum, A. (1998-99). The social compact in American history. (In Keeping the promise: Intergenerational strategies for strengthening the social compact, a special issue of the Journal of the American Society on Aging.) *Generations, 22* (4), 15-18.

Blum, R.W., Beuhring, T., & Rinehart, P.M. (2000). Protecting teens: Beyond race, income, and family structure. Center for Adolescent Health, University of Minnesota, Minneapolis, Minn.

Berkman, L.F. (1995). The role of social relations in health promotion. *Psychosomatic Medicine 57*, 245-254.

Brody, E. (1981). Women in the middle and family help to older people. *Gerontologist 21* (5), 471-80.

Camino, L. (2000). Youth-adult partnerships: Entering new territory in community work and research. (In Promoting adolescent development in community context: Challenges to scholars, non-profit managers, and higher education, a special issue of) *Developmental Science, 4*, 11-20.

Children's Defense Fund Yearbook 2000. www.childrensdefense.org/ss_child_abuse.html

Cornman, J.M. & Kingson, E.R. (1996). Trends, issues, perspectives and values for the aging of the baby boom cohorts. *Gerontologist 36* (1), 15-26.

Dyckwald, K. (1998). Presentation to the American Society on Aging Annual Meeting.

Federal Interagency Forum on Aging-Related Statistics. (2000). Older Americans 2000: Key indicators of well-being. Washington, D.C.

Fisher, B.J. (1995). Successful aging, life satisfaction, and generativity in later life. *International Journal of Aging and Human Development, 41*, 239-250.

Freedman, M. (1999). *Primetime: How baby boomers will revolutionize retirement and transform America.* New York: Public Affairs.

Hart, P. (1999). *The new face of retirement.* Washington, D.C.: Peter Hart Research Associates.

Hooyman, N. & Kiyak, H. (1999). *Social gerontology: A multidisciplinary perspective.* Boston: Allyn and Bacon.

Kaiser Family Foundation Survey. (1999). Kids and media @ the new millenium.

Kingson, E.R., Cornman, J.C. & Leavitt, J. (1997, February). Bonds that build: An intergenerational strategy for community. *Wingspread Journal,* pp. 20-27.

Lugaila, T.A. (1998). Marital status and living arrangements: March 1998 (update) (Publication No. P20-506). Washington, D.C.: U.S. Census Bureau.

National Longitudinal Study of Adolescent Health. (2000).

Newman, S., Ward, C., Smith, T., et al.(1997). *Intergenerational programs: Past, present, and future.* Washington, D.C.: Taylor and Francis.

Peterson. P. (1999). *Gray dawn: How the coming age wave will transform America—and the world.* New York: Times Books.

Putnam, R. (2000). *Bowling alone: The collapse and revival of American community.* New York: Simon and Schuster.

Reich, R. (1998-99). Broken Faith: Why We Need to Renew the Social Compact. (In Keeping the promise: Intergenerational strategies for strengthening the social compact, a special issue of the Journal of the American Society on Aging.) *Generations, 22* (4), 19-24.

Riley, M.W., Kahn, R.L., & Foner, A. (Eds.) (1994). *Age and structural lag*. New York: John Wiley and Sons.

Roszak, T. (1998). *America the wise*. New York: Houghton Mifflin Company.

Rowe, J. & Kahn, R. (1998). *Successful aging*. New York: Pantheon Books.

Social Capital Community Benchmark Survey. (2001). http://www.cfsv.org/communitysurvey/results.html.

Tocqueville, A. (1840). *Democracy in America*. P. Bradley (Ed.) (1945). New York: Vintage Books.

U.S. Administration on Aging. (1996). *Aging in the twenty-first century*. Washington, D.C.: National Aging Information Center.

Zeldin, S., Camino, L. & Wheeler, W. (Eds.) (2000). Promoting adolescent development in community context: Challenges to scholars, nonprofit managers, and higher education. *Applied Developmental Science, 4*, special issue.

Intergenerational Teaching and Learning in Canadian First Nations Partnership Programs

By Jessica Ball, Alan Pence, Martina Pierre, and Valerie Kuehne

Introduction

The conventional image of the "ivory tower" of mainstream academia reaches back over the centuries, reinforcing the basic foundation of education as the conveying of "universal" truths and knowledge legitimated as the product of scientific inquiry. The same image also underlies a modernist approach to education that is fundamentally based on what learners *lack* rather than what they *bring* to the learning activity. However, with such an approach the ways of others cannot be respected but must be challenged by the one "true" way. In mainstream universities in Canada, as in nations around the world where European expansion and colonialism imposed a cultural majority on an indigenous minority population, Euro-western theories and research dominate the voice of academic credibility. The walls of the ivory tower have themselves become obstacles to hearing, seeing, and interacting with others' truths (Dahlberg, Moss & Pence, 1999).

In sharp contrast, the revitalization of traditional roles of teaching and learning that will be described in this chapter—within the context of a pioneering partnership approach to post-secondary training of child and youth care practitioners in First Nations communities across western

Canada—builds on a post-modernist foundation that respects and values a multiplicity of voices. This chapter will illustrate how the walls of academia were breached by an innovative, process-oriented approach to education in which the design, delivery, and evaluation of childcare training was jointly and successfully co-constructed by First Nations communities and the School of Child and Youth Care at the University of Victoria. The impetus for a series of collaborative partnerships undertaken through the 1990s will be presented in the context of the historical oppression of First Nations peoples in Canada. This will be followed by discussion of key components of the unique Generative Curriculum Model that now serves as a framework for community-based education among First Nations peoples. This program approach demonstrates the capacity to renew and strengthen local commitment and to provide for the developmental needs of young children and families in ways that incorporate their own cultural traditions, values, and practices. Particular attention will be paid to the role of First Nations Elders, whose active participation as co-instructors was instrumental in building bridges across generations, leading in turn to restored cultural pride, cultural knowledge, and cultural identity.

Beyond illustrating the richness of an intergenerational program model, another aim of this chapter is to share some insights about how to go beyond the superficial practices of those mainstream institutions that provide an ineffectual "add on" to Euro-western curricula as evidence of their sensitivity to minority cultures. Even within the realm of partnerships, problems have arisen for Canada's indigenous populations as the more dominant, mainstream partners ultimately require, implicitly or explicitly, the less dominant aboriginal partner to accommodate to majority cultural values. While some First Nations students achieve success in mainstream education programs, most lament their experiences, largely because the dominant discourse of valued theory and practices contradicts, invalidates, or undermines their way of life. Obstacles to learning typically encountered by minority students in adult education programs include: marginalization, invisibility, inferior status, negative expectations communicated by instructors, and a lack of cultural sensitivity among instructors and dominant culture students (Sparks, 1998).

There are, however, welcome signs of change. Early childhood education programs in parts of Canada are beginning to pay closer attention to the importance of preparing students to work with culturally and linguistically diverse children and families. A recent study on how Ontario community colleges are addressing the issue reports on teaching strategies for diversity awareness and action (Corson, 1998). Corson proposes three interconnected concepts of students' learning needs: self-discovery, cross-cultural understanding, and critical thinking skills. These concepts incorporate many of the principles and practices that have been put in place over the past decade through the series of partnerships that will be outlined in this chapter.

The process-oriented educational program that provides the framework for this chapter represents a radical shift from the longstanding "best" practices approach in early childhood education. It is based upon a partnership approach aimed at establishing meaningful, mutual, and ongoing intergenerational teaching and learning in First Nations communities. The process itself is complex, time-consuming, and richly rewarding. The ways in which community-specific cultural traditions and values enter the curriculum through intergenerational teaching and learning will be described, and the far-reaching, positive outcomes that are possible when Elders, instructors, and students work together in co-constructing curriculum, alongside a partnering university-based team, will be identified. As will be shown, the model outlined in this chapter has many possible applications across cultural communities and human service sectors.

First Nations: A Search for Culturally Appropriate Education

First Nations are among Canadian aboriginal peoples, who also include Inuit, Aleut, and Metis. There are approximately 500,000 status (registered) First Nations people living on reserve lands in Canada. In addition, there are an established 750,000 status and non-status First Nations and Metis people living off reserves, in both urban and rural communities. Groups of First Nations are often organized for administrative purposes into band councils or tribal councils representing several communities that are usually clustered together geographically. Constituent communities may or may not share the same cultural and migration history, language, and customs.

Traditionally Elders, who may play an honorary advisory role in community affairs, are relied on to pass down cultural traditions. They are often, though not always, senior citizens or elderly. Each community has its own criteria for recognizing and involving a community member as an Elder. In a large number of First Nations communities, as in many societies around the globe, Elders have lost their status, roles, and traditional functions in community life. This has occurred for a wide variety of reasons, many of which are general across societies and geographies.

Among First Nations in Canada, a particular kind of cultural holocaust has occurred over the past century. Those First Nations communities that survived the first wave of colonists have experienced the destruction of their family life through government policies requiring that children as young as five years old be sent to residential schools away from their communities. Most residential schools forbade the continuation of any manifestation of the child's culture of origin and, very often, denied family ties, including those of siblings living at the same school (Smillie, 1996). Tragically, such fragmentation greatly exacerbated the deterioration of Elders' roles and of intergenerational relationships within families and communities. Although the long era of enforced residential schools for First Nations children is now over, formidable gaps in the transmission of culture and extended familial bonds remain. Many First Nations adults do not know their own traditional culture and language of origin and have attenuated identities as First Nations people (York, 1990).

Not only do aboriginal students still not find their traditions and values respected in most early childhood education curricula, they often encounter negative stereotypes about First Nations people in texts and resources that continue to be presented by educators as authoritative research materials. Increasingly, however, national and regional aboriginal organizations in Canada are negotiating with governments and lobbying to establish economic and administrative control over fundamental services that impact on the health of their communities, including early childhood education and childcare. First Nations people are increasingly vocal about mainstream education programs that are neither transferable nor desirable within their cultural communities (Pence, Kuehne, Greenwood-Church, & Opekokew, 1993).

Culturally appropriate family services are crucial for the preservation of aboriginal traditions and identity, both of which have been under siege for generations in Canada through a combination of deliberate oppression and neglect by all levels of government. As Greenwood notes in an extensive review of aboriginal childcare in Canada, culturally appropriate childcare is regarded by First Nations communities as a necessary support to accessing employment and education opportunities. The virtual absence of these services is seen as a significant barrier to achieving social security, self-sufficiency and economic development goals (Greenwood, 1999).

First Nations Partnership Programs: An Overview

In the decade between 1989 and 1999, seven First Nations community groups partnered with a Canadian university to co-construct, deliver, and evaluate a program of community-based, bicultural course work leading to a Diploma in Child and Youth Care. The distinguishing characteristic of the evolving academic and professional field of Child and Youth Care in Canada is its developmental-contextual perspective. Students study and learn to serve children and families in ways that capitalize on their assets and that support rather than challenge their well being. The program that was developed is a uniquely collaborative approach to post-secondary education for minority culture students and is unprecedented in Canada and, to our knowledge, elsewhere.

The program was initiated in 1989 by the Meadow Lake Tribal Council, representing nine Cree and Dene communities in the province of Saskatchewan. The Council invited Alan Pence, of the University of Victoria, to collaborate on the development of a multicultural curriculum that would prepare Cree and Dene community members to deliver effective childcare programs in and beyond their communities, and in both aboriginal and non-aboriginal settings (Pence & McCallum, 1994; Pence, 1999).

After a review of existing mainstream programs of training, the Executive Director of the Meadow Lake Tribal Council, Ray Ahenakew, asked: "What of us—our Cree and Dene cultures—is in these [mainstream] programs? How are the particular needs, circumstances, and goals of our remote Cree and Dene communities going to be addressed in these programs?" The primary aim of the Meadow Lake Tribal Council was to develop and deliver a training program that would build upon existing cultural strengths. Their practical intent was to prepare community members to create child and family services that resonated with the cultural values, traditional knowledge, contemporary practices and objectives of their constituent First Nations communities. As Ahenakew emphasized: "We must rediscover our traditional values of caring, sharing, and living in harmony—and bring them into our daily lives and practices."

The training program that led to the creation of the First Nations Partnership Programs, and that became the catalyst for the Generative Curriculum Model (Pence & Ball, 1999; Pence et al., 1994), evolved from the addressing of these concerns. It began with an acknowledgement of the poor record of education and social programs imposed upon aboriginal peoples in North America by external agencies lacking in core aboriginal representation and with a vision that core elements of the curriculum and the program delivery would come from within the Cree and Dene communities to which the students belonged and, for the most part, where they intended to work.

In those communities, and in all subsequent partnerships between the University of Victoria and First Nations communities, Elders were identified as the people who best know the social, historical, and cultural contexts and goals for the children with whom childcare practitioners eventually work. Similarly, the role of Elders as the guardians of the culture had been highlighted in numerous reports by aboriginal organizations, including the first national inquiry in Canada to explore the needs and the meeting of those needs by existing childcare services of off-reserve status and non-status First Nations people. In the words of the Native Council of Canada, childcare "can be a vehicle through which cultures can be retained and transmitted from generation to generation" (Greenwood, 1999). Elders emerged as the natural choice for co-constructing and co-teaching the First Nations Partnership Programs curriculum. An Elder who participated regularly in the Mount Currie First Nation partnership noted:

> Our weekly meetings with students help us all to remember and pass
> along our culture [from] before the White Man came and remind us of
> how we raised our children, how we want them to grow, and who they
> will become as First Nations people.

Since the initial partnership with the Meadow Lake Tribal Council, there have been six further partnership programs, all located in rural areas of western Canada (British Columbia and Saskatchewan), including: Cowichan Tribes, Mount Currie First Nation, Nzen'man' Child and Family Services, Onion Lake First Nation, Tl'azt'en Nation, and Treaty 8 Tribal Association. The populations of our First Nations community partners have ranged from 800 to 3,000 individuals living on or near the reserve lands where the main community is situated. The seventh training program was completed in mid-1999, and partnerships are being considered with two more First Nations communities.

Previous reports on the First Nations Partnership Programs have explicated the principles that have guided program development and delivery across seven geographically dispersed and culturally distinct Canadian First Nations communities (Ball & Pence, 1999a; Pence & Ball, 1999b; Pence, Kuehne, Greenwood-Church, & Opekokew, 1993). Briefly, these guiding principles are:

1. Community initiative and involvement in all aspects of program delivery.
2. Bicultural respect.
3. Co-construction of curriculum (Euro-western tradition and community-specific tradition).
4. Community development through partnership.
5. Children as the focus within an ecological context.
6. University accredited Child and Youth Care education ladder.
7. Broad scope of human service career applications.

The following section will illustrate how these principles were put into practice.

The Generative Curriculum Model

Community contributions

First Nations communities engaged with the university-based team in mutual learning, sharing of skills, and collaborative construction of concepts and curricula. These were delivered in the students' own communities, using a flexible framework, called the Generative Curriculum Model, to support an intergenerational teaching and learning process. The first of the guiding principles ("community initiatives") translates into commu-

nity-directed action: the First Nations partner in the training program plays
the central role in all aspects of program planning, delivery, and evaluation. The community partner recruits students, instructors and other resource people, especially Elders, who contribute significant portions of
the curriculum content of each course, as well as some of the methods of
teaching and learning that themselves are embodiments of their aboriginal
culture. Topics most frequently addressed by Elders include: constructions of childhood and child development; children's roles in their families, peer groups, schools, and larger community; and the socialization
and care of children and youth. In the words of a student in the First
Nations Partnership Programs initiative with Mount Currie First Nation:

> This program is unique in giving me the chance to learn from my Elders
> what I need to know about who I am and my culture's ways of being
> with children. I couldn't learn this from any textbook, and I couldn't
> reach out to the children in my community ... without knowing what the
> Elders can teach me through this program.

University contributions

The guiding principles are further interwoven through the Generative
Curriculum Model in its "all ways" respectful teaching and learning about
different cultural perspectives. The curriculum content is bicultural: in
addition to learning from Elders, students are introduced to research-
based theory and practices of child and youth care and development.
They are exposed to some traditional Euro-western teaching strategies,
and they are asked to engage in the kinds of learning activities and evaluation procedures found on typical Canadian university campuses. Thus,
both the messages and the media from each partner enter the training
process. A student in our partnership program with Mount Currie First
Nation put it succinctly:

> Being in this program is like having the best of both worlds. We love to
> learn about what researchers have found out about child development
> and such from our textbooks, and we love to learn more about our own
> culture and how we can use it to help the children of our community.

The 18 courses that make up the training program are structured using
an "open architecture," with room for the voices of students, Elders, and
others in the community to participate fully in the active, constructivist
teaching and learning process. The knowledge and ideas about child and
youth care and development that students come away with are generated,
as it were, in the space between the two (or more) cultural groups. One of
the three instructors in the partnership with Mount Currie First Nation,
who was also a community member, noted:

We don't have all the answers. In a generative program, we can enjoy learning about what research on child development has shown and what methods seem to be helpful in certain situations. And we can delve further into our own history and traditions, and see how these can help us with our children.

As might be expected, given the name itself, the Generative Curriculum Model is characterized by a high level of participation and a large degree of indeterminacy. Precise details of the organizational structure, content, and goals of the child and youth care training program are deliberately left open-ended at the beginning of each partnership in order to make room for community participation in creating the course framework and generating curriculum content. In this way, each program is a unique co-creation of the particular partners. At the same time, all of the partnerships have been guided by the principles outlined earlier, with the most central being community-driven program delivery and collaborative intergenerational construction of curriculum.

Program highlights

The First Nations Partnership Programs and the model on which they are based have been very successful in several key areas and have gained national and international recognition. There are several reasons for this. First, program completion rates across the seven communities have ranged from 60 to 100 percent, far exceeding typical completion rates of 0 to 40 percent among First Nations students in other post-secondary programs across Canada. Second, over 95 percent of partnership program graduates have remained in their own communities to work in human service areas. This runs counter to the "brain drain" experienced by many rural First Nations communities when students are forced to leave home to undertake mainstream post-secondary education. Third, initiatives on the part of program graduates to promote the health and development of children and youth in their communities have been widely accepted and actively supported by the resident children, parents, and Elders. This contrasts with the community resistance that is frequently experienced when First Nations students return home and attempt to implement mainstream training programs learned in isolation from their communities. Fourth, evaluations of the programs have yielded evidence of far-reaching positive impacts on cultural pride, community cohesion, parenting effectiveness, and the development of a supportive community environment for children and youth (Ball & Pence, 1999a,b; Pence & Ball, 1999). Fifth, many Elders involved in the partnership programs have been reinstated to their traditional place as transmitters of culture, language, and dignity (Pence, 1998).

A core element of the Generative Curriculum Model is its ability to use intensive intergenerational experiences to reintegrate into the community those who have been isolated from it: the student who has gone away to pursue education or training and the Elder whose valued role has been forgotten.

A comprehensive research investigation was conducted in 1998-2000, partly to determine the effective components of the First Nations Partnership Programs that led to these unprecedented positive outcomes. Program evaluation identified the importance of the roles played by Elders and the mediating role played by an Intergenerational Facilitator.

Conditions Enabling Successful Intergenerational Processes

Community-driven program delivery

Successful intergenerational teaching and learning depends upon the initiative of the First Nations community in choosing to partner with the university and to participate in delivering the program in its own setting. The student cohorts enrolled in each training program ranged from 10 to 22 community members. Students were not required to leave their families or their roles in their community in order to take the program because it was delivered entirely in the community. Instructors were recruited by the communities and lived in or near the community where the program was delivered. An Intergenerational Facilitator, recruited from within the community, was responsible for coordinating regular meetings between Elders and students and facilitating effective dialogue, including discussions between Elders and course instructors on co-teaching.

The logistics of Elder involvement reflected variations among programs in terms of location and the diversity of constituent cultural communities. In some programs, such as those with the Meadow Lake Tribal Council, Cowichan Tribes, and Treaty 8 Tribal Association, students came from several different First Nations in the region. Elders from all of the communities to which the students belonged were recruited to participate in the program. This meant that some Elders traveled a considerable distance to attend the classes, and many different cultural traditions and languages were represented. In other partnerships, such as those with Mount Currie First Nation and Tl'azt'en Nation, the participating Elders all lived in the largest, centralized community and spoke the same traditional language.

In our experience, Elder involvement cannot be mandated when a program is initiated from outside the community. In the First Nations Partnership Programs, participation by dozens of Elders was the result of their gradual orientation to the nature of this community-initiated program and the rationale for their involvement. Community members made the invitations following culturally specific protocol. Individuals with whom the Elders had a prior relationship of trust made practical arrangements. The

Elders' sharing and dialogue with students and instructors were predicated upon mutual trust, obligation, and an acknowledgement of their common future as First Nations people.

Effective intergenerational teaching and learning is engendered when the program structure and content is sufficiently open and flexible to welcome both the content and form of Elders' participation. The nature of their contributions can neither be precisely prescribed nor predicted. The ways in which their contributions will be received also cannot be pre-ordained. As a native scholar who addressed the issue from an Elders' perspective has commented: "Elders have teaching challenges to deal with.... The legends and stories [of the Elders] have to be retold, reshaped, and refitted to meet contemporary seekers' changed and changing needs" (Couture, 1996, p. 52).

When Elder participation is construed as merely an intriguing addendum to the main body of curricula, little of value is likely to transpire. A growing number of post-secondary programs in Canada are jumping on the band wagon of cultural sensitivity, inviting one or two aboriginal Elders to give a "guest presentation" in a university setting or to perform a ceremonial function or two. This kind of limited and de-contextualized activity is decorative at best and can be destructively patronizing. It bears no resemblance to the ongoing, mutually transformative process that can and does occur when Elders are reinstated — through genuine interest and mutual engagement — in their traditional roles as men and women with the wisdom and experience to nurture younger generations and to pass on their valued knowledge, memories, spirituality, and skills (Ball & Pence, 1999a, b; Pence, 1999).

Students, for their part, needed time to absorb the Elders' offerings and to grow into their own roles as learners and as facilitators in the process of teaching, learning, and nurturing the relationships between the oldest and youngest generations. An Intergenerational Facilitator explained:

> The circle has been broken for so long, our ancestral traditions have been put aside for so long, the students need time, especially in the beginning. Time to recover who they are. Time to see that they are being asked and being given an opportunity to inherit all the accumulated wisdom of all the generations of people in our Nation who have gone before them. Time to grow into being the leaders in our community that they will become.

The intergenerational facilitator

Learning from Elders, even in a First Nations context where this is a common tradition, does not just happen automatically. Our experiences have shown that even when Elders are ready and willing to participate in and out of class meetings with students, there is no guarantee that something of mutual benefit and satisfaction will ensue. A bridge was needed to facilitate mutual engagement and to assist with the development of effective communication over time.

This bridging function was performed effectively by an Intergenerational Facilitator in each of the partnerships. These individuals held positions of trust and respect within their communities. In four of the partnerships, this role was filled by Elders or "Elders in training." The Intergenerational Facilitators were clearly vital from the outset, but what was not fully anticipated was the role that each of these Intergenerational Facilitators would play in helping to overcome misgivings by some course instructors and some students about the unfamiliar practice of placing the experiential wisdom of Elders alongside scripted curriculum materials offered from outside the community.

Within each cohort in the seven partnership programs, students were distributed along a bipolar dimension with regards to their initial receptivity to Elders' contributions. Typically, some students expressed fairly strong attachment to particular Elders and identification with their culture and community. Other students expressed fairly strong ambivalence about their communities and doubts about whether Elders' teachings could have any value or relevance to themselves, their families, or their future careers in child and youth care. Many of these students explained that they had enrolled in the program in order to gain the mainstream perspectives that they expected to find in university accredited courses. In two partnering communities, a majority of students stated that, initially, they saw the training program as a way to become independent, as their way out of their community and culture of origin.

At the conclusion of each partnership program, 95 percent of the students remained in their communities. Most are now committed to helping revitalize the cultural health of their home communities and improving the conditions of children in them. However, without the bridging functions performed by the Intergenerational Facilitator, it is likely that some of the students' initial feelings of alienation from the First Nations context and the generative nature of the curriculum would have persisted.

All of the First Nations community organizations that entered into a partnership for delivering the training program did so, in part, because they hoped that the involvement of Elders would create opportunities to retrieve and record their cultural histories and traditions and to bridge the gap between generations. In each program, the Intergenerational Facilitator was a member of the First Nations community to which all or most of the students belonged. The roles and responsibilities of this position encompassed many different aspects of intergenerational teaching and learning, including:

1. Seeking the participation of many Elders, including Elders from each of the communities to which students belonged.
2. Following cultural protocol for inviting the Elders and providing gifts to thank them for their participation.
3. Making practical arrangements for Elders' participation (e.g., transportation, meals, lodging).
4. Encouraging students to be receptive to Elders' invitations to meet outside the classroom. Some Elders preferred having students visit them at home to discuss course work.
5. Showing students how to act respectfully towards Elders in culturally congruent ways.
6. Helping with translation from a traditional First Nations language to English and vice-versa, as needed.
7. Helping students with the development of questions for Elders that pertained to course topics.
8. Generally promoting good communication and a good feeling between the students, instructors, and Elders.
9. Being available for students to react to the content or form of an Elder's contributions — to refute, debate, and discuss their teachings. As discussed, some students had somewhat negative or mixed reactions to some Elders' statements, at least initially.
10. Helping students to tolerate ambiguities in what Elders said. When Elders teach through stories, the lesson is often implicit or indirect and the learning is latent. Students have reported that months after a session with an Elder they suddenly understood the point.
11. Helping students to accept apparent contradictions between ideas presented in the university-based part of the curriculum and ideas presented by the Elders.
12. Modeling and reinforcing for students their own process of becoming bridges between the oldest and youngest generations, in accordance with traditional cultural roles, whereby Elders are mentors and guides and children are recipients of their wisdom and nurturance.

Outcomes

Reconnecting generations

As a result of the regular participation of Elders throughout the program and the supportive role of the Intergenerational Facilitator, students not only learned more about the traditions and values of their culture, but also forged relationships with older members of their community, often for the first time. A student in the partnership program with Tl'azt'en Nation, in north-central British Columbia, remarked:

Having the Elders coming to the program on a regular basis is really a good idea because we are learning their knowledge, and we are also getting to know them. I always wanted to learn from an Elder, but I was too shy and they weren't really ever around. Now I can walk with the Elders, and we can continue the talking from our class about the old ways and how these can still be used to help us with our children today.

The Meadow Lake community member who played the role of Intergenerational Facilitator commented on enhanced intergenerational rapport and communication in terms of systemic community change:

The students, recognizing the special wisdom of the Elders, began to consult them on personal as well as course-related matters. Today we have Elders involved in most community programs. In the past we seldom involved Elders. The childcare training program is where it all started.

Personal and cultural healing

Instructors have underscored the tremendous personal and cultural healing that students, instructors, Elders, and others involved in the program experienced as a result of mobilizing the whole community in explorations of childhood and in determining how best to support the development of children in their own community. Former students have reported increased cultural identity, self-esteem, parenting effectiveness, and confidence as community leaders as a result of the program. As the Intergenerational Facilitator in our partnership program with Cowichan Tribes said simply: "When the students get the elders' teachings, they are touching the ground and finding their roots."

It is generally agreed that a stable and strong identity and positive self esteem are important foundations for effectively socializing children and youth. But how do these qualities come about if one is divorced from the strengths of traditional care-giving in one's own cultural community? In our partnerships, we saw how the involvement of Elders brought all students, even the most disenchanted, into a circle of belonging to a nurturing community of other people who shared many of their sorrows and joys and who had the strength to support them through their personal healing, growth, and career development. In this regard, we have found that traditional constructs of "cultural sensitivity" and "cultural appropriateness" are wholly inadequate to capture the depth and significance of the experiences of participants in a training program grounded in intergenerational relationships — of respect, teaching, learning, sharing, and support — that are embodiments of the students' own cultures. One of our partners in the Mount Currie First Nation asserted: "We need our elders [in order] to regain our roots — our sense of ourselves and our beginnings — so that we can help our children set their feet on the path to a healthy future."

Enhanced parent-child relationships

Many students reported that they had learned from the Elders new ways of being with their own children and other children in their care. In the words of the Intergenerational Facilitator in our partnership with Cowichan Tribes:

> Elders' teachings have made the students more conscious. It has really improved parenting skills. Elders ask: 'Did you hear me? I know you're listening but did you really hear? Are you practicing what you heard?' And the students go home and practice what the elders told them about how to encourage their children and how to be patient with them.

Echoing this, a student in the program at Mount Currie declared:

> Patience. That's the most important lesson I learned from the elders. They taught us other things too, about our language and some of the ways of surviving back then, and crafts we can do with children now — that kind of thing. But patience is what they showed us, and I learned from them how to be patient with my kids.

Similarly, a student in our program with Meadow Lake Tribal Council said:

> The Elders taught me to listen to children. I always used to take the controlling seat...and now I allow my children to talk about their choices, and I listen to them and let them make some of their own decisions. And I think that's good. It teaches them some independence and some responsibility.

The ripple effect of Elders' involvement is further illustrated by an example drawn from the partnership with Mount Currie First Nation. Many parents in the community want their children to undergo traditional puberty training, which they believe engenders self-discipline, goal setting, cleanliness, and spirituality. Many of these parents, however, cannot look to their own adolescence for guidance. Because of their residential school experience, they did not undergo this traditional training. Many, in fact, were forced to renounce their cultural heritage, thus losing their connections to Elders and to the Elders' roles as teachers. Some leaders of the Mount Currie First Nation saw the partnership program as a chance to bring the Elders back into their natural teaching roles, in accordance with their Lil'wat culture. They hoped to increase knowledge in the community about rites of passage, such as puberty, as well as to learn from the Elders about other aspects of child rearing.

A revered Elder, Marie Leo, accepted an invitation from the Intergenerational Facilitator to meet with students in the partnership program to discuss traditional Lil'wat child rearing practices, including puberty rites. These discussions were both videotaped and recorded in students' notes as part of their course work. During the program, Leo gave the following account of her experience:

> I really enjoy it, going over there and answering questions that the students give us. It's really needed for the young people to remember our ways, how we raised our children and how we disciplined them. And we talk about it in our language so that we can get it right. I hope the students learn from us that it is not our way to scream at a child, 'cause a screaming mother has a screaming child later. A child needs to hear gentle ways, and needs to be talked to, even laughed with, when they're acting up. They need a lot of understanding. There is a lot of support for these young students to learn, and not just learn our ways, but learn all kinds of ways from everyone, like [those of] my old friend who is East Indian, and my old Chinese friend, and others of us who are old in this community. Even if these people didn't necessarily grow up here, we all have something to teach these young students. Even though we're not teachers, we're like Argyle socks — we're all diamond and intertwined.

Culturally grounded practitioner training

As discussed earlier, the majority of students who participated in First Nations Partnership Programs completed the program, and all but a few graduates have remained in their own communities to work in human services, mostly in childcare and development programs. Clearly, there is immeasurable value to First Nations communities when trained childcare practitioners remain in the community to work, initiate new programs, serve as role models, and generally share their knowledge and skills. Program graduates have been hired for a range of occupations, including: staff and supervisory roles in daycares, Aboriginal Head Start programs, preschools, and kindergartens; teachers' assistants; learning support workers; home-school liaison workers; youth activities coordinators; and college and continuing education advisors for other First Nations students.

Because students in the partnership programs learned through dialogue and practice within their own community, rather than in isolation, what they contribute as leaders in human service development and in their own families resonates with the cultural outlook and approaches of their community. Former students have emphasized the value of being able to discuss with their Elders a range of traditional and contemporary ideas about what children need to develop optimally and how best to foster children's well-being in their own community. Dialogue with Elders has provided, and continues to provide, opportunities to assess alternative approaches for their appropriateness to the culturally specific goals for children that parents and Elders in the community want and are most likely to support. A frequent theme in the accounts of former students about their program experience is that they gained knowledge and skills during their training that did not represent ideas they associated with education received at a distance, at mainstream institutions. Most of those latter ideas the Elders and other community members described as "foreign," "impractical," "irrelevant," "totally white," or "culturally contradicting."

As a community-based administrator for the partnership with Treaty 8 Tribal Association in northeast British Columbia remarked:

> We can consider what mainstream theories say, and if we choose to believe them and use them in our work, that doesn't make us less Indian. And if we choose to assert the importance of our cultural traditions and ways of raising children, that doesn't make us wrong. This program recognizes and encourages this give and take, pick and choose. It doesn't cage us and expect us to act like Europeans, to act as if we're assimilated.

Conclusion

The training programs described in this chapter contain powerful intergenerational interventions through ongoing and direct Elder involvement in student learning, as developed by a community member in the role of an Intergenerational Facilitator. Riley and Riley (1994) have described opportunities for community members to participate in grappling with issues that face them in their everyday lives as "opportunity structures" and argue that more of these structures must be created for older adults to contribute meaningfully to their societies. The First Nations Partnership Programs provide such structures at the foundation of training; as a result, the participating Elders in partnering communities truly can be "primary contributors to the constantly continuing process of building community stability and development" (Kretzman & McKnight, 1993, p. 51).

Program participants have spoken eloquently about the many ways in which the focus on intergenerational teaching and learning has contributed to the revitalization of traditional roles, helping to restore and reconstruct their cultural identity, cultural knowledge, and cultural pride. Many community members have described how the involvement of Elders in the training programs has helped the community as a whole return to its cultural and spiritual beginnings, becoming more culturally directed in creating child and youth care services that further the goals of healthy development and cultural continuity across generations. Their clear and strong words add support to the growing chorus of voices now advocating for intergenerational approaches to enrich the personal and social fabric of all societies (Calhoun, Kingson, & Newman, 1997; Kuehne, 1998-99). A student in the Mount Currie First Nation program asserted:

> We can't learn everything from our books. We also have to learn from our Elders as to how to raise our children, and then they will know how to raise their children, and it just goes on from there."

In the end, as one community-based administrator said: "The elders have the hope for our people. When we listen to what they want to pass on to us, they pass on their hope to us."

References

Ball, J., & Pence, A.R. (1999a). Beyond developmentally appropriate practice: Developing community and culturally appropriate practice. *Young Children*, March, 46-50.

Ball, J., & Pence, A. (1999b). Promoting healthy environments for children and youth through participatory, bicultural, community-based training partnerships. *Notos: Intercultural and Second Language Council Journal, 1* (1), 26-33.

Calhoun, G., Kingson, E., & Newman, S. (1997). Intergenerational approaches to public policy: Trends and challenges, (pp. 161-173). In S. Newman, C. Ward, T. Smith, J. Wilson and J. McCrea (Eds.) *Intergenerational programs: Past, present, and future.* Washington, D.C.: Taylor & Francis.

Corson, P. (1998). Preparing early childhood educators for diversity. *Interaction, 12* (2), 30-31.

Couture, J.E. (1996). The role of native elders: Emergent issues (pp. 41-56). In D.A. Long and O.P. Dickason (Eds.), *Visions of the heart: Canadian aboriginal issues.* Toronto: Harcourt Brace.

Dahlberg, G., Moss, P., & Pence, A. (1999). *Beyond quality in early childhood education and care: Postmodern perspectives.* London: Falmer Press.

Greenwood, M. (1999). Aboriginal childcare in review (Part One). *Interaction, 13* (2), 17-20.

Kretzman, J. & McKnight, J. (1993). *Building communities from the inside out: A path toward finding and mobilizing community assets.* Chicago, IL: ACTA Publications.

Kuehne, V.S. (1998-99). Building intergenerational communities through research and evaluation. *Generations, 22* (1), 82-87.

Pence, A.R. (1998). On knowing the place: Reflections on understanding quality care. *Canadian Journal for Research in Early Childhood Education.*

Pence, A.R. (1999). "It takes a village...", and new roads to get there (pp. 322-336). In D. Keating and C. Hertzman (Eds.), *Developmental Health as the Wealth of Nations.* New York: Guilford Press.

Pence, A.R., & Ball, J. (1999). Two sides of an eagle's feather: Co-Constructing ECCD training curricula in university partnerships with Canadian First Nations communities (pp. 36 - 47). In H. Penn (Ed.), *Theory, policy and practice in early childhood services.* Buckingham, UK: Open University Press.

Pence, A.R., Kuehne, V., Greenwood-Church, M., & Opekokew, M.R. (1993). Generative Curriculum: A model of university and First Nations co-operative post-secondary education. *International Journal of Educational Development, 13* (4), 339-349.

Pence, A.R., & McCallum (1994). Developing cross-cultural partnerships: Implications for childcare quality research and practice (pp. 108-122). In P. Moss and A. Pence (Eds.), *Valuing Quality in Early Childhood Services: New approaches to defining quality.* New York: Teachers College Press.

Riley, J., & Riley, M. (1994). Beyond productive aging. *Aging International, 21* (2), 15-19.

Smillie, B.G. (1996). The missionary vision of the heart (pp. 21-40). In D.A. Long and O.P. Dickason (Eds.), *Visions of the heart: Canadian aboriginal issues.* Toronto: Harcourt Brace.

Sparks, B. (1998). The politics of culture and the struggle to get an education. *Adult Education Quarterly, 48* (4), 245-259.

York, G. (1990). *The dispossessed: Life and death in native Canada.* Toronto: Little, Brown.

Notes

1 Funding for research on the Generative Curriculum Model on which this chapter was based was provided by Childcare Visions, Human Resources Development Canada, the Lawson Foundation, and the Vancouver Foundation.

Intergenerational Programs and Possibilities in Hawaii[1]

By Matthew S. Kaplan, Ph.D. and Joseph W. Lapilio, III

Introduction

As in many other regions in the United States, Hawaii is home to an active intergenerational movement characterized by a host of diverse initiatives. Senior adult volunteers contribute to student learning in schools, students visit nursing homes and other adult care facilities, community centers organize intergenerational crafts and story-telling activities, and faith-based organizations coordinate efforts to support isolated, frail elders.

Hawaii is also home to intergenerational festivals, awards ceremonies, training workshops, conferences, college certificate training programs, and a statewide network of organizations and individuals devoted to promoting intergenerational programs and policies throughout island communities. The result is an impressive web of organized activity aimed at strengthening and preserving the integrity of intergenerational relationships in people's lives.

To explore Hawaii's intergenerational movement and consider some likely directions it will take in years to come, it is vital to attend to Hawaii's unique cultural landscape, its history, and its current demographic and social trends. To begin with, Hawaii is the gateway to the United States for a large immigrant population coming from nations throughout the Pacific/ Asian region. In addition, as one of the 50 United States, it is the destination of an increasingly steady migration of people from the North American continent. It is estimated that by 2003, one-half of Hawaii's one million residents will be people born in some location other than Hawaii (Hawaii Community Services Council, 1999).

In addition to Hawaii's substantial European (including mainland United States), Chinese, and Japanese populations, it has, if not large, at least statistically significant Filipino, Korean, and Southeast Asian populations. It could in consequence be viewed as an East-meets-West microcosm.

Further, Hawaii is simultaneously home to an indigenous Pacific Island culture with its own rich history and identity. Citizens of native Hawaiian ancestry, still about 15 percent of the population, are the descendants of voyagers in historically separate migrations from other Polynesian islands, around 500 A.D. and again from 1100 to 1500 A.D. (Sing, 1986.)

This meeting of peoples and worldviews has yielded one of the most interesting and diverse multicultural populations in the world.

Though Hawaii is known for its tolerance and diversity, its history is filled with turbulence and conflict. First Western contact took place in 1778. Within 40 years, by the time the first King Kamehameha had died in 1819, Hawaii's essentially feudal society and stone age culture was united and transformed into a European style monarchy with institutions modeled on both the British and United States systems of government. In 1893, the last remaining monarch, Queen Liliuokalani, was overthrown by a group of Americans who felt their business interests were threatened (Herman, 1999). By 1900, Hawaii was a territory of the United States. In 1959, it was admitted into the union as a state. Struggles for cultural identity and the very survival of Hawaii's indigenous culture continue today in various forms.

In the context of a resurgence in recent years of interest in strengthening and reaffirming positive aspects of Hawaiian cultural values and sense of spirituality, some important intergenerational programs and practices have developed which promote cultural perspectives, celebrate cultural values, and work to transmit cultural knowledge. These initiatives use storytelling, dance, cultural crafts, healing arts, and other modalities to bring people together across generations in a manner that emphasizes elements of the Hawaiian cultural heritage. Participants gain a sense of connectedness to a cultural timeline (cultural continuity) and likely receive the benefits that psychologists associate with the sense of belonging that comes with an intact sense of cultural identity.

There are other dynamics that also have a profound influence on Hawaii's intergenerational landscape. For example, Hawaii is undergoing some of the same demographic changes as other places; i.e., there is a distinct "aging society" trend. According to the Executive Office on

Aging, from 1980 to 1990 the number of persons in Hawaii aged 60+ grew by 52.5 percent as compared to a 14.9 percent growth rate for the total population. Furthermore, when extending current population trends to the year 2020, Hawaii's 85+ group is projected to increase by 242 percent, the second fastest growth rate in the nation (behind Nevada's 245 percent). As the population ages, there will likely be considerable interest and debate in the years to come about how to generate active roles for seniors.

At the same time, Hawaii is facing a pattern of rapid growth in its young population. Today, one half of all residents 19 years old and younger are under the age of five. With growing numbers of very young and very old, Hawaii is faced with a challenge and an opportunity. From a deficits perspective, these population groups present a growing challenge as they will compete for limited resources to address their needs. From an assets perspective, the existence of these two diverse groups represent an opportunity for collaboration and engagement between generations and a chance to transmit values and culture from elders to youth.

Concerns in regard to certain modes of Western influence in Hawaii also has a bearing on the public's support for intergenerational program strategies. Chief among these are chronic social problems, fragmented human service systems, and the declining quality of life of socially dislocated young people and senior adults. In the aftermath of recent episodes of youth violence such as that at Columbine High School,[2] echoes of the national question, "Can this happen here?" resonate throughout Hawaii.

Fortunately, in Hawaii we do not see the kind of "breakdown" in intergenerational relations that is making headlines in U.S. mainland newspapers. There are various reasons for this, including the high level of respect that people have for the traditions and values—and the elders who transmit these—in the many cultures that make up Hawaii's multi-cultural landscape. Hawaii is home to people from cultural backgrounds which accentuate values related to intergenerational respect and continuity. For example, the Confucian ethic of filial piety propagated in many local Asian families conveys a sense of loyalty and responsibility to elderly family members. This often translates into a preference for maintaining intergenerational households, even when it entails caring for ill or frail family members at home despite formidable economic and social obstacles. And the host culture of Hawaii has a long tradition of respect for the *kupuna*, the elders, as teachers of both practical tasks and spiritual values.

In the remainder of this article, we will highlight some of the many intergenerational initiatives taking root in Hawaii and present some suggestions for additional intergenerational activity. Since there is so much intergenerational activity going on, we will attempt merely to demonstrate the diversity of such initiatives rather than to provide an exhaustive list. We believe that such an examination of how the theme of intergenerational connection and reconnection is played out in

Hawaii can provide insights into how diverse philosophies, policies, complexities, and quality-of-life concerns shape modern life in Hawaii. At the same time, it is our hope that by placing Hawaii under an intergenerational-studies lens, new ideas will be generated for addressing some of Hawaii's most enduring problems.

Intergenerational Intervention from a Native Hawaiian Perspective

Members of indigenous cultures with histories of discontinuity/fragmentation seem to experience a disproportionate number of problems in terms of family relations (e.g., incidence of abuse), health, educational performance, and employment. This is the case for Native Hawaiians as well as Native Americans, Aborigines of Australia and many other indigenous peoples. Native Hawaiians constitute between 12.5 and 18.8 percent of the total population,[3] but they represent 38 percent of the prison population (Herman, 1999) and 45 percent of the teenage mothers (Sing, 1997). Also, compared to other ethnic groups in Hawaii, they are the lowest academic performers in public schools[4] and the highest alcohol and drug abusers among high school seniors (Sing, 1997). They also have the highest percentages of homelessness and unemployment, the highest proportion of health risks, and the lowest life expectancy (Herman, 1999).

Traditionally, social agencies tend to treat these problems separately. If somebody is homeless, their focus is on finding them a home; if somebody has a reading problem, put them in a remediation program. Alternatively, particular needs or difficulties as experienced by Native Hawaiians can be viewed holistically, as integrally tied to the experience of cultural dislocation. In this formulation, culture is seen as the central venue through which people can find their relationships to each other, have a sense of self identity and self respect, and discern how they fit into the world (and beyond).

Dr. David Sing, director of "Na Pua No'eau" (The Center for Gifted and Talented Native Hawaiian Children), based at the University of Hawaii at Hilo, has been a powerful spokesperson for the importance of nurturing intergenerational contacts for strengthening and reaffirming positive aspects of Hawaiian cultural values and sense of spirituality. He presents a "fly a kite" metaphor for a conceptual framework for linking the problems experienced by indigenous peoples to the experience of cultural dislocation (Sing, 1997). The kite represents the child and its flight represents the child's knowledge and aspirations. The string, the foundation for holding the kite, represents the child's "source." This includes family and culture. If this connection is severed, the kite flies wild.

Sing sees the main intervention objective as the instilling in young children of a Hawaiian perspective. They can then use this as a foundation from which they can embrace life's challenges, including learning subjects as diverse as history, technology, and values. Senior adults have an invaluable role to play as conveyers of culture. A common phrase in Hawaiian reflects a tradition of respecting the power and prestige of elders: "*na hulu kupuna*" ("our precious elders"). In the Hawaiian community, as in other traditional Asian-Pacific cultures, the elder (kupuna) is respected, holds a high position in the family, and plays a prominent role in terms of passing on stories, teaching language, and conveying cultural perspectives. When younger generations lose touch with, or stop respecting, the experiences of the older generations, members of both generations are disconnected not only from each other but also from an important dimension of their culture.

The resurgence, in the last 25 years, of Hawaii's indigenous culture has fueled efforts to rejuvenate Hawaiian arts, language, medicine, religious practices, and territorial integrity[5] (Herman, 1999). In hula, a prime example of a cherished cultural tradition, practitioners are finding a deep sense of cultural significance in their art form. This sentiment is conveyed by Keolalaulani Dalire, recent winner of the Miss Aloha Hula contest, as she described her feelings about hula and her lifelong quest to learn more: "This is a reawakening for me and for all of us, the Hawaiian people, to regain what they have lost in the past" (*Oi*, April 9, 1999, A-6). Hula, as other Hawaiian cultural arts, provides a link to the past (or the *piko*) and helps to provide a place, or reference point, for those who practice it.[6]

The current struggle to restore Hawaii's indigenous language is an important aspect of this cultural resurgence. Since the language we speak is interwoven with our sense of heritage, it is important not to trivialize language. Many indigenous people have suffered the indignation of losing their language and, with this, an important aspect of their cultural distinctiveness. Elizabeth Kauahipaula, an activist in the Hawaiian language resurgence movement, remembers being beaten by teachers for speaking Hawaiian. She also recounts teachers making home visits, telling Native Hawaiian parents that speaking Hawaiian at home had a negative impact on their children's academic performance in school (Whitney, 1999).

From an historical perspective, these experiences reinforce the view that the Hawaiians did not lose their language; it was taken from them. In 1880, 150 schools taught in Hawaiian, but in 1897, four years after the overthrow of Queen Liliuokalani, only one was left (Whitney, 1999). It wasn't until the 1960s that interest developed in a systematic attempt to resurrect the Hawaiian language. By the end of the 1970s, the renaissance of the Hawaiian language had brought it back into the schools, including the University of Hawaii, but it wasn't until 1986 that the Legislature passed a bill that removed laws that made instruction in Hawaiian in both public and private schools illegal. Where only a dozen years ago only a few elderly people spoke Hawaiian, now there are young people graduating from high school language immersion programs having been taught all of their topics in Hawaiian (Whitney, 1999).[7]

Another indication that the Hawaiian language is alive and growing is its presence on the internet. Whitney (1999) states:

> Internet searches can be done on Ka Ho'okele 4.05, a Hawaiian language Web browser adapted from Netscape Navigator. Anyone can download Ka Ho'okele and a Hawaiian language font installation from Kualono, which is at www.olelo.hawaii.edu. (p. 46).

Another force that is helping to strengthen Native Hawaiian cultural consciousness is a tradition of defiance that has been kept alive for more than 100 years. Since the overthrow of Queen Liliuokalani in 1893, many remarkable individuals have fought diligently, often with great personal sacrifice, against educational, governance, and human service policies that have oppressed the Hawaiian people and denied the legitimacy of their cultural distinctiveness as an important resource, a way of life, and a source of pride and strength.[8]

Native Hawaiians' voices have found expression through political activism, literature, songs, chants, and alternative economic and community development. Among Hawaii's most popular songs are those that refer to the struggles of Hawaiians at the time of the Queen's overthrow. Songs, such as *Kaulana Na Pua, Onipa'a* and *Hawai'i Aloha* were initially solidarity songs to protest the overthrow and annexation of Hawaii by the United States.[9] The resurgence of *hula kahiko* (the more ancient forms of hula) includes expressions of not only pride but determination. Whether through hula, mentoring, or other means, this tradition of activism is kept alive by the transmission of activist skills and values from generation to generation.

A prime example of how cultural revitalization, Hawaii-style, is embraced as an intergenerational challenge is the adventure of *Hokulea*. Beginning in the 1970s, the rebirth of instrument-less ocean navigation through the voyages of the Polynesian voyaging canoe, *Hokulea*, brought together the Hawaiian community in building the vessel and in its numerous journeys throughout Polynesia. During the voyages to Tahiti, Rapa Nui, and Aotearoa, 6,000 youths in schools across the state plotted the canoe's course and built on the metaphor of voyaging to design a vision for Hawaii's future. Using this vision, adults assisted in developing a plan for Hawaii decision-makers. The project, *Ke Ala Hoku*, is becoming a national model for the use of outcomes and benchmarking.

Intergenerational Programs and Organizations

School-based intergenerational programs

Hawaii is home to some large-scale school-based intergenerational programs. One initiative, clearly influenced by the Native Hawaiian cultural renaissance, is the "Kupuna Program," managed by the Department of Education's Hawaiian Studies Division. Focused primarily on the early elementary population, native elders (*kupuna*) are hired part-time to share their stories, songs, and arts and crafts with children. While the program is under potential assault in a cash-strapped state, because of it thousands of young children have regular exposure to elders and are able to make connections to their past. Through experiences such as these, coupled with the training from home and family, many elder Hawaiians are called "aunty" or "uncle" by children to whom they are not related and whom they do not even know.

Two other influential senior volunteer programs are "Senior Adults Volunteering in Education" (SAVE), administered by Helping Hands Hawaii, and the Tutu Tutorial Program, sponsored by the Assistance League of Hawaii.

There are also numerous small programs, many of which typically do not receive much media attention but which nevertheless effectively enliven students' exposure to academic subjects and local history. For example, the SASSIE Program (Seniors and Students Sharing Intergenerational Experiences) brings a small group of Mililani (Honolulu) senior adults into Kipapa Elementary School to enhance student learning and appreciation of Hawaii's plantation era local history. The vision of SASSIE organizers is to relocate Kipapa School Building "B," the last remaining plantation-type school building on Oahu, to Hawaii's Plantation Village in Waipahu, where it would be converted into an innovative intergenerational sharing and historical learning center.

A program called FELLOWS (Fellowship and Lifelong Learning Opportunities at Waialae School) represents a "senior center within a school" approach for cultivating senior adults as educational resources. Based in Waialae Elementary School (in the Kaimuki neighborhood of Honolulu), the FELLOWS Center serves as a magnet for recruiting and training senior adult volunteers to perform a variety of functions at the school. These include basic tutoring, participating in special school events, mentoring, and engaging the students in discussion about the local community and issues of citizenship. Program partners include Seniors Actively Volunteering in Education and the Hawaii Intergenerational Network.

The Hawaii Intergenerational Network has also developed a senior mentoring initiative for preschool-aged children who have emotional or behavioral difficulties. With funding recently approved by the state legislature

($100,000 for each of two years), the Network and various community organization partners will train 25 senior volunteers, match them with 50 children aged 2 to 5 years attending four preschools, and facilitate mentoring relationships that provide the children with nurturing support appropriate to their emotional or behavioral difficulties. The model is also designed to be family oriented. Mentors will whenever possible be compatible with the children's families. Factors such as culture and language and even the neighborhoods in which they live will be considered. Family strengthening will be promoted through ongoing communication and conferences with parents, volunteers and coordinators. Parents will also meet quarterly as a group with mentors and coordinators to discuss appropriate modeling practices.

The inverse of senior adult volunteerism is youth volunteerism. Grounded in the same spirit of community service, many school-based initiatives recruit and train young people to provide meaningful services for senior adults. Punahou School (private, non-denominational, K-12), for example, has an innovative community service program in which students visit seniors in adult care facilities and nursing homes as one option for fulfilling their mandatory community service requirements. As part of this initiative, Dr. Felice Brown, the director of Intergenerational Rainbows, created and initiated the "Rainbow Connection" course which she taught for several summers at Punahou with fifth through eighth grade students. After an intense training period, students visited skilled nursing facilities daily for six weeks, using clowning, puppetry, the arts, music, and magic as motivational tools for engaging the seniors. Beyond the positive impact the students had on the seniors' lives, the students themselves experienced profound growth and enhanced self esteem as a function of learning that they could make a positive difference in other people's lives (F. Brown, personal communication, 1999).

Intergenerational festivals

The past few years have witnessed many firsts in Hawaii's growing intergenerational movement. In 1999, American Savings Bank began sponsoring the annual "Keiki Kupuna Festival," a milestone event taking place at Seagull Schools' Kapolei (leeward Oahu) Campus. Activities included the creation of family trees to trace people's heritage, a keiki-kupuna look-alike contest, and a host of hands-on activities conducted throughout the Kapolei facility through which participants of all age groups engaged each other in crafts, discussion, song, and computer play.

According to Jeff Wagner, one of the facilitators of this event,

> The seniors as well as the children embrace the activities with a sense of
> "awe" and a sense of sharing... There are no fears, no stereotypes, no
> "grumpy old people" who hate kids. They (the children) find just the

opposite; the seniors are very gentle and loving. They tell wonderful stories and sing all kinds of songs. Some even tell jokes as they play games with them.

Wayne Minami, President and CEO of American Savings Bank, further captured the spirit of the event: "The kupuna have so much to share with our keikis about our treasured heritage and history. The sharing and caring between the generations will sustain a thriving community in Hawaii" (Wagner, 1999).

The intergenerational connection theme is expressed in other festival-type events as well. For example, each year the Kohala High School (North Kohala, Island of Hawaii), in partnership with health agencies and community members, hosts the Kohala Intergenerational Health Fair. The activities, which target youth and senior adults, include: workshops on traditional and alternative healing, free testing and health screenings, student dramatic performances highlighting the gift of good health, senior adult presentations on traditional arts, and a concert by popular local bands, highlighting the theme of drug-free expression. Referring to the Health Fair held March 17, 2000, David Fuertes, a high school teacher and longtime community volunteer, stated:

> We envision the school as a dynamic hub of our community, bridging the generations through mentorships and outreach, strengthening our unique and rich Kohala community, preserving traditions and creating new traditions to endure in the hearts of our youth (Kohala Intergenerational Fair, 2000).

The Lualualei Starlight Storytelling Festival, held annually on the Waianae Coast of Oahu, is another example of a generation-bridging event. Planned by Nettie Armitage-Lapilio and hosted at a public beach park, the festival is usually scheduled for five consecutive nights, featuring a different storyteller each night, under the stars. A truly grassroots event, the audience is filled with families who bring their dinners and blankets in order to enjoy the night with their children. According to the organizer, "Opportunities like this, that bring families together to share a common event, have become rare. But the overwhelming response to our event clearly shows a hunger to return and strengthen these opportunities" (N. Armitage-Lapilio, personal communication, May 2000).

Intergenerational advocacy

A framework for establishing an intergenerational advocacy initiative in Hawaii is being developed through a unique partnership between Kokua Council for Senior Citizens and St. Andrew's Priory. Nine St. Andrews Priory students have been organized as a parallel board of the Kokua Council. Although this youth advisory board does not have fiduciary responsibility, they attend Kokua Council's monthly meetings and help provide testimony, write testimony, and decide which legislative issues require action for Kokua Council follow-up. This initiative represents an innovative strategy for building upon and extending Kokua Council's fine tradition of advocacy work on behalf of Hawaii's senior adult population, while at the same time expanding opportunities for young people to learn how to influence the legislative system as it affects the quality of life for both youth and seniors.

Another advocacy initiative that has gained momentum in Hawaii (as well as the U.S. Mainland) is tied to the issue of grandparents' rights. *Na Tutu*, an ad hoc committee of the Windward Oahu Family & Community Education Council (FCE), is dedicated to supporting legislation that will allow minor children who, for various reasons, are under the full care of grandparents, aunts, godparents, stepparents or close family friends, to receive needed care and support within a family environment. With a history dating back to a videotape conference held on January 11, 1999 in which the Windward Oahu FCE participated,[10] *Na Tutu* has grown into a formidable collaboration of organizations concerned with the issues facing grandparents, family members, and any adult raising children other than their own. Through numerous meetings with state legislators, and with an innovative strategy of giving out "Na Tutu dolls" to legislators, the group successfully lobbied passage in the Hawaii State Senate of a grandparents' rights bill similar to the ones passed in some other states (e.g., Kentucky and Indiana). The bill is currently moving through the State House of Representatives.

It is also important to include in this section efforts by native Hawaiian groups and individuals aimed at affecting state policies that have a bearing on the quality of life of native Hawaiian families. It is not uncommon to find large groups of native Hawaiians, with all generations represented — including *keiki* (children), *makua* (adult generation), and *kupuna* (elders) — camped out at the state legislature participating in public demonstrations, or perhaps even engaged in actions of civil disobedience (e.g., beach "squatter" communities).

Community service

On Lanai, elders, who have taken the challenge to repair two centuries of environmental damage, actively work with young Hawaiians on the island by visiting classrooms, telling their stories, and taking them to reforestation sites to help plant new vegetation and tend to that already planted by the preservation project. Considering that the level of environmental damage will require several generations of Lana`i residents to repair, the intergenerational and multi-agency focus of this initiative is quite appropriate. The project is called *Hui Malama Pono O Lanai*, translated as "Restore the Island of Lanai."

Several intergenerational initiatives with a community service thrust can also be categorized as "faith-based initiatives." A noteworthy program is Project Dana, which enlists volunteers of all ages to provide an array of services for frail elderly and disabled persons, including home visits, telephone visits, respite assistance, hospital and care home visits, minor home repairs and light housekeeping, and transportation assistance. With its name derived from the Sanskrit word for selfless giving, Project Dana is an interfaith cooperative effort based in the Moiliili Hongwanji Mission. Project Dana's administrator, Rose Nakamura, has the singular ability to see her world through an intergenerational perspective. Each need she encounters triggers an intergenerational response. For example, when a single working mother with young children moved into the neighborhood, Nakamura introduced the family to an elderly widow in the same building. Such matches result in great benefits for both parties.

Project Dana also coordinates efforts with the Kailua Hongwanji Temple to provide services for individuals in Honolulu and on windward side of Oahu. Sixty-five agencies, including churches, hospitals and the Executive Office on Aging are members of Project Dana's Oahu network. Project Dana trains volunteer coordinators from partner organizations and from church congregations interested in initiating or strengthening their own ministries of caring. All new volunteers receive training and education in an orientation program that promotes respect and compassion for the individuals who receive care.

Another faith-based initiative that spans the generations is FACE (Faith and Action for Community Equity), a coalition of 23 religious institutions representing 3,000+ constituents from the Catholic, Protestant, Buddhist, and Jewish faiths.

Although intergenerational exchange is not one of its fundamental goals, through its mission of finding non-controversial yet life-supporting community improvement ideas, this coalition regularly focuses on issues affecting the young and the elderly. For example, FACE launched a campaign to ban advertisements aimed at raising youth alcohol consumption.

FACE has also been effective in improving bus stops for seniors and reducing traffic hazards for elder or handicapped pedestrians who need more time to get across streets. To address the issues and search for remedies, FACE holds monthly and annual meetings of local residents (of all ages) and politicians.

A statewide network

The Hawaii Intergenerational Network (HIN) was created in 1993 and incorporated as a membership non-profit organization by the State of Hawaii in 1996 for the purpose of promoting and enhancing intergenerational programs and activities throughout the state. According

to Generations United, the premier membership-based national organization that focuses solely on promoting intergenerational strategies, programs, and policies, Hawaii is one of approximately 20 states with a statewide intergenerational network. Like most of these other statewide
intergenerational coalitions and networks, the Hawaii Intergenerational
Network functions to promote information exchange, provide technical
assistance, and advocate on behalf of intergenerational programs and
policies at the state level. This entails distributing a newsletter on a regular basis, sponsoring seminars and conferences, and producing resource
materials (e.g., an "occasional papers" series), all with the goal of generating excitement and building the knowledge base needed to support
intergenerational initiatives in Hawaii.

   Unlike most other statewide intergenerational networks, however, HIN
takes a direct role in planning and implementing new intergenerational
programs. Beginning in 1998, HIN began forming partnerships with other
organizations for the purpose of establishing "demonstration projects"
and using these initiatives to communicate to the public and the professional community the value of intergenerational methodologies for addressing various educational, human service and community development needs. HIN's ultimate strategy for these demonstration projects is to
facilitate their eventual evolution into self-sustaining entities, with col-
laborating local organizations taking ownership over program administration functions. Through a strategic planning process conducted with the
HIN Board of Directors in 1999, a key decision was made to further develop HIN's demonstration projects strategy as the organization's central
tool for educating the public and the professional community about the
benefits of intergenerational programs. Three demonstration projects are
now in operation, and HIN is in discussions with other organizations to
establish two new projects.

   HIN currently has 55 individual and organizational members. Beyond
this list, there are over 100 "Friends of HIN," with whom HIN representatives communicate frequently. These represent key collaborators, contributors, and supporters of HIN in its mission to promote and strengthen
intergenerational programs in Hawaii.

Intergenerational awards and recognition

   In conjunction with the annual Keiki-Kupuna Festival event, described
above, HIN conducts an award ceremony to recognize exemplary intergenerational programs and program organizers. In a similar though unrelated
vein, the theme for the Mayor's 33rd Senior Recognition Program (1999) was
"Recognition for Intergenerational Service Programs"; 12 such programs in
Honolulu were honored alongside an impressive group of outstanding senior volunteers. The rationale for selecting award recipients was described
by the Honolulu Committee on Aging (Elderly Affairs) as follows:

To celebrate the theme of the International Year of Older Persons, "Towards a Society for All Ages," and to affirm that partnerships of all ages are needed to nurture a healthful society, the Honolulu Committee on Aging will give special recognition to programs that involve different age groups in meeting needs, advocating and producing improvements, providing services, and sponsoring experiences or training that equip people to meet life's challenges.

Program Possibilities

Henkin and Kingson (1998-99) speak of the potential for intergenerational programs and policies to "help keep the promise — that is, to strengthen the nation's social compact and, by doing so, to advance a more civil, civic and caring society" (pp. 6-7). In a similar vein, we envision new intergenerational programs and policies that could help strengthen the "social compact" in Hawaii. In this section, we lay out a few intergenerational intervention ideas for building more caring communities and contributing to a better quality of life in Hawaii.

As noted in the Introduction, Hawaii is a busy port of entrance for immigrants from Asia. In Hawaii, as in many other areas in the United States, immigrants face a unique set of challenges. In line with the anti-immigrant atmosphere that has been sweeping the nation over the past four years, a plethora of federal and state legislative initiatives aim at reducing the services and benefits provided for legal immigrants. This is also the case on the local front. In the mid- to late-1990s, agencies providing services for refugees and immigrants experienced budget cuts far greater than those faced by other agencies. Such cuts in services exacerbate the difficulties experienced by immigrants groups at both ends of the age scale. Already financially vulnerable due to language problems, senior adult immigrants become even more socially isolated, and a disproportionate number of young immigrants turn to local gangs and illegal activity.

One intergenerational approach that is likely to be effective in supporting both young and elderly members of families immigrating to Hawaii is the SHINE program. Students Helping in the Naturalization of Elders is an intergenerational program initiative designed by Temple University's Center for Intergenerational Learning[11] as a strategy for enlisting college students in service delivery efforts targeting ethnically diverse senior adults. With funding provided by the Corporation for National Service and the Department of Education, SHINE demonstration projects are currently operating in nine cities, one of which is Honolulu.

Another stream of thinking about intergenerational program possibilities emerges from consideration of one of the biggest concerns of most people living in Hawaii (at the time of writing); i.e., the stagnant economy.

The local economy has been influenced more directly by the lull in Japan's economy than the economic boom taking place on the U.S. mainland over the past 5-7 years. In addition to great interest on the part of communities and state government agencies, such as the Department of Business Economic Development & Tourism, to generate economic activity, there is often an intentional effort to weave an intergenerational theme into economic stimulation packages. The Executive Office on Aging is a central partner in many economic development discussions. This agency, with assistance from the University of Hawaii, initiated a visioning and strategic planning process in 1996 called "The Hawaii Summit: 2011 Project." The initiative involved a cross section of individuals, government officials, non-profit service providers and business leaders in an 18 month process of identifying key issues related to aging and developing alternative visions of the future. In efforts to find creative approaches to encourage business growth and development, the need to address demographic changes, particularly the aging of the "Baby Boomer" generation (Kim and Foley, 1999) was consistently mentioned.

In many of the community planning initiatives that are influenced by the *Project 2011: Incubating Small Businesses* concept, much of the dialogue is centered on finding alternatives to mainstream economic activity. Alternative forms of tourism, for example, are being developed to highlight indigenous culture and create opportunities for education of the youth (local and visiting) by elders who are seen as holding the most knowledge about the local cultural heritage. A three-day Waianae Coast Community-based Tourism Conference was held on January 30, 1999. The vision endorsed at its end emphasized the important role local senior adults are likely to play in terms of serving as storytellers, hula instructors, fishermen, arts and crafts experts, and conveyors of the aloha spirit. Other neighborhoods could benefit from a similar process.

Conclusion

From a Hawaiian perspective, it is hard to distinguish the intergenerational field from what the Hawaiians mean when they say "aloha." Intergenerational engagement is part of a value system that emphasizes caregiving, love, and respect. Diverse and abundant, Hawaii's intergenerational initiatives, and the continuity and unity between the generations that they symbolize, represent an important stabilizing force in Hawaii. As we enter into a new millennium with new opportunities for thinking creatively about how service programs are formulated and funded, it makes sense to continue to explore ways to build upon the interdependencies between the generations and work to establish stronger support systems between them.

Although intergenerational programs are generally well received by the public, whether they receive the necessary public and private investment to survive is another question. In the words of Bob Disch, an intergenerational program activist at the Hunter College Brookdale Center on Aging in New York City, support for intergenerational initiatives is often "a mile wide and an inch deep." His point is that despite the fact that intergenerational program strategies often excite the public with warm images of community cooperation, productive aging, and interpersonal caring, such initiatives are typically on frail financial footing. Underfunding also seems to be the case in Hawaii. Many of the initiatives noted in this article are on "soft money"; i.e., they survive from grant to grant. Yet some promising developments are unfolding, such as the recent appropropriation by the state legislature referred to above.

Although we contend that more and more stable funding is needed to move the intergenerational imperative forward in Hawaii, we also advocate structural change in the way social programs are conceived and developed. Because major government funding streams are often earmarked for youth-only, aging-only, and other single-purpose initiatives, even successful, popular intergenerational programs are rarely integrated into ongoing service systems. Thicker threads of interagency cooperation are likely to make it easier to institutionalize innovative intergenerational initiatives.

Effective programs could and should be replicated, and systems need to be set up to provide professionals and lay persons with more access to information about programs that have been field-tested and found to be effective in various settings in other parts of the country. Members of the public, the philanthropic community, and the corporate community have key roles to play. With more forethought and resource allocation, Hawaii can take a leadership position in demonstrating to the rest of the country and to other nations constructive ways for instilling healthy interaction patterns between the young and elderly.

References

Akana, A. (1918). *The sinews for racial development.*

Hawaii Community Services Council (1999). *Scanning Hawaii: Forces for change.* Honolulu: HCSC.

Henkin, N. and Kingson, E. (1998-99, winter). Introduction: Keeping the promise. *Generations, 22,* 4, pp. 6-9.

Herman, R.D.K. (1999). Hawaii at the Crossroads. In D.W. Woodcock (Ed.). *Hawaii: New geographies* (pp. 71-84). Honolulu: University of Hawaii-Manoa Department of Geography.

Kim, K. and Foley, D. (1999). *Project 2011: Baby boomers and retirement: Challenges and opportunities.* Honolulu: Executive Office on Aging, State of Hawaii.

Kohala Intergenerational Fair (2000, March 12). KHS, elders in community, many volunteers plan big "wellness fair." *Hawaii Tribune-Herald,* p. 29.

Lum, C. (1999, January 31). Waianae seeking its own style of tourism. *The Honolulu Advertiser*, A-25.

OHA (1996). *Native Hawaiian Data Book*. Honolulu: Office of Hawaiian Affairs.

Oi, C. (1999, April 9). Dancing across the generations. *Honolulu Star-Bulletin*, pp. A-1, A-6.

Silva, N. K. (1997). Ku'e!: Hawaiian Women's Resistance to the Annexation. *Social Process of Hawaii, 38*, 2-15.

Sing, D. (1997). The Hawaii connection. *Journal of Aging and Identity*, 2(4) 285-293.

Sing, D. (1986). Raising the achievement level of native Hawaiians in the college classroom through the matching of teaching strategies with student characteristics. Unpublished doctoral dissertation, Claremont Graduate School, Claremont.

Wagner, J. (1999, spring). The First Annual Keiki Kupuna Festival: Some personal reflections. *Hawaii Intergenerational Network Newsletter, 2*, pp. 5-6.

Whitney, S.K. (1999, July). *Ho'ola 'olelo* Hawaii: Saving Hawaiian. *Honolulu Magazine*, pp. 35-37, 45-51.

Notes

1 The authors are indebted to Dr. Larry LeDoux and Dr. Houston Wood of Hawaii Pacific University and Dr. Oscar Kurren of the University of Hawaii at Manoa for their comments on earlier drafts.

2 On April 20, 1999, the nation was stunned when two teenagers from Columbine High School in Colorado killed 12 other students and a teacher and wounded about two dozen others before committing suicide.

3 Sing (1997) notes that the figure of 12.5 percent is provided by the U.S. Census whereas and 18.8 percent is provided by the State Department of Health (OHA, 1996).

4 It is interesting to note that before 1893, the population of the Kingdom of Hawaii had the highest literacy rate in the 19th-century world — 90 percent were literate.

5 It is estimated that there are over 40 Native Hawaiian groups actively promoting restoration of the native Hawaiian Nation (Herman, 1999). In Hawaii, the political struggle for sovereignty is affecting the cultural and psychological terrain of the Hawaiian experience.

6 In Hawaiian culture, there are three locations on the body that provide the individual with genealogical reference points. The soft spot on the head of an infant, in Hawaiian called the *manawa*, is the link to heaven and the *aumakua* or ancestors. The *piko*, or navel, links the child to the parent generation, or *makua*. Genitals link the child to the future generation. These establish responsibility to past, present, and future (N. Armitage-Lapilio, personal communication, May 24, 2000).

7 In 1983, an assistant professor of Hawaiian Studies at University of Hawaii at Hilo and six others established "Aha Punana Leo," based on the Maori preschool concept of "Kohanga Reo" ("the language nest"), which introduced preschools based on the "immersion" concept (Whitney, 1999, p. 37). Now, Aha Punana Leo receives millions of dollars in federal and state grants each year, employs 130 people, administers nine preschools statewide, and co-administers (with the State

Department of Education) an elementary and a junior high school. The University of Hawaii now offers both bachelor and master of arts degrees in Hawaiian language and provides a center for development of immersion curriculum materials. The Department of Education runs an additional 14 immersion schools, although they are typically underfunded and with limited resources (Whitney, 1999).

8 Unfortunately, most Hawaiians today are unaware of the literature of early Hawaiian revolutionaries in the early 1900s who used their writing skills to persuade others to adopt skills and behaviors aimed at saving the Hawaiian nation (e.g., Akana, 1918). The silence to which these early 20th century activists are assigned results in a belief that everyone, including Native Hawaiians, agreed and rejoiced in the annexation of the Republic of Hawaii as a territory of the United States. Amazingly, petitions signed by 90 percent of the Native Hawaiian population opposing annexation were recent recovered. These reached 100 years into the future and added fuel to contemporary efforts to achieve some form of sovereignty for Native Hawaiians (Silva, 1997).

9 Hawaii Annexation Petitions which were filed in 1897 can be found in the Library of Congress.

10 This videoconference was sponsored by the National Network for Family Resiliency of the Children, Youth and Families Network of the Cooperative State Research, Educational and Extension Service; University of Wisconsin Extension Cooperative Extension Service; Purdue University Cooperative Extension Service; American Association of Retired Persons; Foster Grandparent Program; and the University of Hawaii at Manoa College of Tropical Agriculture and Human Resources Cooperative Extension Service. The video was entitled "Grandparents Raising Grandchildren: Implications for Professionals and Agencies."

11 Temple University's Center for Intergenerational Learning (Philadelphia, Pennsylvania) was created in 1980 to foster intergenerational cooperation and exchange through the development of innovative educational and service programs involving people of all ages.

Intergenerational Initiatives in Singapore: Commitments to Community and Family building

By Leng Leng Thang[1]

Introduction

A small city-state about the size of Chicago situated at the southern tip of the Malay peninsular in Southeast Asia,[2] Singapore has a population of 3,217,500 people.[3] A multi-cultural society, it is 77 percent Chinese, 14 percent Malays, 7.6 percent Indians and 1.4 percent other ethnic groups.

From its humble beginning as a small fishing village through colonization by the British in 1819, Singapore has evolved to become a thriving "more advanced developing nation"[4] today. Over the three decades since its independence in 1965, the nation has attained impressive economic growth and a high standard of living. Symbols of affluence such as sky-scrapers, modern shopping complexes stocked with imported merchandise from all over the world, and a comprehensive transportation network including highways and mass and light rapid transit systems put Singapore among the ranks of large, sophisticated metropolitan cities.

The long-ruling People's Action Party (PAP),[5] which has played a pivotal role in Singapore's successful economic development, has evolved from the survivalist economic pragmatism of its first two decades — which included authoritarianism and overt state intervention— to a communitarian ideology in which collective interests are placed above individual ones (Chua, 1995). The new vision for Singapore, called "Singapore 21," launched by Prime Minister Goh Chok Tong in August 1997, speaks of strengthening Singapore's "heartware" and reflects the new communitarianism in its definition of five key objectives:

- Every Singaporean matters.
- Strong Families: Our foundation and our future.
- Opportunities for all.
- The Singapore Heartbeat: Feeling passionately about Singapore.
- Active Citizens: Making a difference to society.

This shift away from sheer economic pragmatism to concerns with matters of the "heart" indicates a realization of the need for correct values and guide posts to address problems that are commonly faced by societies with increased affluence and mobility.

One of those problems is the distancing of the generations in the society, and this chapter focuses on concerns generated by this phenomenon. It begins with a background survey of demographic trends and patterns of social changes in Singaporean society. The second section, which provides an overview of intergenerational program approaches, is followed by a detailed description of one intergenerational initiative to serve as a window for understanding the nature and extent of intergenerational initiatives in Singapore.[6] Finally, the chapter discusses the underlying rationale and current directions of intergenerational initiatives in Singapore.

Changing demographic trends and social patterns

Age-integrated initiatives are consistent with emerging awareness of the aging trend in Singapore's demographics. Over the past three decades, the country has undergone a rapid decline in both fertility rate and mortality rate. The median age of the population provides a clear indication of the its maturity over time: in 1970, the medium age was 19.7 years; it jumped to 24.4 years in 1980 and 31.8 years in 1995. It is expected to reach 41 years by 2030. It is projected that there will be a phenomenal increase in the number and proportion of elderly (defined as those 60 years and above) in the next century. By the year 2030, the elderly population is expected to increase by more than three times, from the present level to 1,055,000 persons, accounting for more than a quarter of the population (Cheung and Thang, 1997).

The rapid aging of the population is brought about by several major factors including the aging of the postwar baby boomers, an increase in life expectancy, and a decline in the birth rate. By the year 2030, the postwar baby boomers who have constituted the "youthful" age structure — now aged 30 to 44 — will have moved on to the 65+ age bracket.

With improvement in the standard of living, they are also expected to live longer. The life expectancy among average Singaporeans has increased markedly, from 65.1 and 70 for males and females respectively, in 1970, to 75 and 78, respectively, by the year 2000.

The aging of the population is further accelerated by a decline in birth rate since the late 1950s. The decline in annual births from about 60, 000 during 1957-60 to about 40,000 in early 1980s was due in part to the success of family planning programs introduced between 1965 and 1974. In 1986, the number of births fell to a record low of 38, 000. Two factors contributed to this. First, 1986 coincided with the 'Year of the Tiger' in the lunar calendar, a year regarded as an inauspicious one for marriage and childbearing. Secondly, there may have been a postponement of births during this period as a result of an economic recession that started in 1984 and intensified in 1985-86.

Since 1987, with the introduction of a pro-natal population policy, the number of births has increased, and it has been fluctuating at around 50,000 in recent years. However, the total fertility rate (TFR) still falls below the replacement level. Assuming the current TFR of 1.7 continues, by 2010, as a result of the fall in the number of females of childbearing ages (because of the past fertility decline), there will only be about 36,000 births, a figure substantially less than the present 50,000 level (Cheung, 1999).

Along with demographic changes, the society has also undergone significant changes in household and social patterns. With declining fertility and a trend toward more nuclear families, the number of family members per household shrank from 4.9 in 1980 to 4.0 in 1995. At the same time, three-generational families, once a norm among Singaporean households, also declined. As a society and culture which places elderly care primarily within the familial realm, these changes in household demographics justify concern about the availability of eldercare.

Mitigating that concern may be the fact that the rate, in Singapore, of co-residence of the elderly with their children — which was 85 percent in 1995[7] — remains constant compared with other Asian countries such as Japan and Taiwan. It is important to look at co-residence rate as an indicator of the availability of family care for elderly in the society. However, it may not be accurate to assume elder care merely because elderly individuals share one roof with their children. Albert Hermalin, a sociologist noted for his research on aging in Asia, has cautioned that "people living together may not take care of each other." He urges researchers to focus on ties between the generations (*The Straits Times*, 20 March 1999).

Indeed, elderly who live with their children may not necessarily depend on them. For example, it is a norm in Singapore for unmarried children to live with their parents partly due to high housing costs. And healthy elderly parents staying with their married children may be providing support for their children through childcare and housework (Hermalin, 1995).

The high rate of participation of women in the Singapore labor force also reduces their capacity to provide caregiving. The female labor force participation has increased tremendously, from 22 percent in 1965 to 52 percent in 1996. As a result, double-career couples have more than doubled from 112, 000 in 1980 to 252, 000 in 1995 (Cheung, 1999). To cope with the demands of caregiving, it is not uncommon for families with frail elderly to engage foreign domestic maids as full-time caregivers. At the same time, there have been increasing demands for various day care services to support working women, including childcare, before and after school care, and elderly day care.

On the positive side, although there will be more frail elderly in the 65-years and older population, they will have improved health and a healthier living style. We can also look forward to more active elderly who are expected to stay healthy, achieve higher educational levels and be more financially independent. In 1995, 10.8 percent of the elderly population had at least secondary education; by 2030, this will increase to 62.2 percent. Already more elderly are living alone, or with a spouse only, from 10 percent in 1990 to 15 percent in 1997. It is projected that by the year 2045, one-quarter of the elderly in Singapore will live away from their children, either on their own or with their spouses (*The Straits Times*, 10 Nov 1998).

Their increasing independence shows that, with more resources and higher life expectancies, more of the elderly are unwilling to perceive retirement from the work force as the onset of disengagement from the society. Rather they are increasingly searching for productive ways to spend their retired years, and they look forward to fruitful engagement in their own hobbies, travel, and voluntary work.

Although elderly who choose to do voluntary work may involve themselves with the young generations, most elderly activities are age-segregated and provide few opportunities for interaction with the younger generations. We are witnessing an emerging group of active elderly who are literate and healthy. However, it is not uncommon for communication between the old and the young to be hampered by the fact that many of today's elderly are illiterate or speak only Chinese dialects unfamiliar to today's younger people.[8] Although they constitute a diminishing group, unfortunately they are the basis of the common stereotypical image of the elderly in Singapore, an image that is further reinforced through the media and public perceptions. For example, a popular comedic character, "Liang Po Po (Grandma Liang)," who also appeared in a bestselling local film, characterizes the elderly grandmother as naïve and illiterate. The character has aroused dissatisfaction among the elderly and has caused public criticism of the media's promotion of negative depictions of them.

These social phenomena and trends are the background to the establishment of a range of intergenerational initiatives in Singapore. Besides providing a solution to the elder- and childcare dilemmas faced by dual-career couples, the models described below, particularly the age-integrated centers, serve to address the onset of generational disengagement in Singapore that has arisen with changing social circumstances.

Intergenerational Initiatives in Singapore

Compared to the United States, intergenerational programming to date has received relatively little attention in Singapore. This is largely due to its cultural and social perception of intergenerational interaction as happening only within the familial context. Nonetheless, changing social patterns and the emerging population of active retirees have resulted in an increase in a variety of intergenerational activities nationwide. These initiatives can be divided into three categories.

Initiatives from the young

Initiatives in which youth provide a service for the elderly are the most common types of intergenerational programs. These include school programs whereby students visit old age homes to provide services such as cleaning the premises, serving meals, and performing songs and dances to entertain the residents.

Since the 1998 introduction, by the Ministry of Education, of a community volunteer program that requires students to spend six hours in community work per year, more schools have "adopted" old age homes for community work. However, as these programs are either onetime events, or short-term contacts (typical twice or three times a year for a student to fulfill six hours of required community work), they are not conducive to establishing rapport between individual students and elderly residents. A secondary school teacher who was in charge of a volunteer program to old age homes recalled that while there were some favorable responses, there were also instances of students who said their brief experience reinforced their negative stereotypes of old age.

Initiatives from active retirees

Fortunately, the stereotypes of retirement and the elderly have begun to change as more highly educated retirees explore the opportunities for making a contribution in their after-employment years. This has positive implications for intergenerational programming. For example, the Retired and Senior Volunteer Program (RSVP) inaugurated in October 1998 emphasizes retirees' involvement with the young. One of its pioneer projects is a mentoring program in two primary schools, providing after school care to latchkey children from low-income families. During the twice-weekly three-hour contact, the senior volunteers supervise the children in their homework, play games and do handicrafts with them. News interviews with the participants show that the senior volunteers and the children have developed a bonding with each other as a result of consistent interaction. While the elderly feel that their lives are enriched by the ability to help others, the children benefit from the patience of their senior mentors and enjoy the warmth and care showered upon them. Recent news reports highlight images of the children celebrating the seniors' birthdays as a way of showing their appreciation (*The Straits Times*, Nov. 1, 1998).

The Information technology age has also benefited intergenerational interaction. The computer-literacy course conducted by RSVP is popular among the elderly, many of whom view their learning how to email and "surf" the net as ways to facilitate more interaction with their children and grandchildren. Through information technology, they can now communicate with their offspring overseas instantaneously at the touch of a button.

Cross-agency collaborations

Initiatives in this category take a collaborative approach, involving participants and program staff from several centers or services that coexist side-by-side, either by coincidence or as a deliberate effort (Kuehne, 1999). As planning for intergenerational activities requires extra time and effort on the part of the staff, such initiatives can only be possible when staff at both services realize and believe in the benefits of intergenerational programming for their clients. Due to time and manpower constraints, however, very few childcare and elderly services centers situated near to each other have high levels of age integration, although many do have occasional interaction such as joint celebrations of special events and festivals. There is thus a need to promote intergenerational programming on a more regular basis to maximize their proximity to each other.

The Tampines 3-in-1 Family Center, in the Tampines district, and the Ayer Rajah community and services complex in the western part of Singapore, are the only age-integrated facilities in the country. Both were opened on the same day in March 1999, the latter by the Prime Minister. The Ayer Rajah center is a three-story complex hosting the elderly and child care center in the same compound as the community center for residents.

The Ayer Rajah complex is a model of a collaborative approach by two different organizations: the Ayer Raja elderly care and childcare services. They have shared the same premises since the early 1980s, and moved together to their present location. Even before the move, the two services occasionally organized age-integrated activities. After moving to the new multilevel complex, the old and young have more casual contacts with each other as they now share the same dining hall during meal times. In addition to joint festive activities, more age-integrated activities such as *qigong* exercise and games are planned.

However, Ayer Raja faces constraints associated with its management structure. As the youth and elder services come under different sets of management, programs for intergenerational integration can only be an "extracurricular" activity. Rather than being part of the objectives of each service, such activities are possible only through the goodwill of the teachers and caregivers. The Tampines 3-in-1 Family Center, having overcome such constraints by uniting all services under one collective management structure, is better able to collaborate different services more effectively for regular age-integrated activities.

Considering the level of forethought and planning involved in developing it, as well as its extensive scale and record of successes, the Tampines 3-in-1 Center is arguably one of the most significant intergenerational endeavors to be found in Singapore. For this reason, and because of its ramifications as a model for similar initiatives in a number of countries, this initiative is examined in detail below.

Tampines 3-in-1 Center

The Tampines 3-in-1 Family Center[9] was officially open by the Prime Minister in March 1999. In its attempts at broadening the connection between the old and the young — not only in terms of its present activities, but also in its plans to harness active retirees — Tampines 3-in-1 is a model for all the efforts to expand intergenerational initiatives in Singapore.

Situated in Tampines, a large housing estate in the eastern suburb of Singapore, the family center provides three service centers under its care umbrella: day care for persons aged 55 years and older, childcare for two-and-a-half to six-year-olds, and before- and after-school care (BFSC) for children aged seven to 12. The center stretches through the first level of three blocks of high-rise public apartments. The three service centers are linked by covered walkways, and they face a common courtyard that has a landmark clock tower, a basketball court, benches for the residents, and a covered playground.

The childcare and before- and after-school care centers operate from 7 a.m. to 7 p.m. five and one half days each week. The aged care program has slightly shorter operating hours, from 7:30 a.m. to 6:30 p.m., and is closed on weekends. While transport for children to and from childcare and BFSC is family-arranged, elderly in the aged care program can opt for paid transport provided by the center. There are 96 and 160 children[10] in childcare and BFSC respectively. The aged care has an average daily attendance of 35 elderly. Including the 38 staff in three centers, the kitchen has to prepare lunches for about 340 people daily. The two cooks receive assistance from volunteers who help prepare the food. Volunteers also help to serve meals and interact with the children and elderly.

It may not be unusual to find services for different age groups situated in such close proximity to each other in Singapore, given the country's high density of 5,965 persons per square kilometer. However, Tampines 3-in-1 Family Center is unique for its active promotion of age-integration. The center strives to provide a program in which the young and old are brought together to participate in activities that promote mutual care and friendship, so that the preschoolers and young children may gain a positive insight into the aging process as they are surrounded by the warmth and understanding of loving "grandparent" figures. The age-integration program is a daily affair for the elderly. For an hour or so every day, a group of children visit the aged care portion of the facility for joint activities.

While the older children play chess and other board games with the elderly, the younger ones may join the elderly in doing jigsaw puzzles, coloring or other handicraft. Elderly who are literate read to the children. Young children are also involved in helping some elderly in their physiotherapy by picking up the beanbags that they have thrown into a basket. As the children count the beanbags and differentiate their colors, the activity becomes a learning experience for the young as well as physical exercise for the elderly. For two afternoons a week, the children participate with the elderly in music therapy.

During school holidays, more age-integration activities are possible. These include special relay games for participants at all three services, intergenerational outings to the zoo or local museums, and picnics. Festive and seasonal events provide even more opportunities to enhance age-integration. There are joint celebrations for various events such as national day, grandparent's day, and birthdays. To celebrate the International Year of the Older Persons, in 1999, the center organized a special three-generational concert.

During traditional festive celebrations, elderly are invited to host storytelling sessions for the children on the origins and background of the festivals. There are also hands-on activities for all, including making lanterns and moon cakes during the Chinese mid-autumn festival and making rice dumplings during the dragon boat festival. These traditional activities, once common in large Chinese families, have long disappeared with the advent of young nuclear families. Their revival in an age-integrated setting not only provides fun and interaction, it is also significant in passing down traditions to the young in a manner that is consistent with the role of grandparents in a three-generational family.

The fulfillment of age-integration in the center is largely attributed to the vision of its executive director, Mrs. Amy Fong. She first became aware of intergenerational programming during a visit to a community-based age-integrated learning center in Phoenix, Arizona in 1994. Motivated by the family-like interaction between the children and their elderly child caregivers, she began to promote, on her return to Singapore, the concept of an age-integrated center. The concept was supported by the Member of Parliament for Tampines, Mr. Mah Bow Tan, who believed that such an age-integrated center would help solve the problem of aged care faced by the families in the district and would help to bind the community together. Work on creating it began in July 1996.

Fong admits that it took determination to sell the new idea to the community. When the 3-in-1 center idea was first introduced at the community center in 1996, even the staff had to be convinced that intergenerational contact is essential for the well being of all generations.

Parents posed a barrier too. Their negative stereotypes of the elderly as senile and sick resulted in concerns that interacting with the old would bring disease and danger to the children. In addition to overcoming these objections, Fong also noted that some elderly experienced initial withdrawal and felt intimidated by the young. They were afraid that the children might despise them for being slow and weak. Children also took time to overcome their fear of getting close to the elderly. As some elderly spoke only dialects no longer spoken by the children today, there were initial difficulties in communication. Nevertheless, nonverbal gestures such as smiles and the holding of hands proved to be an effective means of communication for both generations who gradually improved communication through constant contacts.

Despite such challenges and the lengthy learning curve, in the four years since it started the Tampines 3-in-1 Center has succeeded in making age-integration an acceptable concept in the community. More parents now register their children in the 3-in-1 program precisely because of the opportunities it affords for age-integration experiences.

The staff observes that through intergenerational contact, children learn about the process of aging and become willing to slow down to accommodate the elderly. Simply by addressing the elderly as *gong gong* or *ah mah* — the dialect terms for grandfather and grandmother — the children cultivate a sense of family warmth. The elderly, too, benefit from the liveliness of the young and derive a sense of usefulness from the opportunity to share their knowledge with them. One elderly grandmother who was formerly a schoolteacher, volunteered to read to the children and, when interviewed, stated that she enjoyed the task.

Besides alternate generational programs, the center also encourages intra-generational interaction such as pairing up primary school children with preschoolers in a reading program and involving the senior volunteers not only with the children, but also with more infirm elders.

Currently about 70 volunteers work at the center, most of them retirees or housewives.[11] The members commit themselves to a set number of hours of volunteer work a week, depending on their own time.

To attract more volunteers from the community, the center set up, late in 1998, a friendship club for volunteers and potential volunteers. The club is housed in a room near the general office and offers karaoke facilities at an attractive rate to the members. The volunteers also use the premises for classes — in English conversation and Mandarin conversation, for example — for fellow members. Besides their work at the 3-in-1 Family Center, the friendship club members once a month prepare lunches and organize performances at two old age homes that the Family Center has adopted.

Fong hopes to develop the friendship center into a center for the community. Among the plans for expansion is a resource library for residents. She also hopes to set up training services for retirees who want a second career with the young, such as working flexible hours as teacher's aides in childcare centers. However, that proposal has met with skepticism, reflecting the still prevalent stereotypical image of intergenerational contact— the relegation of the elderly to the receiver-end of service rather than recognizing their potential to contribute.

Perspectives on Intergenerational Initiatives

The nature and characteristics of intergenerational programs under the above-mentioned three categories—youth-initiated, elder-initiated, or collaborative—appear to conform to the characteristics identified by Kuehne in her paper on the contributions of intergenerational programs to community building (1999). She summarizes three approaches to intergenerational programs in the community: the "collaborative approach," the "emphasis on assets and capacity," and the "focus on relationship and culture." While the first and third approaches are found in the three types of intergenerational initiatives described above, the "emphasis on assets and capacity"— which focuses on the strengths of both the young and old in community building — is still relatively uncommon in Singapore.

The cultural perception of age grades and age hierarchy among Asians suggests an explanation for the paucity of intergenerational initiatives that enable the young and old to work together as "buddies." Conformation to traditional perceptions of age hierarchy would mean that the elderly, as pioneers in life, should be respected and treated with higher status as seniors. Thus, they are perceived as belonging to a supervisory level, even if they should work with the young. Moreover, in Asian culture, retirement is still commonly perceived not only as one's exit from paid work, but also as symbolic of one's retreat from an active lifestyle. Taken together with the stereotype of the elderly as people who need to be cared for and respected, it is no wonder that volunteer or community work by retirees is considerably undeveloped in this region as compared to American communities. Although efforts by groups such as RSVP do signify a change in attitudes among the elderly, a major cultural shift of perception is necessary if Singaporean society is to harness the great potential of programmed intergenerational exchange.

Both scholarly writings (for example, works of psychologist Erik Erikson and anthropologist Margaret Mead) and cultural traditions across cultures point to the desirability of ties between generations, recognizing these as natural as well as psychologically, socially and economically important. In general, intergenerational programming is developed as a response to age segregation in society, thus implying a recognition of the benefits of past patterns of generational engagement in the family and community.

As intergenerational programming often focuses on the larger engagement of the generations, most, if not all programs, are community-focused. As Mrs. Fong of the 3-in-1 Family Center said:

> What is community? In the past, community was *kampong* (village), with doors open and children playing at neighbor's house. Now, people shut their doors. You don't have the feeling of community anymore.

One of the objectives of the Tampines 3-in-1 Family Center is to recreate the feeling of community. This is why the center is committed to building a community through various intergenerational activities, and why it is expanding its community volunteer program. It serves as an outstanding example of the contribution that age-integrated facilities can make in terms of community building.

Besides the goal of "community building," intergenerational initiatives in Singapore depict the cultural, social and national emphasis on the *family*, an emphasis consistent with and growing from the "Singapore 21" vision to build strong families. The Prime Minister's statement of that vision includes the following principles:

- Strong families give meaning to life, and are an irreplaceable source of care and support.
- Within a strong family, our children can grow up healthy and confident, able to meet the future and fulfill their dreams.
- *Our elders can also enjoy dignity and respect, and pass down the values and lessons they have learned in life* (1999).

The cultural and social dimensions of family building in intergenerational activities are suggested by the use of terms such as "big family" and "family-like setting," terms which accurately describe age-integrated services. They give a human-emphasis and positive image to the institutions providing those services. The Tampines 3-in-1 services, for instance, is called the "family center," and it emphasizes the institution as "a home away from home." At the same time, it also stresses its setting as one of "modal family care" — i.e., a setting in which one can learn family-centered values through integration across generations and active intergenerational participation in traditional celebrations.

Such *big family*-oriented ideals in age-integrated services suggests wider implications on the changing conceptualizations of what constitutes a family. Henkin and Kingson's (1999) discussion of retooling the family notes the need to support the family and community through more flexible kinship and kinship-like configurations at different points in the course of life. They further comment that:

> Perhaps as researchers at Trends Research Institute suggest, a new definition of family as "groups of interdependent people with shared values, goals, and responsibilities and a long term commitment to one another and their community" will emerge in the next century (Celene, 1997; c.f. Henkin and Kingson, 1999).

Such a trend is supported in a study of extra-familial cross-generational ties in the *daikazoku* (big family) context in a Japanese age-integrated facility (Thang, 1999). However, in Singapore, the "big family" is emphasized as a supplement to, not a substitute for, the family's responsibilities in caring for its members. This was highlighted by the Prime Minister in his speech at the official opening of the age-integrated facilities at Tampines 3-in-1 Family Center and Ayer Rajah community and services complex in March 1999. In his addresses at both age-integrated facilities, the Prime Minister stressed his support for the three-in-one concept because "these centers make good use of space in land-scarce Singapore." His message to the Tampines center applauded the community for its "resourceful way of integrating the needs of caring for the children and the elderly."[12] However, he also expressed anxieties on the declining role of family in providing care, and he claimed that community services could never replace the family's moral obligation to look after its young and elderly. His message was clear: as supplemental family care, these services should not weaken family ties. In the speech, he also suggested:

> Getting experts trained by the Community Development Ministry to hold one-day sessions for people who send their family members to these centers. These sessions would not only remind them of their obligations, but offer pointers on how to look after elderly parents, especially the sick (*The Straits Times*, March 8, 1999).

Such recurrent emphasis on the family and its responsibilities for both the old and young are reflected in recent events that promote intergenerational interaction within the family. The Community Development Ministry sponsored multigenerational camps for three-generational families during Senior Citizen's Week in November 1998. The state's promotion of family values and family cohesiveness also includes events to promote grandparent-grandchildren relations.

Conclusion

In conclusion, this examination of intergenerational programming in Singapore shows it in a state of emergence in this society. It also shows the attempts by policy makers, welfare service administrators and the public to grapple with the idea and explore how best it can fit into the existing cultural, social and political climate of the society. The discourse highlights the need for practitioners and researchers to come together to share their experiences and formulate systematic training and workshops to promote and plan intergenerational programming appropriate to their particular social context.

Intergenerational initiatives in Singapore have taken different forms as the elderly not only serve as recipients of care from the young, but also as mentors to younger generations, particularly when the retirees are healthy and educated. We can expect more intergenerational program activity within the family-building domain noted above.

Acknowledgments

The author wishes to express special thanks to the following individuals for their kind assistance in the writing of this paper: Mrs. Amy Fong and Miss Eunice Tan of Tampines 3-in-1 Family Center and Mrs. H.B. Foong of Ayer Rajah Day Care Centre.

References

Cheung, P. & Thang, L. L. (1997). Aging situation and its problems in Singapore. In *Aging people in transition: Papers of international symposium on a comparative study of three cases in Asia: Korea, Taiwan and Japan* (pp. 217-230). Tokyo: Advanced Research Center for Human Sciences, Waseda University.

Cheung, P. (1999). Needs and challenges of new demography. In L. Low (Ed.), *Singapore — Towards a developed status* (pp. 194-209). Singapore: Centre for Advanced Studies, National University of Singapore and Oxford University Press.

Chua, B.H. (1995). *Communitarian ideology and democracy in Singapore*. London: Routledge.

Hang, C.H. (1999). What it takes to sustain research and development in a small, developed nation in the 21st century. In L. Low (Ed.), *Singapore — Towards a developed status* (pp. 25-36). Singapore: Centre for Advanced Studies, National University of Singapore and Oxford University Press

Henkin, N. & Kingson, E. (1999). Advancing an intergenerational agenda for the twenty-first Century. *Generations, 22* (4), 99-105.

Hermalin, A. I. (1995). *Aging in Asia: Setting the research foundation*. East West Center: Asia-Pacific Population Research Reports.

Kaplan, M. & Thang, L. L. (1997). Intergenerational programs in Japan: symbolic extension of family unity. *Journal of Aging and Identity, 2* (4), 295-315.

Kuehne, V. S. (1999). Building intergenerational communities through research and evaluation. *Generations, 22* (4), 82-87.

Registry of Births and Deaths (1998). *Report on registration of births and deaths.* Singapore Immigration and Registration.

Singapore Department of Statistics (1990). *Yearbook of statistics — Singapore, 1990.*

Singapore Department of Statistics (1998). *Yearbook of statistics — Singapore, 1998.*

Thang, L. L. (1999). The dancing granny: linking the generations in a Japanese age-integrated welfare centre. *Japanese Studies, 19* (2), 151- 162.

The Straits Times. Various issues.

Notes

1 On the Dept. of Japanese Studies faculty of the National University of Singapore.

2 The total land area of Singapore is 648.1 square kilometers.

3 1999 figure for Singapore citizens and permanent residents only. The total population is 3,893,600 including foreigners. (Statistics Singapore, http://www.singstat.gov.sg).

4 Singapore was classified by the Organization for Economic Cooperation and Development (OECD) as a more advanced developing nation on 1 January 1996 (Hang, 1999).

5 The People's Action Party, founded by Lee Kuan Yew and others as a coalition of several different political movements, has governed Singapore since 1959 when the country achieved internal self-government from the British.

6 Participant observation and informal interviews with the staff, elderly and children were personally conducted at the Center in July and September 1999.

7 Taken from the National Survey of Senior Citizens in 1995. The rate shows elderly 60 years and over who are living with at least one child.

8 Many first generation Chinese migrants to Singapore speak their own local Chinese dialects. As a result, a Chinese has to learn several dialects in order to communicate effectively with others in the wider Chinese community in Singapore. To cut across dialect barriers, former Prime Minister Yew, in 1979, initiated the annual Speak Mandarin campaign. The campaigns have been successful and have promoted the speaking of Mandarin in place of dialects. The education system in Singapore, which emphasizes bilingualism, also encourages today's younger Singaporeans to only speak English and their mother tongue (Mandarin, Malay or Tamil). (http://www.gov.sg/spkmandarin/history/history.html#f)

9 The 3-in-1 Family Center is a community project of the People's Action Party (the ruling party) community foundation, Tampines East Branch, and is cosponsored by the Northeast Community Development Council and the Ministry of Community Development.

10 Singapore schools run two sessions: the morning session is from 7:30-1 p.m., and the afternoon session is from 1:15-6:30 p.m. Students in the morning session of school come to BFSC after their school, while students from the afternoon session come from home in the morning. There are 90 students in the morning and 70 in the afternoon.

11 The friendship club has members ranging from age 40 to 70+. Some of them are parents of children who are attending the BFSC.

12 Quoted from the Prime Minister's message printed in the booklet "Tampines 3-in-1 Family Center: a place for living, loving and learning" published by the center for its official opening on March 7, 1999.

Intergenerational Programs and Practice in the Marshall Islands: Implications for Cultural Preservation

Hilda C. Heine

Introduction

In many societies, intergenerational activities play a significant role not only in transmitting the culture from generation to generation but also in preserving the fabric of society itself. In Pacific Islands communities such as the Marshall Islands, intergenerational activities include the teaching of songs, storytelling festivals, chanting lessons, tattooing, sharing of traditional healing knowledge as well as family apprenticeships in traditional canoe building and sailing. Learning to predict the weather through reading clouds and wave patterns, learning different fishing styles and skills, even learning the art of love from seasoned and skillful teachers — all are activities that bring together the older and the younger generations. Furthermore, intergenerational activities allow the young to be mentored in essential community and cultural values that form the foundation of belief systems and value structures. These activities provide a sense of continuity that bridges the cultural and traditional knowledge gap between different generations.

These intergenerational learning activities, or *ekkatak jen, im ibben, rutto ro,* are unique in that they are provided in contextual settings, often on a one-to-one basis, by a respected elder serving in a mentoring role. In that respect, they can be classified as either non-formal education, that is "worthwhile learning that is organized but not institutionalized," or informal education, "worthwhile learning that is not organized nor institutionalized" (Thaman, 1999). The education system of Pacific societies, including that of the Marshall Islands, was comprised of these types of learning activities, *ekkatak,* before the advent of formal education in the form of schooling. These *ekkatak* strengthened participants' understanding of the proper place of such knowledge and skills in the larger society and their importance in keeping the society intact. These activities also helped to build a stronger sense of belonging in younger members of the community and served as a lesson to them of their proper place in their world. The increased understanding of cultural roots, heightened knowledge of important societal values, and better appreciation of the role of family and relationships in keeping the fabric of the society intact are all part of intergenerational initiatives aimed at promoting cultural continuity.

Today, institutions such as museums, libraries, and schools have replaced traditional learning, *kilen ekkatak,* the apprenticeship method of passing knowledge from one generation to another. They have also replaced traditional venues where the older and the younger generations came together to share and learn. In the Marshall Islands, these modern institutions are still considered foreign and are not valued as integral parts of the communities. Efforts to bring traditional and modern learning together in these non-traditional settings are often fragmented and launched with limited resources. Furthermore, the lack of cultural context that connects their existence and their values to island settings and values almost guarantees their general failures.

Museums, for example, are places to house artifacts that depict what a group of people values and how they live their lives. Many of the lauded values they preserve are no longer living values and unless sustained efforts to connect them to modern lives are made, they are meaningless. Unfortunately, attempts to teach younger generations about these values often occur in a vacuum. This lack of contextual learning for younger members of the community accounts for the failure of museums, for the most part.

Formal schooling, and how that is carried out, provides for learning out of context in much the same ways that museum does. The community, including elders who are experts in the values and skills of the community, are not part of the schooling process. This adopted, but entrenched way of *ekkatak,* has made current attempts to involve community and parents in the education process largely failed efforts. Communities such as those in the RMI need to reevaluate the role of formal schooling and move toward a more appropriate system that can be sustained by the community for the purposes of passing on traditional community *ekkatak.* Sustained intergenerational activities, including non-formal and informal *ekkatak,* are needed to slow the pace of social change and help societal members make sense of the rapid changes occurring all around them.

Background Information

The Republic of the Marshall Islands (RMI) is a group of islands (Hau'ofa, 1993) and atolls located in the western Pacific made up of two nearly parallel chains of atolls, the *Ratak* (Sunrise) and the *Ralik* (Sunset). These two chains include 29 low-lying coral atolls and 5 islands between 160-180 degrees longitude and five to 20 degrees north latitude. Together, the RMI comprises approximately 70 square miles of land area and is the smallest of the group of political entities formerly known as the Trust Territory of the Pacific Islands and fifth smallest nation in the world.

The Marshall Islands achieved independence and constitutional government in 1986, and like the other two former Trust Territory entities, the Federated States of Micronesia and the Republic of Palau, entered into a separate relationship with the United States under a Compact of Free Association (1987). The Compact of Free Association between the RMI and the United States provides for external security for the country and funding for the internal operation of the government. In return, the United States maintains exclusive strategic rights over the RMI and is permitted to operate a missile-testing program on Kwajalein Atoll.

A president who is elected by members of Parliament, the *Nitijela,* heads the country. Members of the *Nitijela* are popularly elected every four years and represent each of the inhabited islands in the RMI.

The Marshall Islands' geographic location and remoteness — 2,270 miles southwest of Hawaii and 2,000 miles east of Guam, five hours by commercial jet in either direction — is both a curse and a blessing. It is a blessing in the sense that remoteness helps to slow down the pace of modern development. Its distance from anywhere makes it difficult for tourism and other commercial development to flourish. Economically, the Marshall Islands' government depends, for funding, on military land-use payments from the United States, government employment with Compact funding, and small fishing, agricultural, and handicraft sectors. International aid from such countries as the Republic of China (Taiwan), Japan, Australia and New Zealand also contributes to government coffers.

The RMI population in 1988 was 43,380. Between 1980 and 1988, the RMI experienced one of the highest population growth rates in the world, 4.3 percent. That has been significantly reduced to its current rate of 1.5 percent in 1999. The 1999 census data showed an in-country population of 50,840; 65 percent of this population live in urban centers of Majuro and Ebeye, making RMI one of the most urban populations in the entire Pacific. More than 50 percent of this population are youth 18 years and younger. In addition to the in-country count, approximately 8,000 Marshallese reside overseas, mainly in the United States.

The growth rate in the past 20 years has made it difficult for institutions such as schools, hospitals, and youth programs to meet needs of clients. There are currently not enough public schools, either primary and secondary, to enroll all school age children. The private schools have taken on an important role in meeting the needs for education. However, the 1988 census showed 10.3 percent and 35.3 percent of youth between the ages of 6-13 and 14-18, respectively, not attending school.

Inter-island migration contributes to the pressure of overcrowding in population centers such Majuro and Ebeye. Out migration to the United States, since the onset of the Compact, has provided an economic escape hatch and has helped to keep unemployment under control. Even so, according to the 1999 Census, the current unemployment rate in the Marshall Islands is 30.9 percent. A negative consequence of out-migration is the loss of valuable human resources to RMI as a young and developing nation.

Since the Compact of Free Association went into effect in 1986, approximately 8,000 Marshallese have emigrated and established communities in Oregon, Arkansas, Oklahoma, Texas, Arizona, California's Orange County, Hawaii and Guam. While the allure of big cities is part of the attraction, Marshallese also emigrate in search of better schools and health care for family members, and job opportunities. Whatever the reason, emigration challenges islanders' ability to keep their culture intact. Furthermore, the ability to engage in traditional intergenerational activities, the primary means of preserving Marshallese culture, is weak in overseas communities due to their small size and the young age of community members.

Factors impacting social change

Despite the relative isolation of the Marshall Islands, cultural and social changes are sweeping across the society like tidal waves. Though very expensive, modern air transportation and advanced telecommunication have made the link to commercial centers such as Hawaii and Guam easier. Cellular telephone, video and cable television have also contributed to this fast rate of change. The ability to connect across great distances has put the people of the Marshall Islands in closer proximity to the latest fads found in metropolitan cities. Video movies and cable television have themselves become a source of social and cultural tension between the young and older generations, who have mixed feelings about the meaning of progress and how to regulate its pace so as not to create social and cultural chaos in the community.

The introduction of a money economy has also greatly weakened the importance of the extended family. With the modern concept of social security and saving accounts in commercial banks, the importance of the family as a form of social security in old age is becoming less relevant. Nuclear families seem to make far more sense in a cash economy.

Young Marshallese returning home from the newly established Marshallese communities in the United States are less Marshallese and more American. Sadly, many have only a superficial knowledge of what it means to be Marshallese. The Compact itself has thus become another catalyst to the current social and cultural changes taking place in the Marshall Islands.

These patterns of social changes have impacted the culture in deep and far-reaching ways. Some of the key cultural concepts, principles and values that kept the Marshallese people resilient are beginning to give ways under such strong pressures. However, as in olden times, and like other Pacific Island countries, "there is capacity to indigenise the forces of global modernity and turn them to their own ends" (Hooper, 2000). Indeed the knowledge that adaptation to these forces is taking place, as had occurred in earlier times, speaks to a resiliency that is inherent in the Marshallese people and their culture.

The cultural context

The *Iroij,* or chief, is a distinguishing characteristic of Marshallese society. While chief systems exist elsewhere in the Pacific region, the Marshallese *Iroij* system is unique in being tied closely to land inheritance and land rights. A key cultural feature of this chief system is the concept of sharing and communal land ownership.

The land inheritance system is also based on this concept. Members of the clan communally own *wetos*, land parcels, and have equal rights to proceeds from the land; however, an individual member of the clan cannot sell a parcel of land. Landlord rights belong to the whole clan and are passed down from one generation to the next, through the mother's side.

Membership in clans is also determined through the mother side. As a matrilineal society dominated by women, the women's role is a significant one in the Marshallese culture. Land rights, clan membership, even one's place in the community as a whole are determined by one's mother. While the men are expected to go to war, the women's role is significant in making peace. Women are expected to marry men from other clans and bring back the riches of the marriage to share with the members of their own clans, their own extended family. Thus, women are also a source of economic well-being for the clan.

The introduction of foreign concepts such as land leases and the sale of specific land rights has become one of many sources of tensions between traditional and modern ways in the Marshall Islands. Men have always served as spokespersons for women when it comes to land decisions. This is carried over into decisions about the leasing of land or the selling of certain rights on land. Because women are not party to most of this decision-making, their rights are often ignored. This threat to the power of women over land rights is a threat to one of the fundamental pillars of Marshallese society, land inheritance.

The concept of sharing is important in traditional Marshallese society and epitomizes the culture in its broadest sense. Sharing is shown in the ways communities traditionally come together to build houses and canoes and to assist on occasions of birth, sickness and death. In this system, the success of an individual member is a success of the clan as well. The reverse is also true, as a member's inappropriate actions may cause embarrassment to the whole clan. Such embarrassment may have long-term consequences. Each clan comes to be known for certain idiosyncratic behaviors, and these identifications can be passed down from one generation to the next. For example, the author belongs to a clan whose members are supposed to be so "dense" that when it's going to rain, they are known to take out house contents for airing under the sun. Whether the idiosyncrasy is true of any individual member is not important. As a member of a certain clan, one is "famous" for that clan's idiosyncratic identifier.

The clan or extended family, as described above, plays an important role in Marshallese society and is one of the foundations of traditional Marshallese culture. It too is changing as the clans, the *jowi*, are slowly being replaced by nuclear families. While family ties are still strong, there are long-term effects associated with this structural change. For example, the significant clan identification, noted earlier, is diminished as nuclear families are less likely to know their extended family relations.

The weakening of extended family support and family cohesiveness does more than create tensions between traditional and modern value systems. The extended family played a significant role in keeping the community in harmony and ensuring equitable resolutions of social conflicts and tensions between family members. It also acted as the social security system for aging family members and the fundamental means of passing on traditional knowledge and values through in-formal education. Younger members of the extended family cared for the elder family members who taught children the values and skills of the family and the culture through intergenerational communal activities. Everyone in the family had a role to play, responsibilities to carry out, and security in the structure they helped nurture.

The weakening of the extended family, therefore, as urban centers become westernized, is having a far more serious consequence to the well-being of the society than most Marshallese are ready to admit or accept. The decay of the extended family and its critical role in assuring a clan safety net provides an example. The family safety net encouraged and assigned child rearing responsibility to parents and other family members.

Despite parental shortcomings or failures, the family net assured the development of appropriate cultural values in the child's formative stages of growing up. Social problems such as increasingly high incidences of domestic violence, suicide among young males, malnourished children, teenage pregnancies, alcohol abuse, divorce, and prostitution, are just some of social problems that are a consequence of the decline of the extended family structure.

The weakening of the extended family has also diminished a sense of reciprocity and communal sharing that is pivotal in traditional societies. The small size of earlier Marshallese communities meant that everyone knew each other and cared for each other. When a house was built, or a canoe was launched, the entire community was involved, without expectation of any compensation. The practice is called *kumit*: everyone helping to assure completion of a project. Reciprocity was silently understood as a given. This Marshallese concept of volunteerism was an integral part of livelihood and social relationships on these islands. Where *kumit* was once a popular practice, the very concept of it is now no longer understood by the younger generation in the urban centers.

Cultural Continuity and Change

Pacific Megatrends in Education, a publication of Pacific Resources for Education and Learning (PREL), identifies seven megatrends that will affect education in the Pacific region over the next 10 years. One of the seven is "Increased Westernization but Retention of Culture and Language." While the study acknowledges increases in Westernization on parts of many small Pacific Islands nations, including the Republic of the Marshall Islands, it also acknowledges an increased tendency to look to one's own culture to seek solutions and insights. Many of the islanders who rushed to welcome "Western ways" as solutions to all Pacific problems have understandably come to the realization that not everything western is necessarily good, or good for everyone.

The intersection of indigenous cultures with Western culture often meant that traditional ways of learning and interacting with other members of the society are replaced. In the case of the Marshall Islands, intergenerational activities were, for the most part, replaced by newer and more modern ways of maintaining and passing on cultural knowledge and skills (museums, schools, churches etc). As the activities themselves were as much an integral part of Marshallese culture as the knowledge and skills transmitted through them, the people's sense of self-esteem disappeared along with their cultural practices and arts.

This began with the first sustained contact of the culture with the West. The Boston missionaries who introduced Christianity to the Marshall Islands all but forbade all forms of Marshallese arts including dance and tattooing. (Recently, however, consistent with the prediction of *Pacific Megatrends,* a cultural renaissance of sorts is beginning to revive those arts and skills and, with them, Marshallese self-esteem.)

Intergenerational activities and learning, *ekkatak jen, im ibben, rutto ro*, once the primary means of passing on traditional values, knowledge and skills, were replaced by the West's more "efficient institutions": schools, churches, and hospitals. In the traditional Marshallese societies, the elders had a very important role to play in the small but complex societies of the islands. They were respected for the knowledge and wisdom that came from years of rich and varied life experiences. This knowledge was passed down to younger members of the *"bwij,"* or lineage, through intergenerational activities such as canoe and house building for boys and weaving cooking for the girls. The intergenerational activities were thus an integral part of the life of the *bwij* and the larger Marshallese society.

As a people with no written language, Marshallese, *Ri-Majol,* preserved and passed on knowledge from generation to generation through oral stories, legends, chants, songs, and even tattoo patterns with meanings quite unique to different classes and genders within the society. It was the *bwijs* responsibility to ensure that knowledge, in some cases unique to that *bwij* alone, was passed on to the next generation. In a sense, the *bwij* was the guardian of that knowledge and was responsible for the functions that schools, churches, hospitals and even police departments perform in Western and contemporary Marshallese society. In this way, intergenerational initiatives provided the continuity that linked generations of Marshallese from the past to the present and across the island chain.

Members of any given *bwij* are commonly scattered throughout the 26 inhabited islands and atolls, so knowing one's *bwij* was always the way family connections were kept intact and new relationships established. Today that function would be more beneficial since so many members may be located outside the Marshall Islands. Unfortunately, the practice seems to be in decline, and knowing ones *bwij* is becoming limited to preventing intermarriages between members of the same clan. Where once the *bwij* was keeper and transmitter of cultural knowledge and tradition, including having the overall responsibility for community intergenerational initiatives, today the *bwij* is restricted to conveying information about one's relatives, rank in society and stereotyped characteristics.

Intergenerational Initiatives

The responsibility for intergenerational activities, *ekkatak jen, im ibben rutto ro*, in traditional times belonged to the elder members of the extended families, and the continuity of traditional knowledge was preserved and passed on in an apprenticeship mode. That took place in informal rather than formal settings. In these settings, limited attention was given to such things as number of contact hours, length of training, and standards for training. Apprenticeship standards are assessed through the knowledge and skills demonstrated by the apprentice. While today these *ekkatak,* may be about learning modern rather than traditional skills (for girls, cooking or washing using electrical appliances, and for boys, fishing using a motor boat), how they are taught within families and clans pretty much follow the traditional method of mentoring by family elders. This learning process is quite distinct from the academic learning process that is inherent in formal schooling. The distinction also underlies the transmission of important knowledge and techniques that were highly prized and regarded as well kept secrets.

How knowledge was passed on to others was an inherent component of intergenerational activities. Moreover, the intergenerational approach allowed master elders to guard prized knowledge by selecting the future guardian of that knowledge. Knowledge was viewed by Marshallese as a personal possession carrying with it responsibility for its preservation and transmission. To illustrate this, noted Marshallese navigators passed their knowledge and personally developed systems on to one of their children or to someone specifically adopted because of special interest and aptitude. Some who were considered master navigators oversaw the teaching of others in their extended family, giving rise to shared systems and ongoing "schools" that traced back to a master. The history of Marshallese navigation makes noteworthy mentioned of the fact that a child selected by a navigator to carry on the knowledge could be a male or female, and in fact, at least two masters cited by the Marshall Islanders were women (Archer, 1995).

The teaching and the learning of such traditional skills as navigating, sailing, canoe and house building, food preparation, roofing/mat/basket weaving, fishing, among others, integrate cultural and environmental values in both content and the manner in which they were taught. An intergenerational approach to teaching and learning these skills was woven into the fabric of the culture. It was in this spirit of responsibility and guardianship that knowledge and cultural continuity was passed on through generations.

Although modern institutions have, to a large degree, replaced this traditional way of transmitting knowledge and cultural continuity, there are efforts in the Marshallese community to bring the elders together to share their intricate skills and transmit cultural values in the process. Within families and clans, *ekkatak jen im ibben ritto ro* is still a viable way of transmitting intimate family knowledge. Another is the *Waan Aelon in Majol,* which is just one of several examples of large-scale, community-wide intergenerational activities in the Marshall Islands.

Waan Aelon in Majol

The *Waan Aelon in Majol* (Canoes of the Marshall Islands), or WAM Canoe Project uses elders to train youth in canoe and boat building, traditional house building and other traditional skills. Its goal is to preserve the history of the Marshall Islands through the promotion of voyaging and canoe building and navigation, prevent the loss of canoe and boat building skills by using master builders to train youths, and preserve the viable cultural and economic resource base of the Marshall Islands through promotion of canoes as the choice for inter-island transport, fishing, food gathering, and recreational sailing.

The WAM training center is located on the main island of Majuro in the populated center of Delap and is constructed completely of traditional building materials. Here master house and canoe builders are identified and employed as teachers in a program that has, at any given time, from 10 to 20 boys aged 17-21 learning traditional canoe and house building under the masters' supervision. Some of the young men are enrolled in WAM's peer educators program designed to provide lifeskills to a wider population of young people in an island setting. Plans are in place to recruit trade masters in women's traditional handicraft and to open the training program to young women.

WAM generates employment opportunities for youth in cottage-industry building jobs and aims to increase job opportunities in traditional construction and other areas. The center offers, for example, a venue for making and selling canoe models and other handicraft. Further, the WAM Center illustrates to the community how economic sustainability can be achieved through its use of renewable energy in the form of trade winds and sun.

A cultural awareness component of WAM began in 1999 for elementary school children from five public and two private schools. Students are taken to the WAM center three times a week. There, they are given canoe illustrations, so that they can learn the various parts of the canoe, and they hear stories and legends about these canoe parts and about navigation and sailing. Finally, the master canoe builders spend the last 15 minutes of each visit reviewing the different parts of the canoe in both English and Marshallese.

Between 1989 and 1995, in partnership with the Alele Museum's *Waan Aelon Kein* Project, WAM constructed more than four different traditional types of outrigger canoes, including the Jaluit *malmal,* the Likiep *taburbur* and the Namdrik, Ailuk and Enewetak voyaging canoe, the *walap.* These outrigger canoe types differ in types of materials used in construction, types of lashing, and design, which may be either contemporary or traditional. WAM also assisted the government of the Marshall Islands in its participation and presentations at the 1992 Sixth Festival of Pacific Arts in Rarotonga in the Cook Islands and subsequently the Seventh Festival of Pacific Arts in Apia, Western Samoa. (At the Rarotonga festival, the

Enewetak voyaging canoe, the Walap, was officially deemed the fastest traditional craft in the entire Pacific.)

Between 1994 and 1996, WAM partnered with Youth to Youth in Health (YTYIH), a non-profit organization with a mission to provide health, education and cultural programs to Marshallese youth through songs, theater and skits. WAM established a maintenance and rent-to-sail training program for Majuro youth utilizing *Laninmentol,* a nearly 50-foot-long voyaging canoe built in Ujae Atoll in the early 1990s. The use of *Laninmentol* for rent-to-sail promoted interest in canoe building and sailing, a skill that had almost been lost a generation earlier. More people are now building canoes for fishing and for inter-lagoon transport in the outer Marshall Islands. Moreover, traditional and community leaders are among the serious participants of the canoe competition, lending more credibility and value to canoe sailing.

WAM's focus on teaching youths and recording traditional building and navigational skills has sparked a renaissance of canoeing and voyaging in the Marshall Islands. The Outrigger Hotel Marshall Islands now sponsors an annual Outrigger Cup each May that brings participants from all over the Marshall Islands. In the process, WAM has generated pride in the culture and its values. Many of the skills that would have been lost forever as members of the older generation die, are being taught to the younger generation and, at the same time, recorded in videos and print for future generations.

Lutok Kobban Alele

Lutok Kobban Alele (Pour out the Valuable Content of the Basket) is an annual event sponsored by the Marshall Islands Museum, *Alele,* with assistance from the central and local governments. Designed to promote awareness, appreciation, and respect for the culture, the museum is named after the *Alele,* the Marshallese basket in which a family stores its valuables. *Alele* is the closest Marshallese word or concept to the idea of a museum, where a community stores its historical and commemorative articles for future generations.

Alele Day is an official holiday in the Marshall Islands. It takes place on the last day of the last week of August, *Lutok Kobban Alele* week, a week when the community comes together to celebrate, honor, and remember Marshallese culture and traditions. Every school participates, making various presentations in the school and in the community that are designed to teach the young to appreciate and respect the culture. Throughout the week, the government radio station broadcasts traditional stories, *inon,* as well as chants and songs, and the TV station shows local dancing by different community groups.

Lutok Kobban Alele week closes with a parade of floats around the island. Schools, community groups, government departments and businesses participate in this islands-wide parade. Each entry tries to depict the cultural themes of the week in the most creative, fun and meaningful way, and entrants compete for the First-, Second- and Third-place prizes that are given to the creators of the best floats. Many schools participate in the parade and often win prizes.

In addition to the annual event, the *Alele* sponsors a year-round program for children to learn about the culture as well as a radio program where elders present traditional skills and concepts, tell stories, and explain origins and values.

Youth to Youth in Health

YTYIH, mentioned above, is a non-profit, non-governmental organization that was originally a part of the Ministry of Health, Division of Population and Family Planning. Started in 1986, it has continued to successfully grow and attract funding from international organizations.

This programs trains peer educators (13-25 years old) to lead health education and cultural promotion outreach activities, counsel youth clients at health clinics, and share with elementary, high school, and out-of-school youth information about family planning, contraceptives, sexually-transmitted diseases, nutrition, suicide prevention, the hazards of alcohol consumption and smoking cigarettes and other topics of concern to the community at large.

While the focus is on youth, by youth, elder members of the community are often brought in to teach the peer educators. The focus is on training youth as peer educators, because youths are more receptive to their peers. This is the basis of the program.

One of the goals of the YTYIH program is to "combine the promotion of cultural identity and pride, awareness of health needs and youth responsibility as the basis for empowering youth to be 'change agents' throughout the Marshall Islands." As agents of change, the peer educators transmit their message via outreach activities and through media and video productions, slide shows, radio programs, skits, and print materials such as posters and leaflets. With the vast majority of Marshallese population under 25 years of age, it makes sense to involve youth in health and cultural promotion.

Currently, there are YTYIH chapters in about two-thirds of the islands and atoll communities in the Marshall Islands. Their message of health promotion and cultural empowerment is likely to continue to resonate vibrantly throughout the small nation.

School initiatives

Various schools have ongoing intergenerational activities in which community elders and parents teach cultural knowledge and skills to school children. At Assumption High School, a private school in Majuro, master fishermen teach schoolboys traditional fishing methods. A group of elders take the boys over long weekends to lagoon islets where they spend a couple of days learning how to make lures, identify types of fish and crabs appropriate for various fishing styles, weave fish baskets, and make *mweo*, braided ropes from coconut fronds, for catching fish. The processes are video taped for future learning when such outreach experiences may not be possible.

Likewise, skilled women teach girls how to weave mats, baskets, hats, and various hair pieces that are common in the Marshall Islands. The process of selecting, cleaning, and preparing the coconut or pandanus fronds for weaving is time-consuming and can be arduous. Yet, it is an important process in the weaving and making of handicrafts,

These activities generate continuity in values and skills from generation to generation. However, lack of funding has often limited their scope and creativity. More importantly, the learning of these skills out of context, often in urban settings, generates little meaning and appreciation for them among the younger generations. The competition with TV, video, and now computers also make it difficult to sustain such programs.

Implications for Promoting Cultural Continuity

While the above discussion suggests that a number of efforts are being made to stimulate the revival and preservation of traditional Marshallese culture, it would be an error to think that these efforts will be adequate to the task. A number of clear themes emerge for both public consideration and policy-making:

- Existing initiatives are relatively spontaneous, are not part of a coordinated effort or master strategy, and are not assured of continued support. Specific programs to promote cultural continuity are needed and must be organized, coordinated and sustained. The extent to which such programs can be supported, privately and by government, depends on the level of public awareness of the significant language and cultural loss that has taken place to date.
- As a people, the Marshallese are diminished without a vibrant culture and living language. The invasiveness of western culture through the media must be contained. Efforts to stop the erosion of culture and language should be given primary attention by government and traditional leaders, the *Iroij*. The preservation of Marshallese pride, along with Marshallese social and chiefly systems, rests on the survival of the Marshallese language and culture.
- Government must develop policies that support and promote cultural programs. The current "development" agenda for the government must place a high priority on preserving that which is valued in the

Marshallese culture, including *Kajin Majol*, the indigenous language, and protecting the environment. Policies that promote development and preservation of traditional values, skills and crafts, songs and dances need to be praised and positively supported to influence "tipping points" where the positive context influences pride and value and these become widely practiced, applied and promoted; policies governing language use in governmental functions and documents need to be strengthened and enforced.

- The *Alele* Museum should be given additional resources to expand its programs to the country's smaller communities and to schools and to be a visible force in the society.

Change is inevitable. It is incumbent on the cultural guardians, however, to be mindful of the patterns of changes and to help members of the community make sense of them in meaningful ways. New ways of doing things can be helpful and do not always have negative impact on the fabric of society. It is how new changes are interpreted, embraced, and applied in the lives of individuals that makes a difference in the long run.

In the Marshall Islands, where fast-paced changes are disrupting the fabric of society, an implication for policy makers might be support for organized initiatives such as the *Waan Aelon in Majol* (WAM) and YTYIH project. Here, elders, guardians of the culture, provide authentic, sustained, and meaningful learning experiences for the younger generation. This type of intergenerational activity, where young men learn by watching elders perform traditional work, is authentic learning in the Marshallese cultural context. This teaching strategy allows a youth to listen to the elders on a day-to-day basis and to learn traditional and cultural nuances by observing cultural activities and actually "living the culture." Such activities are critical to the survival of Marshallese traditions and cultural values.

Culture is made meaningful through interaction in particular cultural contexts. Therefore, in order for Marshallese values, skills and arts to endure the test of time, they must be taught in real, meaningful, natural, and contemporary contexts. Learning about the culture from books and other written transmissions, while useful, often does not convey the cultural nuances that are an integral part of the knowledge and skills to be learned. In other words, learning about culture in imposed settings devoid of meaningful contexts, becomes meaningless and chances for cultural survival minimized.

References

Archer, M. (1995). *Models and maps from the Marshall Islands: A case of ethnomathematics.* Historia Mathematica. Academic Press.

Hammond, O. (2000). PREL briefing paper: Pacific megatrends in education.

Honolulu, Hawaii: Pacific Resources for Education and Learning.

Hau'ofa, E. et al. (1993). *A new Oceania: Rediscovering our sea of islands*. Suva: University of the South Pacific 25th Anniversary Publication, in association with Beake House.

Hooper, A., ed. (2000). *Culture and sustainable development in the Pacific*. Canberra, Australia: Paragon Printers.

Office of Planning and Statistics (1999). *1999 Census of Population and Housing, Republic of the Marshall Islands*. Majuro, Marshall Islands.

Thaman, K. H.. (1999). A matter of life and death: Schooling and culture in Oceania. Keynote Address, Innovations for Effective Schooling Conference, Auckland, New Zealand.

Intergenerational Programs in Japan: Symbolic Extensions of Family Unity[1]

Matthew Kaplan[2], Ph.D. and Leng Leng Thang, Ph.D.[3]

Overview

In the context of Japan's rapidly aging population and concerns about changing family values, living arrangements, and lifestyles, this article notes the growing popularity of intergenerational programs and examines their implications for supplementing family support systems. Discussion centers on the results obtained from two distinct research projects conducted by the authors on intergenerational programs in Japan. One research initiative was exploratory in nature and conceived with the aim of charting the etiology of intergenerational programs on a national level. The other was an ethnographic study of one age-integrated institutional setting. In both endeavors, the authors encountered a prolific use of family metaphors and references to family-like support in descriptions of how intergenerational program intervention benefits the participants. In part, this suggests a certain amount of nostalgia for traditions and symbols reflecting the cultural ideals of family stability and unity.

Significant demographic and social trends in contemporary Japan have distinct implications for influencing the future landscape of intergenerational relations. In particular, there is a rapid growth in the proportion of elderly people, a pattern toward age-segregation in living arrangements, and an increase in negative attitudes toward the aged. In the context of these trends, there will likely be considerable interest and debate in the

years to come regarding the changing nature of intergenerational relationships, within and beyond families, and the degree to which problems
associated with such changes can be minimized or ameliorated. This paper
aims to augment this dialogue by focusing on the role of intergenerational
program initiatives for supplementing familial support systems. We believe the diversity and prevalence of intergenerational initiatives in Japan
and the powerful symbolism they convey of intergenerational continuity
and unity represent an important stabilizing force within Japanese society.

Below we present integrated results derived from two distinct research
studies on intergenerational programs in Japan. One initiative was exploratory in nature and conceived with the aim of charting the etiology of
intergenerational programs on a national level, and the other was an ethnographic study of one age-integrated institutional setting. In both research endeavors, the authors encountered a prolific use of family metaphors in descriptions of the perceived value of programmatic intervention
for the participants. Among the more interesting family-as-metaphor
themes encountered were "rental families," "event grandparenthood," and
"collective grandparenting." This finding is considered in the context of
cultural ideals that emphasize the primacy of "family" and family-based
systems of support in people's lives. Subsequent discussion addresses
certain ironies that emerge when conceptualizing intergenerational programs as vehicles for promoting family-like feelings and relationships,
particularly when they are implemented in institutional settings where
daily life is strikingly dissimilar to pre-institutional community-based living.

Aging in Japan: A Nation in Transition

The demographic landscape in Japan is in an era of drastic change. The
"aging society" trend is picking up strong momentum. Based on current
trends and statistics, the percentage of the population in Japan that is 65
years of age or older was 14.1 percent in 1994 (Statistics Bureau, 1996) and
is anticipated to increase to 25.8 percent by the year 2025 (Kono, 1994).
This places Japan as the nation with the most rapidly aging population,
and it is anticipated that Japan will have the most aged population in the
world in the twenty-first century (Kono, 1994).

The "aging of Japan" phenomenon is often presented and perceived
as a burden to society, with today's younger generations being the ones
to shoulder that burden (e.g., Oshima, 1996). In a recent *Time* magazine
article, entitled "The Silvering of Japan," the author states:

> The implications of the trend (of the aging population) are frightening; it
> is likely to limit future economic growth, drive up health costs and stick
> future generations with the immense cost of overhauling an outdated
> social infrastructure. The silvering of Japan has begun to rip apart the

cohesiveness of families and place heavy emotional burdens on a society in which life is stressful enough as it is (Makihara, 1994, pp. 49-50).

Pessimistic views toward aging are also found in survey results. According to a survey on Japan's "long-life society" conducted in 1991 by the Public Relations Office of the Cabinet Secretariat, only 37 percent of women in their 20s had positive associations and looked forward to enjoying a life with ever-increasing longevity expectations. They perceived life to be "dull" and "wretched" for elderly people (Fujitake, 1992). Similarly, studies that focus on how children and youth perceive elders generally conclude that the attitudes of Japanese youth towards the elders are characterized by negative stereotypes (Koyano, 1989). International comparisons of young people's perceptions of elders place Japanese youth as holding the most negative views (Koyano 1993) and having the weakest commitment to caring for their aging parents (Makihara, 1994).

Negative stereotypical images of the aged in Japan can also be found in the mass media (Koyano, 1993; Holtzman & Akiyama, 1985; Ehrlich, 1992). Ehrlich (1992), who studied how elderly people are characterized in Japanese films, notes that immediately following WORLD WAR II, films typically depicted the elderly as revered, respected, and exhibiting a steadfast quality. Though faced with harsh realities, they transcended their difficulties (at least in a spiritual sense). In contrast, when elderly people are portrayed in modern Japanese films, they are often presented as being "isolated and disenfranchised." With a backdrop of illness and disease, such films typically convey a tone of hopelessness and bleak pessimism. Ehrlich states:

> In Japanese cinema, the image of the elderly tends to either symbolize an ideal past, now lost or rapidly on the verge of extinction, or else it serves as a mirror of the illnesses of the present (p. 272).

As an indication of the decline in traditional values of respect for elderly family members, in recent years, the news media has been quick to seize upon the themes of "silver harassment," which refers to the abuse or neglect of elderly people, and "lonely deaths" ("*kodokushi*"), which refers to elders left uncared for by absentee relatives and local agencies that aid the elderly. (E.g., see "Elderly Bashing," 1994; "Lonely deaths," October 28, 1996.)

This is an alarming contrast to the idealized images of respect and care for Japanese elders which dominate social scientists' writings on Japan (for example, Palmore, 1975, and Palmore and Maeda, 1985). Koyano (1989) attributes this discrepancy between ideal and actual images to the "*tatemae*" and "*honne*" mentality of the Japanese; "*tatemae*" refers to the ideal, culturally defined, normative meaning of things and "*honne*" refers to the actual meaning or feeling of things. *Tatemae*, as Palmore (1975) has observed, is manifested in the "silver seats" which exist on every train; the Respect for Elders Day held every September 15; and the Law for the Welfare of the Elderly (enacted in 1963) which declared in Article 2 that "The elderly shall be loved and respected as those who have contributed toward the development of society for many years, and shall be warranted a healthful and peaceful life" (Koyano, 1989, p. 342). *Honne*, on the contrary, is characterized by negative images of elders as silly, senile, weak, and stubborn (Koyano, 1989).

To further explore societal transition with implications for the aging revolution taking place in Japan, it is important to examine changes in family structure. A key demographic trend considered by some Japan specialists to indicate that the institution of the Japanese family is undergoing fundamental change is the shift in household composition. In 1960, 90 percent of people over 60 years of age lived with their families (their children) as compared to only 60 percent in 1991 (Ozawa, 1991). Such a decrease in multi-generational households means that a growing number of the expanding aged population are living alone or only with their spouses.

Living alone can be an imposing life circumstance for many senior adults (even though, in comparison to the United States, fewer elders are living alone—only 13 percent of the elderly population in Japan live alone as compared to 40 percent in the United States [Sodei, 1991]). A growing number of elders living alone in Japan experience social isolation (men more than women) and financial and housing situation instability (women more than men) (Sodei, 1991). Moreover, Japanese are found to have less contact with their children (and grandchildren) than other nationalities when they do not live together (Management and Coordination Agency, 1990).

The factors that are making it more difficult for families to stay together in multi-generational households warrant attention, particularly in situations that require support for older family members. The decrease in shared living arrangements has been attributed to many factors, including the trend toward fewer children per couple (older adults with few or no children may have no choice but to live alone), more geographic mobility, an attitude change on the part of older adults favoring independent living (Sodei, 1991), and the progress of industrialization and urbanization (1994). In urban areas, less space for housing contributes to the disproportionate number of senior adults living alone. In rural areas, where traditions for multi-generational living are more ingrained in people's lifestyle preferences (Kase, 1995), an even higher percentage of senior adults live alone. These data are perceived to pose a serious threat to family continuity (Hendry, 1995), but it is more readily attributed to underdeveloped economic conditions which trigger out-migration of young people to the cities, leaving elderly people behind (Sodei, 1991).

Lebra (1984) notes that the question of who will care for ailing elderly family members often leads to divisive quarrels among relatives, particularly when the wives of eldest sons are unwilling or unable to assume this responsibility.[4] Lock (1993) extends this discussion and anticipates an escalation in such family quarrels as a result of increases in longevity, a concordant increase in the number of years spent providing care for elderly relatives, and the growing age of caregivers.

Of relevance to the discussion of changing patterns in caring for the elderly is the rapid growth in the diversity and number of institution-based living options available for senior adults. These range from nursing homes (for frail seniors) and low-cost homes (for relatively mobile seniors) supported by national and local governments to a wide variety of private retirement housing which has become a booming business in meeting the demand of middle-class seniors (Kinoshita and Kiefer, 1992).

In comparison to Western countries, there is less of a tradition of relying on human service system support and more of a stigma attached to receiving assistance outside of the family, including social welfare agency assistance. Bethel (1992), in her study of an old people's home run by the social welfare system, notes that for many senior adults institutionalization represents a failure to conform to the Confucian ideal of being cared for by family members.

Yet, it is debatable whether the trend of increased elder care options outside the family represents a violation or rejection of the Confucian ethic of filial piety. Insofar as values associated with filial piety and a sense of loyalty and responsibility to the family are deeply rooted in Japanese history and culture, there are those who argue they are likely to persevere (e.g., Kumagai, 1986; Hamilton, 1988). Such values are ingrained in the socialization process and are reflected in religious practices[5] and even in the Japanese language. (For example, the level of formality used to address family members is determined by relative positions in the familial hierarchy, determined, in part, by one's age and sex).

Kumagai (1995) posits that the modern Japanese family is neither solely traditional nor modern but rather exemplifies a dual structure, incorporating elements of both the traditional (which is more prominent in rural settings) and the modern (which is more prominent in urban settings). It would seem though that the stability of this duality is in flux. When family support systems persevere, they are often fragile in the face of many of the demographic, social, and economic forces in play in modern Japanese society.

Modern Japan is at a crossroads. It is increasingly recognized that traditional forms of family life are often not enough to counter the feelings that many elderly people have of isolation and uncertainty as to their roles in society, nor is it enough to alleviate the anxiety and pressures experienced by many children and youth who are encountering vast expectations and pressures in regard to education and career preparation (Fukuzawa, 1994; LeTendre, 1994; and Okamoto, 1994).

In the remaining sections of this article, the focus shifts to intergenerational programs, i.e., human service initiatives designed to promote age-integrated activity beyond the family unit. In addition to providing a review of the breadth of intergenerational program models in Japan, we consider their significance for addressing quality of life concerns for the nation's growing population of senior adults and for conveying, not replacing, the cultural ideals of family continuity and unity.

Research Methods

This paper represents a collaboration of data collected by the authors in two distinct research projects focused on intergenerational programs in Japan. With the common objective of gaining insight into the social significance of intergenerational programs in Japan, both projects began with a review of available interdisciplinary scholarly materials, newspaper articles, popular arts and literature, and television documentaries describing how different generations communicate or fail to communicate with each other, and how, as a result of various types of intervention, the generations are brought together in a collaborative fashion.

In one of the research initiatives, conducted by the first author and a team of researchers in Japan,[6] additional methods included: a series of preliminary interviews with professionals knowledgeable about young-old generational interactions in various contexts, 12 site visits, and three case studies of specific intergenerational programs. The preliminary interviews and site visits were used to accumulate narrative detail about why and by whom different types of intergenerational initiatives are established. In total, descriptive data was collected on 50 intergenerational initiatives which reflect geographical and program-type diversity.

For the final phase of this study, profiles were drawn for three intergenerational initiatives; two of these mini-case studies focused on examples of prevalent school-based intergenerational models, and the third was of a program called "Rent-A-Family," run by a Tokyo-based business consulting agency, in which senior citizen clients rent the services of actors (known as "entertainers") to play the parts of their children and grandchildren and share family-like experiences.

The other research initiative, conducted by the second author,[7] also began with a series of preliminary interviews and site visits with professionals in the intergenerational programming arena. This study included visits and observations conducted at five age-integrated facilities and telephone interviews conducted with staff at 12 other age-integrated institutions in the Tokyo Metropolitan area. Ultimately, an intensive ethnographic field study was conducted at one age-integrated institution called "Kotoen," Japan's oldest and most established age-integrated center that combines an old-age home with a nursery school. At Kotoen, the elders are relatively mobile, which greatly facilitates their interactions with the children, and the children are actively encouraged to interact with them. A participant observation approach infused with informal interviewing, a review of documents and artifacts, and video recording were used to examine patterns of social interaction, activity, and perceptions held by caregiving and nursery staff, volunteers, college interns, parents, and senior adults and children at Kotoen.

Intergenerational Programs in Japan: Diverse and Multi-faceted

In Japan, intergenerational programs are termed "intergenerational interaction activities" (*"setaikan koryu katsudo"*). Defined as people from various ages getting together to do something in an extra-familial setting, they have a connotation of three-generational interaction including the middle generation (Saito, 1994, p. 161). However, the programs typically involve cooperation, interaction or exchange between people over 60 years of age and people under 21 years of age, with little, if any, involvement of the middle generation.

In Japan, as in the United States, intergenerational programs are often conceived as a means to address negative consequences associated with intergenerational segregation (in residential, educational, and recreational aspects of living). Although the trend toward intergenerational segregation in Japan is less severe than in the United States (certainly the case in terms of living arrangements), this process is still seen as having a negative impact on the social support and life enrichment opportunities available for children and youth as well as for elderly people (Aoi, 1992; Aging Integrated Research Center, 1994).

Experimentation with regard to intergenerational programs in Japan (as well as in the United States) has also been catalyzed by other concerns. Intergenerational initiatives are often seen as presenting a strategy for: providing productive roles for senior adults; combating "ageism;" promoting pro-social values on the part of youth; promoting intergenerational understanding and mutual support in the face of changes in family structure; and mobilizing the talents, skills, energy, and resources of the young and the elderly.

In Japan, some initiatives are connected with national programs administered by separate ministries; many more are local initiatives planned and implemented by local government agencies, non-governmental neighborhood governing associations (known as *"chonaikai"*), and other community organizations such as youth and elders' organizations and clubs.

Intergenerational programs are also varied in terms of the benefits afforded to the participants. Depending on the setting and the underlying program goals, they contribute to participants' sense of community, solidarity, and cultural identity and help people to pursue their educational objectives, arts and recreation interests, desired states of health and welfare, and environmental preservation and community development goals. Furthermore, these programs help participants attain a sense of religious and spiritual well-being (Kaplan, 1996).

A rich array of intergenerational initiatives exists in Japanese schools (public and private), community settings, and institutional facilities. Many intergenerational activities hinge on the traditional, cultural, and historical knowledge of the elders. Elders visit schools or children's clubs to teach children about "conventional" Japanese traditional crafts such as origami, bamboo crafts, rope crafts, and traditional childhood games. In addition, they talk about the past, typically sharing their childhood experiences, discussing local history, and sharing their perspectives on activities that convey "*furusato*" (old community, hometown) flavor. Such intergenerational exchange promotes a sense of cultural continuity on the part of the youth who gain more understanding and respect for historical traditions and a greater perspective for how postwar modernization has transformed Japan (and the world) in the course of a generation.

Many intergenerational programs are designed with the goal of promoting children and youth understanding and awareness of the social welfare needs of the elderly. In such initiatives, the young participants generally visit old-age institutions or elders living alone in the community and provide some sort of companionship or other service.

In recent years, more and more communities intentionally create spaces for the old and young to interact, such as building "elders' space" in children's playgrounds (Hyogo Prefecture), establishing a children's library in an old-age home (Saitama Prefecture), and placing swings and slides in the open ground of old-age homes (Thang, 2001). In like fashion, it is becoming more common to find day service centers or other elderly services set up in classrooms of schools and nurseries that have vacant space (due to the declining birth rate in Japan).

Under the sponsorship of government health and social welfare agencies, some interesting examples of "joint facilities" exist in which services for senior adults and services for children and youth are provided in the same facility. These facilities often cite practical reasons such as the effective use of limited land and resources and the "emotional" reason of providing "*fureai*" ("heart warming contact") to both the old and the young as the main purposes for this combination.

In some joint facilities, administrators see the different age groups as merely co-existing and make no efforts to integrate them in activities beyond the occasional joint event or fire drill. In others, like Kotoen (discussed in more detail, below), the driving force of the entire institution is its ideology of intergenerational interaction, infused with careful planning and programming efforts (Thang, 2001).

Another set of intergenerational programs in Japan can be categorized according to their private sector genesis. The demographic and social changes occurring in Japanese society generate new business opportunities. Rent-A-Family, a unique service developed by Japan Efficiency Headquarters ("Nihon Kokasei Honbu") in 1990, targeting elderly people who have limited kinship ties or who are not totally fulfilled by them, serves as a good example.

In terms of how the participants of intergenerational activities benefit, Aoi (1992) notes that the psychological significance for older adults is tied to getting the opportunity to work on behalf of children and youth. He reiterates a theme presented by intergenerational program specialists in the United States (e.g., see Newman and Brummel, 1989): that meaningful intergenerational contact helps the senior adult participant develop a sense of "(ego) integrity."[8]

Human development is indeed a lifelong process and in Japan emphasis is placed, from various fronts, on the value of living one's entire life fully. A popular concept that has important connotations for healthy living in one's latter years is *"ikigai"* ("purpose in life"); to have *ikigai* is generally perceived as a desirable attitude toward life. This perception contrasts with states of dependency and helplessness (Thang, 1997). The emphasis on active, healthy aging gives birth to involvement in intergenerational activity such as "volunteer therapy," where the act of helping others is seen as having important implications for keeping senior adults physically and mentally healthy (Tokyo Volunteer Center, 1993, p. 9).

Intergenerational initiatives enrich the lives of the young as well as the elderly participants. The Annual Report on the National Life for Fiscal 1992 (Economic Planning Agency, 1992) makes this point:

> If nuclear families increase at the current rate, and the numbers of grandchildren also decrease as a result of the general decline in the number of children, then occasions to spend time with grandchildren will also decrease. Thus, it will be more and more vital to create places within each community where old people and children can meet, as is already done in some areas. It will provide children with an opportunity to get to know views and opinions different from those of their parents, as well as a unique opportunity for social development quite different from that provided by association with peers (p. 204).

Official support for intergenerational programs in Japan first appeared in aging policy under the "measures for learning and social participation" in the 1986 "Policy Guidelines for a Long-lived Society." Often seen in the framework of the "lifelong learning" movement, a wide spectrum of learning experiences created for people across the life span (Okamoto, 1994; Thompson 1996), intergenerational programs are included as one of the six pillars of the Ministry of Education's (1991) "comprehensive projects to promote '*ikigai*' of elders." Such projects are often sponsored through specific national programs such as the Model Municipality Project (Saito, 1994).

The new Fundamental Law on Policies for Aging Society adopted by Prime Minister Hashimoto's Cabinet in July 1996 reflects an interest in intergenerational programming. This law, which replaces the 1986 Policy Guidelines, states:

> In order to build energetic local communities as well as to help the elderly play an active role in them with something to live for, the elder's environment in social activities will be facilitated. To achieve this goal, opportunities will be provided for the elders and young generations to promote mutual exchange, and voluntary activities of the elders will be supported (Maeda, 1996, p. 131).

The diversity and multi-faceted significance of intergenerational initiatives in Japan represent a powerful stabilizing force for offsetting some of the uncertainties associated with the demographic and social changes noted above. Furthermore, the growing popularity of many intergenerational program models suggests that they reflect an unmistakable yearning for intergenerational re-engagement in Japan. In the next section, we explore a key dimension of the growing appeal of intergenerational programs that we did not expect to find: the symbolism they convey of family continuity and unity.

Intergenerational Programs and the Symbolism of Family Unity

In the literature on intergenerational programs in Japan, the re-uniting of the generations theme often accompanies nostalgic sentiment for the cultural ideal of three-generational living. One report notes how intergenerational activities between frail elders and active youth revitalizes filial traditions that are diminishing. It states that such activities "provide the opportunity for the young to learn how to take care of their own aging parents in the future" (Aging Integrated Research Center, 1994, p. 31).

Both authors of this paper, in their separate research projects on Japanese intergenerational programs, encountered heavy use of symbolism related to family continuity and unity. The second author, in her ethnographic study of Kotoen, a well-established age-integrated institution, found that a central element of how this age-integrated institution is managed and perceived by its participants and the public is tied to its representation as a "big family" or "multi-dimensional family." Similarly, the first author suggests that the public's interest and acceptance of the Rent-A-Family program hinges on its effective invocation of stem-family/kinship-oriented concepts that are familiar and comfortable to its senior adult clientele.

Kotoen

Kotoen is an unusual age-integrated welfare institution that started as an experimental project by a Tokyo welfare organization a decade ago. It combines four different services: a nursery with a capacity of 80, a day service center for 15 elders staying in the community, a nursing home for frail and senile seniors, and an old age home for poor but mobile elders, with a capacity of 50. The main forms of senior-child interactions at Kotoen can be summarized into the following categories: daily morning exercise, which begins after lively greetings from the children and is followed by handshaking and games such as "jang-ken-pong" (paper, scissors, stones); the seniors helping to dress the children (after their afternoon naps); "*Narashi*" (beginning) childcare, in which the center's seniors help care for the one-year-old toddlers; children's visits to the elders' quarters, during which time they participate in joint activities such as drawing, origami (paper folding), clay building, *kami shibai* (paper drama); open childcare, in which groups of elders join the children once a month for an entire day of playing, eating, and sharing free time together; joint celebrations of special events, including traditional cultural events and birthday parties; and other activities such as informal visiting and joint walks (Thang, 2001).

Everything that happens in the center is cast within its philosophy of "*Kotoen daikazoku*," with the goal of striving towards natural interaction resembling a three-generational family. The dream of Kotoen, as we have learned, is to achieve "*fureai*" (heart warming contact) across the generations. The quest to promote intergenerational relations that reflect *fureai* in a big three-generational family manifests itself in many ways, including the establishment of a "*fureai* committee" in 1989 which functions to promote and support alternative generational interactions and placement on a central first floor wall of a large picture of the "Kotoen big family" depicting more than 250 members ranging from 1 to 96 year old. Its logo of a "grandma" in kimono dancing merrily with a couple of children symbolizes Kotoen's philosophy.

Thang (2001) has developed the two concepts of "event grandparenthood" and "collective grandparenting" to represent the nature of intergenerational interaction at Kotoen. "Event grandparenthood" denotes the boundary of grandparenthood in an institution where emotional connections, as in real grandchild-grandparent relationships, are expected to happen within the temporal boundaries of short activity sessions and within the spatial boundaries of an institutional environment. Once outside the frame of the event or activity, life goes on as a typical old-age institution for the elders who lose sight of their grandparenting role.

"Collective grandparenting" refers to the tendency to generalize the concept of grandparenting, beyond one-to-one relationships, to suit the institutional atmosphere of large group activities. Grandparenthood is thus defined as a collective identity, which, within the *daikazoku* framework, allows the children and the elders to take on grandchildren and grandparent roles that transcend their individual selves; they know they will in turn be succeeded by the next generation of elders and children after them. As the elders cheerfully send off the graduates and wait eagerly for the next batch of "grandchildren," the children also view their graduation as the point where they relinquish their Kotoen grandchildren role.

It is ironic that within the framework of living in an institutional setting, where administrative rules and regulations typically serve to instill a regimented atmosphere and constrain spontaneity, the intergenerational contact at Kotoen is nonetheless framed in terms of *daikazoku* and *fureai*. On one hand, there is a disjuncture between ideology and practice. Despite the ideal of establishing a sense of "family," many of the elderly residents and children do not seem to care to foster intimate relations with each other. For example, most of the elders do not know the children's names and could not recall being close to any one child. On the other hand, some meaningful relations have flourished and "spontaneity" has been encouraged to happen through programming.

The "we as a family" feeling has indeed developed spontaneously among many of the elders and children of Kotoen. The passionate involvement of some of the elders and the high frequency with which the elders discuss their common feelings about children reveal the possibility for greater involvement on the part of the elders beyond "event grandparenthood" and "collective grandparenting."

On the macro level, the *daikazoku* ideology suggests a romanticized image of the traditional Japanese family system where three-generations live together harmoniously. Kotoen's image of a "three-generational family" has been repeatedly publicized in the media. (Kotoen has appeared in videos aired on almost all the Tokyo TV networks and in a host of magazines and journals.) The acceptance of the Kotoen ideal by the media and by the public suggests that the ideology does not simply address a private dream, but that it is also a dream yearned for by the wider public. However, this contradicts the present social reality. The truth is, age-segregation is becoming a norm and all indications are that it will become a more established trend in the future.

The ironies faced by Kotoen remind us that we cannot examine an institution outside of its particular cultural temporal context, and sometimes this understanding means coming to terms with the contradictions and recognizing that positive meanings do develop within paradoxical parameters.

Rent-A-Family

Rent-A-Family—another intergenerational endeavor—although based on an entirely different program model than Kotoen, conveys the similar idea that multi-generational family-like experiences can be "constructed" with outside elements. The Rent-A-Family Program, initiated in 1990 by the Japan Efficiency Headquarters, serves as a surrogate family service for senior adults in the Tokyo Metropolitan Region. Clients typically fit into one of four categories: (1) an elderly person who is feeling lonely and wants to be distracted from that feeling, (2) an elderly person who wants a recreational experience, (3) an elderly person who has plans to move in with a younger family member but wants a "preview" experience, and (4) a young or middle-aged adult who wants to give his or her elderly parent(s) a pleasant, supplemental family-like experience (Matsumoto, 1992).

Activities during Rent-A-Family sessions include: preparing and eating meals, "family" walks in the park, discussions about various topics, gift giving, storytelling, singing, "pounding shoulders" (a form of massage), playing *shogi* (Japanese chess), and playing with the "grandchildren" which, for the small children, often involves intimate games with them on the seniors' laps. In some cases, the time is unscheduled in an effort to create an atmosphere of actual family life. Conversation topics vary. A common mode of interaction involves the elderly client reminiscing about the past, "when there were no washing machines" and "when (we) had nothing and had to make things ourselves by sewing and knitting." The clients and the entertainers (in roles) also typically share their life philosophies and discuss job prospects and recreational pursuits.

The Rent-A-Family program is popular; by the end of 1994, there was a waiting list of over 100 families and a publicity list of approximately 100 cases of news media coverage of the program (Kaplan et al., 1998). A common theme presented in media accounts of the program is the notion that even though clients know that the rental family scenarios are not "real," Rent-A-Family experiences often generate much excitement and emotion. It is noted that the clients as well as the entertainers really seem to "enter" their roles, and this sometimes even results in tears (from the clients) at the end of some sessions.

Most of the media attention to the Rent-A-Family program has been positive and fits into discussions about how neither the family unit in modern Japanese society nor the current scope of public welfare programs adequately address the basic companionship and social support needs of many elderly people. Reflecting this theme, the Japan Efficiency Headquarters president is quoted as saying, "(In the past) at least one person in the neighborhood listened to people's problems but nowadays there are so many people feeling that they have nobody to talk to" ("Ichinichi kazoku o haken," 1992).

The program was originally intended to provide nothing more than a leisure-type service. Yet, the high level of interest and enthusiasm has occasionally generated misunderstanding. For example, Yamazaki Tetsu, a Japanese playwright, suggests that Rent-A-Family experiences can provide an attractive substitute for real family experiences. He states:

> If you don't have roots, you can be away from the actual life of reality and move into (experience) different realities and then you can have fun and be cheerful. On the other hand, people who have roots tend to be depressed, but many people prefer to be cheerful or have a happy life. So, we shouldn't root ourselves" ("Rentaru kazoku wa kaunseringu da, 1992, p. 9)

As originally conceived, the program was apparently never intended to replace or serve as a tool for restructuring familial support systems. Yet, Yamazaki Tetsu's comments suggest that the Rent-A-Family concept can be used in a manner that belittles and delimits the importance of (real) family support systems. Families would be restructured; randomness and spontaneity in familial human relations would be removed.

Furthermore, program staff have occasionally made statements (in interviews and in media reports) which "oversell" the program (Rentaru, 1992). They note program benefits for "helping people to realize that they need human love," enhancing self-confidence of elderly clients, and for addressing the psychological needs of people "who experience emptiness of the heart" (p. 9). Although these assertions may be on target, it is premature to make such statements until further research can be conducted.

One should remember that the Rent-A-Family initiative provides participants with a three hour intervention and is thus qualitatively different than programmatic initiatives that involve ongoing interaction and relationship formation between people of different generations. Accordingly, Rent-A-Family does not approach anything that resembles a "solution" to social isolation or loneliness. In fact, the Japan Efficiency Headquarters' program framework serves to prevent the formation of relationships; beyond the formal rental family sessions which clients experience only once or on an irregular basis, clients and entertainers are prohibited from meeting.

Compared to Kotoen, the Rent-A-Family program represents an extreme in intergenerational programs, as emotions become "commodified" and "purchasable." Nevertheless, its entrepreneurial success provides one indication that at least some view it as a needed service. One possible reason for its strong appeal in Japan is that it represents an intervention into elderly people's lives that invokes familiar (comfortable) images of "family." This is perhaps less alien to many Japanese elderly people than public welfare intervention systems for which no tradition exists. Traditionally, the family has functioned as the most vital lifeline of support for elders, and perhaps it is intervention veiled in the family image that is most acceptable for many.

Other programs

Beyond the Kotoen and Rent-A-Family examples provided above, the authors encountered a few other intergenerational programs in which participants' perceptions of program value are cast in terms of a sense of family-like intergenerational congruity and feeling. A case in point is the Hokkaido Intergenerational Recreational Camp program sponsored by the Hokkaido Lifelong Society Foundation and regional and municipal social welfare agencies. This two-day intensive recreational program takes place in four regions in Hokkaido, with three generations represented among the participants—elders, middle-aged adults (mostly parents of the children and staff of the youth and elders clubs), and youth and children (as young as two years of age).

According to comments provided by participants of the 1993 and 1994 day camp programs, even though activities lasted for only two days,[9] the intergenerational communication fostered a heartfelt sense of connectedness and affection. Some participants used the metaphor of "family" to describe their program-related experiences and feelings. For example, a young participant in the fifth grade stated:

> What I found very interesting through participating in this program is that it helped to make "family." Although my friend and I worried whether we could become family with unknown people, the person who became my father was very fun and mother was caring, so I soon forgot that thought (Hokkaido Lifelong Society Foundation, 1993, p. 8).

Another fifth grade student participant stated:

> Our family has four members, it was very fresh to make one big family (although) it was a little strange to feel unknown people to be able to call them mother and father (Hokkaido Lifelong Society Foundation, 1993, p. 13).

A senior adult participant stated:

> They called me "grandma" which made me very happy (Hokkaido Lifelong Society Foundation, 1993, p. 63).

Also along the lines of this "family as metaphor" theme, a staff member from one of the regional social welfare divisions who participated in one of the camp sessions with her daughter, stated:

The participants were having conversations a little bit formally for a while, but (over time) . . . we had more fun and a relaxing atmosphere as if we had one real family. My daughter was happy to have siblings saying, "There are many brothers and sisters!" I believe this was a very good experience for her. . . . Although we were (only) a two-day family, we said good-bye with words, "hope to see you soon" and "say hello when you see me on the street" (Hokkaido Lifelong Society Foundation, 1993, p. 19).

Some participants noted parallels between their program-related and real family experiences. In this regard, a second year high school student stated:

All of my grandparents are fine and I am glad to have taken part in this program before they die. From now on, I will make the most of this experience and take care of elders and my grandparents who built the current society we live in (Hokkaido Lifelong Society Foundation, 1993, pp. 40-41).

In a similar vein, one of the youth group organizers noted:

We also gave massage to each other because we exercised during the daytime. That was when I happened to remember my late grandfather. . . . When my grandfather was alive, we lived on a strict regular schedule, took special care on diet, and above all, my parents were caring so much for my grandparents and told us to do so as well. By participating in this program, I remember these loving feelings towards elders which I almost forgot (Hokkaido Lifelong Society Foundation, 1993, p. 53).

Conclusions

Japanese concern and anxiety over the future of an aging society (including personal feelings of one's own old age) stem from the lack of an updated map by which to redefine and re-situate oneself in a new age of mass longevity. Postwar changes in family structure and the erosion of certain traditional ideals have made the traditional model of old age based on filial piety, valid only a generation before, increasingly obsolete. Until a new model is established to provide a guide, the "heartfelt longevity society" called for in the Management and Coordination Agency report on intergenerational relations (Management and Coordination Agency, 1992) will remain a distant goal.

Intergenerational programming represents a viable, multi-faceted approach for addressing the dilemma of generational disengagement. Although it is clearly understood that intergenerational programs do not provide a perfect substitute for family support, they can provide a meaningful alternative, particularly for those individuals who find traditional family support systems unavailable or insufficient to meet their psychological, social, and physical needs.

At the same time, however, there is some skepticism in regard to whether the promotion of alternate-generational interaction makes sense outside the familial context. For example, when the second author told a government official from a Japanese welfare office about Kotoen, his reaction was "Oh, it's like a drama family (*engeki kazoku*)," implying that such relations sound unreal. In effect, he is asking, "How can a congregation of *tanin* (others) be a family?" Rent-A-Family has provoked a similar reaction. When interviewed regarding his feelings about the program, Yoji Yamada, a famous filmmaker who emphasizes family themes in his movies, objected to the artificiality of the program and further criticized the general idea of reducing natural human interaction to a commodity (Suganuma, 1992). The traditional Japanese view of familial relations, underscored in both sets of reactions, is characterized by adherence to the strict distinction traditionally drawn between the concepts of *uchi* (insider) and *soto* (outsider, others) (Nakane 1970).

Yet, when all is considered, the public's reaction to these and other intergenerational programs has been predominantly positive. In the cases of Kotoen, Rent-A-Family, and the Hokkaido Intergenerational Recreational Camp program — very different types of intergenerational programs — we find it significant that when participants, staff, and observers set out to describe the underlying meaning and value of alternate-generational interaction, they focused on similarities to the warm feelings and support associated with "real" family interaction. This has led us to rethink the concept of the family and question whether intergenerational programs that convey the symbolism of family unity reflect a shift in Japanese conceptions of the ideal family. This ties in with the broader question: can "family" encompass alternate-generational interaction beyond what emerges as a function of marriage or biological links?

In conclusion, although statistics have shown that the proportion of three-generational families is declining in Japan, this does not necessarily indicate that the dream of a nostalgic image of three-generational families is dwindling. Rather, we suggest that new questions about what constitutes "family" ushers in a period in which there is a greater likelihood for public acceptance of new modes and constructions of intergenerational interaction.

References

Aging Integrated Research Center (1994). *Sedaikan koryu ni kansuru chosa kenkyu hokokusho* [Research report on intergenerational exchange], sponsored by the Management and Coordination Agency. Tokyo: Aging Integrated Research Center.

Aoi, K. (1992). *Choju shakaii ron* [Long life society issues]. Tokyo: Ryutsu Keizai University Publishing Company.

Asano, H. (1994). Health care and welfare services for the elderly in Japan. In Japan Aging Research Center (Ed.), *Aging in Japan* (pp. 88-109). Tokyo: Author.

Bethel, D. (1992). Life in Obasuteyama, or, inside a Japanese institution for the elderly. In T.S. Lebra (Ed.), *Japanese social organization* (pp. 109-34), Honolulu: University of Hawaii Press.

Economic Planning Agency (1992). *Annual report on the national life for fiscal 1992: The arrival of the society with a small number of children.* Tokyo: Author (Social Research Division, Social Policy Bureau).

Ehrlich, L.C. (1992). The undesired ones: Images of the elderly in Japanese cinema. In S. Formanek & S. Linhart (Eds.) *Japanese biographies: Life histories, life cycles, life stages* (pp. 271-281). Vienna: Austrian Academy of Science.

Elderly bashing. (1994, March 10). *Mainichi Daily News*, p. 1.

Fujitake, A. (1992, March 1). Clinging to youth. *Japan Update*, 6, p. 25.

Fukuzawa, R.E. (1994). The path to adulthood according to Japanese middle schools. *Journal of Japanese Studies*, 20(1), 61-86.

Hamilton, S.F. (1988). *The interaction of family, community and work in the socialization of youth.* Washington DC: Institute for Educational Leadership, Commission of Work, Family and Citizenship.

Hendry, J. (1995). *Understanding Japanese society.* (Rev. ed.). London: Routledge.

Hokkaido Lifelong Society Foundation (1994). *Koryu no kiseki* [The memories of intergenerational exchange]. Sapporo, Japan: Author.

Hokkaido Lifelong Society Foundation (1993). *Koryu No kiseki* [The memories of intergenerational exchange]. Sapporo, Japan: Author.

Holtzman, J.M. & Akiyama, H. (1985). What children see: The aged on television in Japan and the United States. *The Gerontologist*, 25 (1), 62-68.

Ichinichi kazoku o haken [Dispatching one day families]. (1992, October 10). *Nikkei Ryutsu Shimbun*, p. 11.

Kaplan, M., Kusano, A., Tsuji, I., & Hisamichi, S. (1998). *Intergenerational programs: Support for children, youth and elders in Japan.* N.Y.: State University of New York Press.

Kaplan, M. (1996). A look at intergenerational program initiatives in Japan: A preliminary comparison with the U.S. *Southwest Journal on Aging*, 12, (1-2) 73-79.

Kase, K. (November 1995). The nuclear family in postwar Japan (review essay). In *Social Science Japan*, 5, Institute of Social Science, University of Tokyo. (Available: http://www.iss.u-tokyo.ac.jp/center/SSJ/SSJ5/kase.html).

Kinoshita, Y. & Keifer, C.(1992). *Refuge of the honored: Social organization in a Japanese retirement community.* Berkeley: University of California Press.

Kono, S. (1994). Demographic aspects of population aging in Japan. In Japan Aging Research Center (Ed.), *Aging in Japan*, (pp. 5-54). Tokyo: Author.

Koyano, W. (1989). Japanese attitudes towards the elderly: A review of research findings. *Journal of Cross-Cultural Gerontology*, 4 (3), 335-345.

Koyano, W. (1993). Age-old stereotypes. *Japan Views Quarterly*, 2 (4), 41-42.

Kumagai, F. (1995). Families in Japan: Beliefs and realities. *Journal of Comparative Family Studies*, 26 (1), 135-163.

Kumagai, F. (1986). Modernization and the family in Japan. *Journal of Family History*, 11 (4), 371-382.

Lebra, T. (1984). *Japanese women: Constraint and fulfillment.* Honolulu: University of Hawaii Press.

LeTendre, G. (1994). Guiding them on: Teaching, hierarchy, and social organization in Japanese middle schools. *Journal of Japanese Studies,* 20 (1), 37-59.

Lock, M. (1993). Ideology, female mid-Life, and the graying of Japan. *Journal of Japanese Studies,* 19 (1), 43-78.

Lonely Deaths. (1996, October 28). *Newsweek,* 36-37.

Maeda, D. (1996) Social security, health care, and social services for the elderly in Japan. In Japan Aging Research Center (Ed.), *Aging in Japan.* (pp. 85-112) Tokyo: author.

Makihara K. (1994, November 14). The silvering of Japan. *Time International,* 49-54.

Management and Coordination Agency (1992). *Geneki sedai to rojin no communicationo o kangaeru kondankai* [Conference on communication between generations of active duty people and senior adults] (Summary report: Conclusions drawn from a series of five "informal talks" from March 1992 to June 1992). Tokyo: Author.

Management and Coordination Agency (1990). *Rojin no seikatsu to ishiki ni kansuru kokusai hikaku chosa* [International comparative survey on the lives and consciousness of elders: An overview]. Tokyo: Somucho Chokan Kanbo Rojin Taisaku Shitsu.

Matsumoto, K. (1992, November 7). Rentaru kazokuwa naze hayaru? [Why is Rent-A-Family becoming fashionable?] *Fujinkoron,* 136-141.

Ministry of Education, Science and Culture (1991). *Statistical bulletin of education.* Tokyo: Daiichi Hoki Shupan.

Nakane, C. (1970). *Japanese society.* Berkeley: University of California Press.

Newman, S. & Brummel, S.W. (Eds.) (1989). *Intergenerational programs: Imperatives, strategies, impacts, trends.* Binghamton, NY: Haworth Press.

NHK (1989). *Mago hachijunin no daikazoku* [Family with 80 grandchildren], video documentary. Tokyo: Author.

Ogawa, N., & Hodge, R.W. (1994). Patrilocality, childbearing, and labor supply and earning power of married Japanese women. In J.F. Ermisch and N. Ogawa (Eds.), *The family, the market and the state in aging societies.* (pp.105-131) Oxford: Clarendon Press.

Okamoto, K. (1994). *Lifelong learning movement in Japan: Strategy, practices and challenges.* Tokyo: Lifelong Learning Division, Ministry of Education, Science and Culture.

Oshima, S. (1996, July 5). Japan: Feeling the strains of an aging population. *Science,* 273, 44-45.

Ozawa, M. (1991). Child welfare programs in Japan. *The University of Chicago Press Social Service Review,* 65 (1), 1-21.

Palmore, E. (1975). *The honorable elders: A cross-cultural analysis of aging in Japan.* Durham: Duke University Press.

Palmore, E. & Daisaku, M. (1985). *The honorable elders revisited.* Durham: Duke University Press.

Rentaru kazoku wa kaunseringu da [Rental family is counseling]. (1992, September). *Omoshiro Seikatsu* [Interesting Lifestyles], 27, 8-9.

Saito, S. (1994). Shakai fukushi bunya ni okeru sedaikan koryu no genjo — Fukushi kyoiku o toshite [Present conditions of intergenerational interactions in social welfare sphere — Through welfare education]. In Kazuo Aoi (Ed.), *Koerika shakai no sedaikan koryu* [Intergenerational interaction in aging society], (pp. 160-205). Tokyo: Longevous Society Exploration Center.

Sodei, T. (1991). *Elderly people living alone in Japan*. N.Y.: The International Leadership Center on Longevity and Society (U.S.), Ritter Department of Geriatrics and Adult Development, Mount Sinai School of Medicine.

Statistics Bureau (1996). *Quick report on one-percent sample tabulations of the 1995 population census*. Management and Coordination Agency: Tokyo.

Suganuma, E. (1992, April 10) Rentaru kazoku no shakai-gaku [Rental family sociology: Rental children and grandchildren], *Shukan-Asahi*, 97 (15), 162-163.

Thang, L. L. (1997). *Generations in touch: Linking the old and young in a Tokyo neighborhood*. Unpublished Ph.D. dissertation. University of Illinois at Urbana-Champaign, Urbana-Champaign.

Thang, L. L. (1997). Ikigai and longevity among elderly in Okinawa. In S. Formanek and S. Linhart (Eds.), *Aging: Asian experiences past and present* (pp. 251-263). Vienna: Verlag der Osterreichischen Akademic der Wisseschafren.

Thompson, C. (1996) Hitting the yakuba hall: The politics of lifelong learning and community development in Towa-Cho. Paper presented at the Midwest Conference of Asian Studies, Champaign, IL. October 11-13.

Tokyo Volunteer Center (1993). *Senior Volunteers' Coordinators' Manual*. Tokyo: Author.

Notes

1 Reprinted, with additional editing, with the permission of the *Journal of Aging and Identity*, Vol. 2, No. 4, 1997.

2 At writing, Associate Professor of Psychology; Hawaii Pacific University; 1188 Fort St., Honolulu, HI 96813.

3 At writing, lecturer, Department of Japanese Studies, National University of Singapore.

4 Although much of the burden for caring for elderly relatives has been traditionally placed on the shoulders of women, often daughters-in-law (Kono, 1994), there is a trend in which more women are entering the workplace and developing rewarding career paths. This places conflicting demands on women.

5 There are numerous religious rites with filial piety themes, such as the regular offerings made and special memorial services conducted at Buddhist altars (*butsudan*) in people's houses to preserve the memory of their ancestors. The *butsudan* symbolize the continuity of family-lines (Hendry, 1995).

6 Other research team members were Atsuko Kusano, Ph.D., Associate Professor, Shinshu University; Shigeru Hisamichi, M.D., Dean, Tohoku University School of Medicine and Professor, Department of Public Health; and Ichiro Tsuji, M.D., Associate Professor, Department of Public Health, Tohoku University School of Medicine. This research was made possible by the first author's receipt of a Fulbright Research Scholarship during the 1994-95 academic year.

7 This research was conducted as her doctoral thesis in partial fulfillment of the requirements of the Ph.D. program in Anthropology at the University of Illinois at Urbana-Champaign. The fieldwork was supported by a one-

year dissertation fellowship from the Japan Foundation in 1995-1996. A full version of the research study was published by Cornell University Press, 2001.

8 Erik Erikson coined this phrase in the 1960s to refer to a positive sense of completeness, meaning, and virtue tied in with one's reflections, in historical perspective, on one's own life.

9 Activities include: playing traditional and modern games, making and flying kites, visiting local facilities such as the planetarium (Tokachi Regional program), telling stories, having round table discussions, cooking and eating meals together, participating in after dinner "candle services," traditional crafts such as origami (folding paper to make various objects), making *waraji* (straw sandals), *takezaiku* (bamboo works), *fureai woku lali* (friendship walk rally), and singing (Hokkaido Lifelong Society Foundation, 1993,1994).

Intergenerational Community Building in the Netherlands:

By Kees Penninx

Introduction

The Netherlands is a small, densely populated country largely below the level of the North Sea, that part of the Atlantic Ocean that separates the British Isles from Europe. Major harbors and airports have turned the Netherlands into a meeting place for people from all over the world. A more modest attitude, however, would be appropriate where the development of intergenerational programs is concerned. There are some interesting initiatives, which will be described in this paper, but in most areas, the knowledge and tools necessary for systematic development and evaluation of intergenerational programs are, as yet, lacking. In this respect the Netherlands has much to learn from nations such as the United States, Canada and the United Kingdom. However, every nation will have to set its own course in determining the interesting possibilities of intergenerational programs within its own culture, social policy and social infrastructure.

This article proposes a possible course for the Netherlands. Hopefully this will encourage discussion on the way in which intergenerational programs can take up a structural position in the social landscape of this country and perhaps also in that of other countries. It starts with a survey of the main demographic, socio-cultural, political and economic trends as well as the main social problems the Netherlands will face at the beginning of this new millennium. It will describe the main areas of social policy and services intended to contribute to the solution of social problems. On this basis five policy themes will be identified, to which the government is going to have to pay attention in the next few years, and in which existing intergenerational programs already provide some fundamental answers. Analysis of the present intergenerational relations in the Netherlands leads us to a description of three characteristics required of Netherlands intergenerational program development: a community development approach, empowerment, and diversity management. On the basis of these program characteristics, local populations, community workers and municipalities can jointly determine the outlines of an intergenerational strategy by means of which young and old can explore and develop further the positive impact they can have on each others' lives, as well as on the social quality of their neighborhood.

In order to live up to this ambition, a national strategy is also required, in which the development of knowledge, scientific evaluation, training and promotion of intergenerational programs go side by side. The last section of this paper offers some strategic clues, both on the local and the national level, for the development and ongoing implementation of intergenerational programs in the Netherlands.[1]

National Trends[2] and Main Social Problems

With 15.5 million people living on 37,300 square kilometers (14,400 square miles) the Netherlands is one of the most densely populated countries in the world. The number of inhabitants will increase to 17.2 million around 2030, after which the population is expected to decline. Current growth is primarily the result of natural increase. In the near future, however, international migration will be the main cause of population growth. This will enhance the multicultural nature of Dutch society.

In the Netherlands, as in the rest of Europe, the proportion of under-20s declined from 36 to 24 percent between 1970 and the present day, and is expected to drop to about 21 percent by 2030. The percentage of people aged 65-plus is expected to almost double from 13 percent now to about 25 percent in 2040. The rapid aging of the Dutch population is expected to reach its peak some 20 years from now, when those born in the post-war baby boom of the 1940s and '50s will reach old age.

Since the 1980s, three important policy changes have significantly altered the nature of the Dutch economy: control of public spending, wage moderation, and reorganization of social security. In contrast to the massive economic success these measures made possible, efforts to reduce social problems lagged. Some of the main social problems are listed below.

Long-term unemployment

Some 3.7 percent of the total working population is faced with long-term unemployment. Approximately 300,000 unemployed people receiving social security and unable to obtain a regular job without considerable effort constitute the hard core of the unemployed. This number is 1.5 times greater among people with less education (6.4 percent) and more than three times as much (11.8 percent) among the population of ethnic minorities.

Dichotomy in social security

The social insurance system built up in the twentieth century has undergone major changes during the past few years. The *Bijstandswet* (the Dutch National Assistance Act) has always served as the final safety net. A part of the responsibility has been privatized; employers and employees take care of the consequences by means of all kinds of supplementary insurances. As a result, there has been selective degradation of social protection. Temporary employees, people who depend on allowances without the prospect of paid employment, and households that do not have a double income are most affected by all this. This includes single elderly people, single-parent families, and persons who have a permanent disability restricting their ability to work.

Violence among the young

The number of criminal offences in the Netherlands has remained fairly stable in the last few years. However, a shift can be observed in the offenders: it is increasingly under-aged youngsters and even young children that commit crime. Young offenders are increasingly found among juvenile women and adolescents from ethnic minorities. New forms of violence have either come into existence recently or have increased in such a way that they pose a problem: e.g., violence at soccer games, harassment at school, and violence against particular groups such as homosexuals and the elderly.

Disadvantaged districts

The original old districts or working class districts in the large cities with increasingly large black and minority ethnic populations face such problems as high unemployment rates, low education level, poor housing, and frequent instances of petty crime. Here, especially, children, youngsters and older people are vulnerable to the consequences of poor quality of life, social isolation, lack of social cohesion, and qualitatively poor provisions. The number of schools with 75 percent or more pupils of ethnic minorities, the so-called black schools, is increasing, especially in the four major cities (i.e. Amsterdam, Rotterdam, Utrecht and The Hague) where black schools have doubled from 15 percent in 1985 to 30 percent in 1994.

Multicultural society: the position of ethnic minorities

In 1992 some 2.3 million people (approximately 15 percent of the Dutch population) were members of ethnic minorities. Most of them were of Surinam, Antillean/Aruban, Turkish and Moroccan extraction. From 1990-1995, the indigenous population showed a growth of 3 percent, whereas these four largest groups of ethnic minorities increased by 25 percent. The unemployment rate among ethnic minorities is enormous; literacy and numeracy test results of school children from ethnic minorities are lower compared to those of white pupils. Ethnic minorities are increasingly isolated and social exclusion is an impending threat.

Caregiving

As a result of the ever increasing demand for care and the on-going decrease of people who are able (or willing) to provide it, a huge caregiving gap has emerged. The gap is caused by a number of factors such as the changing family and work relationships. The traditional work-care division between men and women has changed; moreover, due to the increasing participation of women in the job market, they are not able to take on the role of their mothers in providing care for the elderly and the children. As the government has adopted a policy of substitution and cost control (i.e., less residential and professional care) a significant number of people in need of care or domestic support get none at all. Some 20,000 elderly people who suffer from serious physical handicaps live on their own.

Social Policy and Services

The above describes an ambivalent Dutch society with increasing prosperity for some people offset by serious and persistent deprivation for many others. To complement government policy on employment and social security, social policy in the Netherlands emphasizes preventing people from becoming socially disadvantaged or losing social contact with the community by increasing people's influence on policy and by energizing vulnerable groups so that they can participate more independently in society.

Because people and groups living in disadvantaged situations often experience different types of problems simultaneously, agencies for housing, care, welfare, and income must work together to help them explore opportunities and find the assistance they need. An overview of the Dutch landscape of social services shows the need, especially at the local level, for policy-makers to create an integrated approach to deal with social problems.

Approximately 400,000 professionals and 2.7 million volunteers work in the fields of care and welfare in the Netherlands. The structure of this sector reflects an institutionalized tradition of target-group policy. The young, the handicapped, senior citizens, and black and minority ethnic groups are the main target groups for which assistance structures and institutions were created.

Youth services

Youth services encompasses child and youth care, preventive youth work, and child day care. It is directed at the early detection of potentially problematic situations. The emphasis is on non- and semi-residential care.

Services for the disabled

Services for the disabled focus on the principle of equal opportunity. Within these policies, physical integration (living in a "normal" neighborhood), functional integration (making use of normal, usual services) and social integration (participating in work and society) are the main issues.

Services for the elderly

Participation in society is the central issue in the field of care and welfare services for the elderly. Older people should be able to live on their own as long as possible, with additional assistance when necessary. Older people who can no longer take care of themselves can be admitted to a nursing home or a residential home for the elderly.

At the local level, there are special welfare organizations for the elderly only. These offer various services, like meals on wheels, social and recreational activities, and physical exercise courses.

Ethnic minorities

Most people in the Netherlands agree that people from ethnic minorities should have access to existing general services as much as possible. At the same time, cultural diversity is acknowledged. For these reasons, the authorities, whether national, provincial, or municipal, often subsidize minority-group organizations. Municipalities have invested in parenting support, pre-school programs, and extra attention for immigrant children in schools. In the area of juvenile delinquency, where children from ethnic minorities constitute a majority, services aim at strengthening and supporting families and responding quickly and adequately to youngsters who get into trouble with the police.

Local community work

Local community work encompasses services such as community centers, youth centers, day nurseries, street-corner work and play facilities. Volunteers do much of the work. Some services even rely on volunteers completely. Most of the work is restricted to a particular area. People go to the community center, the playground, or the youth center for particular services and projects.

Over the past few years, community work has become an increasingly important contributor to the solution of various social problems in neighborhoods, the encouragement of cooperation between different organizations, and the reintegration of individuals and groups into society.

All in all, the conclusion is justified that the Netherlands is a welfare state with an extensive social infrastructure. At the same time it is clear that this social infrastructure is fragmented, that it is being supplied by different funds, and that it has a number of competing centers of power that speak different languages and have different priorities. In this scattered and institutionalized social landscape, a more client-oriented and co-operative approach is needed. In many municipalities, broad, multi-functional welfare organizations, encompassing the whole range of community work previously discussed, are being established.

Since intergenerational work, in combining the needs of more than one group, has the potential of being an integrative and multi-purpose strategy for reducing social problems, it increasingly draws the attention of policy makers and innovative workers in the field. Moreover, intergenerational programs that encourage groups and individuals to take care of themselves as well as for each other and their community at large fit extremely well into current trends and policies.

Intergenerational Programs in the Netherlands: Themes and Examples

On the basis of the social trends and problems indicated above, the priorities in government policy, and the need for integrated approaches to foster social cohesion and inclusion of vulnerable groups like the young and the old, we can distinguish five main policy themes that emphasize the relevance of social innovation by means of intergenerational programs. In this section, we will explain these themes and illustrate how some already existing intergenerational programs can address them.

Theme 1: Connecting systems in an integrated community-building approach

In our aging society, the need to strengthen ties between generations is emerging ever more frequently on the agendas of politicians, employers, unions, and public interest groups that seek to promote the active participation of both younger and older people in community life. Research indicates that in the Netherlands 63 percent of older people have few or no contacts with the young, their own grandchildren included (Walker, 1993). This implies that the image that the old and the young have of each other is determined to a considerable extent by the exterior, by incidents, rumors, and the media.

In many neighborhoods the young and the old spend their time in separate facilities that were created for them: the youth center for the young, the senior center for the old. There are childcare provisions and schools for the younger generations, and senior housing and nursing homes for the elders. This physical confinement of the separate age groups is reinforced by the social subdivision of the services: there are specialized social workers for almost every age group.

In this system of age segregation, separate target groups receive a variety of professional services but are hardly encouraged to have dealings with one another. The impact of this physical and social separation on the way people perceive themselves and others has to be taken into account, especially in low income areas where many different age groups and cultural groups must live together peacefully in their shared neighborhood. Because the younger and older generations spend relatively more time in their neighborhood, this can be an area of shared interests to explore.

Intergenerational community programs provide practical opportunities to break through the artificial boundaries and to address people from both sides of the life continuum who have much to offer to each other. In the Netherlands, starting points have been created for cooperation between local childcare systems and the national sector of care for the elderly. The Dutch experiences with day care for toddlers in residential homes and nursing homes for the elderly are a vivid example of how the intergenerational approach can result in interdisciplinary cooperation between previously separated policy circuits and disciplines of work.

Toddler programs

In toddler programs children two to four years of age visit elderly afflicted with dementia once or twice a week. These programs are carried out in nursing homes where children visit and join the elderly in activities such as singing, gymnastics, and drawing. Toddlers have a positive experience and seem to accept the behavior of the elderly. Over time, the children show an increased willingness to share and work together with the older adults. The elders in their turn benefit from the personal attention and affection not normally available in the nursing home setting. The elderly show an increased level of communication, attentiveness and participation, and do not seem to be affected by their limitations. In this setting, their institutional dependency role is reversed to a role of responsibility and caregiving.

Toddler programs broaden the experiences of the staff of the nursing homes and child day care centers by bringing them into contact with new and different activities and ways of working. They often motivate the toddlers' parents to reflect on their own aging and that of their parents. Finally, toddler programs have positive effects on the social image of the elderly and the care institutions in which they live. Currently, every week a new toddler program emerges somewhere in the Netherlands (Mercken, 1997).

Theme 2: The need to promote social safety and competence

As mentioned before, more and more youngsters are involved in crime. Many older people no longer feel safe in the streets and avoid going out in the evening. In the Netherlands a negative attitude exists against special areas for certain age groups (like America's Sun City) or cultural groups. Instead, improving social safety and competence in more or less mixed areas is a predominant theme in government policy. Decades of investing in the economic and physical infrastructure, as well as in "tough" measures such as more police, burglary prevention, etc., have forced the recognition that investing in the social infrastructure of a community is also important.

Immediately after World War II, the Netherlands started a major building program to provide accommodation to the many young families that wanted to get settled. Today these families have aged, their children have left the neighborhoods, and many of these neighborhoods are beginning to deteriorate. The richer middle classes look for housing elsewhere, usually in the greener suburbs and in new-housing estates. In post-war districts older people with lower incomes stay behind and new groups of residents move in, for the larger part black and minority ethnic families with young children. Many older people say: "This is not my neighborhood any more." In this environment intergenerational programs can bring together younger and older community members for agreed-upon purposes that explicitly benefit one or both groups and implicitly benefit all those who are associated with them and the community at large (Kuehne, 1999). By this cooperation the young and the old learn to develop empathy for each other's perspectives. This is, for example, the case in some neighborhoods in Amsterdam where the *Chore Team* operates.

The Amsterdam Chore Team

The Amsterdam Chore Team is a community program for teenagers sponsored by the Welfare Foundation in Amsterdam-South in cooperation with the Welfare Foundation for Older People in the same area. The program aims at increasing the social skills and confidence of teenagers and changing the stereotypical images that both older and younger neighborhood residents have of each other. The average age of the 52 older participants is 72; the age of the 49 teenagers varies from 11 to 17. The majority of the teenagers are from black and minority ethnic backgrounds;

most of the older people are native Dutch. On an individual basis, the teenagers are assigned to older neighborhood residents for whom they do chores once or twice a week. For this activity they collect points that they can cash in for small sums of money or tickets to events. The older people pay a contribution of fifteen guilders every three months. An interesting element in this program is the motivation shift among the teens. At first, they find it less "cool," to walk with an old lady than to earn their own money. Once involved in the program, the teenagers appear willing to continue to work for "their" grandma or grandpa, even if payment would be stopped (Mercken, 1998).

Theme 3:
The need to promote independent living for the elderly

The Netherlands is in the process of a major policy operation called modernization of care for the elderly. An important part of this is a shift of intramural care in residential homes towards extramural care in the district. Increasingly, older people rely on a semi-independent way of living in the district or neighborhood, if necessary with complementary care and service provision. The number of small-scale, clustered accommodation varieties (service apartments, living and care combinations, etc.) for older people living independently in the district is expected to increase dramatically in the next few years. However, these new accommodations often develop into introverted social islands in which the residents are properly housed and cared for but spend their days without any contacts with the other residents of the district.

Also in the near future a large part of the general housing stock will be adapted to the needs of older people. Older generations will be "coming back" into the neighborhood, and while they will require some community resources, many, who have a lifetime of experiences to share and are willing to do so, will also become resources themselves. This has been demonstrated over the past 15 years by a typically Dutch intergenerational program called the Guilds.

The Dutch Guilds

The Dutch Guilds are volunteer groups of people aged 50 or more who are willing to share their knowledge and experience, free of charge, with anyone who asks them. Whether the demand is for knowledge of computers or genealogy, organizational advice or car engineering, education or personal attention and support for children, most Guilds have it. Being a member of Guild provides older people with a meaningful way to pass the time. Guilds keep them active and socially involved and they contribute to a better general image of the elder generation.

At the moment, there are Guilds in about 90 municipalities providing opportunities for thousands of senior citizens to share their knowledge or give advice to tens of thousands of children and adults. Private persons, clubs and associations, businesses, community agencies, schools and social organizations — anyone can grab the telephone and pose their questions. A Guild mediator passes the question on to a volunteer. The volunteer then contacts the client to make further arrangements. All Guilds produce an information bulletin and use local broadcasting systems to inform customers about their services. An increasing number of Guilds adopt schools, refugee centers, welfare organizations and corporate businesses. These Guilds have set up senior citizens' task forces to solve some of the problems these organizations have to face, like the need for special attention and care for disabled children or children with learning problems.

Theme 4: The need for community support to vulnerable children and young people

Providing community support to vulnerable children, young people and young families is a core theme of national and local social policy. Many organizations are active in this area, such as municipalities, schools, community centers, sport clubs and assistance agencies. Here, seniors could play additional but important roles as informal mentors and tutors, bringing in life qualities that the professional systems are unable to offer. Unlike the shining examples of intergenerational mentor schemes in the United States and in the United Kingdom, where they are often directly connected to formal educational and welfare systems, intergenerational mentoring is not widespread in the Netherlands. For a number of reasons this is unfortunate in a country where only one out of four adults aged 55 to 65 is still in the labor force. One reason is that it has become difficult to recruit enough personnel for schools and childcare centers. Might not some of the well-educated and experienced older adults, who have shifted massively towards a life of recreation and leisure, be interested in some kind of "second career"? Unless opportunities for their involvement are created, nobody will know.

Another reason is that in recent years the Netherlands has attempted to care for the vulnerable young as much as possible by means of regular instead of special education. Additional resources from the school's immediate environment (such as volunteers from the neighborhood) are therefore being welcomed more and more. "It takes a village to rear a child" is a familiar saying nowadays also in the Netherlands. The 55+ generation live in that same village. Following the American example, community schools are being created with doors open to district residents. As yet, however, only the participation of parents has been considered. Why not consider the option of 'grandparent' participation?

Only a handful of professionally facilitated intergenerational mentor programs, enabling older people to connect with children's worries and interest — and therefore also to connect with the future — exists in the

Netherlands. One of them is the Guide Program, a small neighborhood-based mentor program in the city of Rotterdam.

The Guide Program

With the aid of community workers, older people in two Rotterdam neighborhoods formed a team of social guides a few years ago, on behalf of children of immigrants who had recently moved into the neighborhood. The senior citizens acquainted the new young residents with local services and talked with them about everyday life in the neighborhood. The seniors also took their charges to visit health centers and to explore the underground system, a library, and a children's farm. Because this results in a relation of trust, the children have no difficulty in turning to their guide if they have questions or problems.

Initially the senior team was a separate group of volunteers. Later it became part of a more broad-ranged integration scheme in which professionals, trained volunteers, and trainees are involved as well. One of the older volunteers reports:

> I was robbed myself once by a few black kids from around the corner. You just feel so helpless. The police won't do anything for you. Later you start to think: could I have prevented it? You can lock yourself in, but that isn't any good, of course. I wanted to cope with it instead of brooding over it. I wanted to know what was going on in these kids. That is why I joined the *Guideprogram* a few years ago. Right now you cannot imagine how much I have learned from them.

Theme 5: The need to establish a multicultural society

As the Netherlands has become an immigration destination, social integration of people from ethnic minorities has become a top priority in Dutch society. Practical experience demonstrates that various forms of intergenerational neighborhood development can also benefit intercultural integration policy. The Amsterdam Chore Team program enables black and minority ethnic teenagers to interact with vulnerable older people in the neighborhood. The other way round, native Dutch older people can be mentors to black and minority ethnic children by introducing them to the Dutch service provisions and habits, as is done in the Rotterdam Guide Program. Older people can also be of use in second language classes for black and other minority people, as is done in a program called "Let's Talk Together," run by several Guild organizations of older people. And finally, by means of intergenerational community action programs, the neighborhood stories and fantasies of different generations and different cultural backgrounds can be traced, laid down and processed in a way that will result in a joint action program based on shared interests.

A good example of the latter is the Neighborhood Memories program that is now being developed by the Netherlands Institute of Care and Welfare. It demonstrates how the process of intergenerational neighborhood development can go hand in hand with the promotion of intercultural communication.

Neighborhood Memories: An intergenerational future workshop

Adolescents and older adults of differing cultural backgrounds use various narrative and creative methods to explore their memories, perceptions and wishes about the neighborhood in which they live. They draw up a joint vision of the future and then present this to the other neighborhood residents, the agencies and the municipality.

It is a three-stage project. In the first stage older people and younger people of mixed cultural backgrounds discuss — in age-separate groups — stories about life in their neighborhood, village or town, focused by means of objects and photos that they brought along. They gather as much information as possible on aspects of neighborhood life in the past and in the present. On the basis of this, both groups are then asked to make a design for the neighborhood in the year 2010, their own vision of the future, one that meets their wishes. This vision is to be visualized in a newspaper, a scale model, a picture book, a song, a play, or any other form of presentation.

The second stage starts with a meeting in which the young invite the old for the presentation of their plan for the future. There can be no discussion on whether the young people's vision is correct or desirable. This stage is rounded off by a preliminary list of action items that will make the district more livable for the young. Then a meeting follows in which the older people present their vision of the future. This meeting will also end with a list of points of action, this time aimed at a livable district for older people. In follow-up meetings similarities and differences between both visions of the future and lists of action items are discussed. Which wishes are similar? Which are different? Which are irreconcilable? Are people prepared to compromise? On the basis of these talks a joint image of the future is formulated that is backed by both groups. This image of the future contains a number of wishes addressed to the local council, but also a list of action items that the participants want to tackle themselves.

The third stage of the program is a joint presentation for other neighborhood residents, the district committee, civil servants and members of the local council, professionals and other volunteers. With this the project ends. It is important that new activities follow, in which the council, organizations and residents make plans to realize the ideas of the young and the old combined. Therefore during the execution of the project, professionals will have to prepare for the desired follow-up procedure.

Dutch Young and Old: Between Solidarity and Conflict

From the above it can be concluded that there are sufficient policy starting points as well as examples of good practice in the Netherlands for the further development and implementation of intergenerational programs. Important questions remain. How do the young and the old feel about this themselves? Do intergenerational programs fulfill their needs? And what is their opinion of each other? Let's visit some older districts in the Netherlands and see the reality.

- Residents of an early post-war housing development in the city of Den Bosch prevented the placing of playground apparatus for young children in one of the squares in the neighborhood, for fear of youngsters loitering or even taking over the square.
- Older people in a service flat in Rotterdam complained about the nuisance caused by students from a near-by comprehensive school. They created a lobby to restrict the young in their freedom of movement.
- Community workers in Vught had their hands full to persuade the younger and older residents of the town center to communicate with each other after continuous complaints from the older people about the noisy behavior of the young.
- In the town of Veldhoven, after a very old man invited young people in to watch television with him, because he felt lonely, they took possession of the house and took money from him.

Situations such as these are no longer an exception in the Dutch neighborhoods. Here sociologists and urban anthropologists would ask: what is really happening? Are these isolated incidents? Is there more to it? According to sociologists studying the generations, these are not a general pattern in the Netherlands, and the generations are not opposing parties (Diepstraten et. al., 1998). Their research shows that the young and the old rarely reproach each other. They do not begrudge each other a place in the labor market or the housing market, and if there are any problems they think it perfectly normal to help each other. But they do reproach the government. Many young and many older people as well feel that in important areas such as income, jobs, education and health care they are being put at a disadvantage by the government. They also share the opinion that politicians hardly listen to them. The image that the young and the old are natural enemies, that they refuse to have anything to do with one another, is opposed with energy in these studies. Intergenerational programs can help here to create frameworks in which the young and the old can explore their separate and joint interests in all openness and can take action on the basis of these on behalf of a common goal, such as a livable and safe living environment.

New initiatives arise regularly, such as The Future Gang, a community program devised by a group of Moroccan adolescents in a low-income area in the city of Haarlem. They wanted to show the other residents in their neighborhood that there is more to young people than crime. Their program, though not deliberately set up as an intergenerational program, nonetheless has many characteristics of good intergenerational programming and is now being implemented in a number of other cities.

Older people in the Netherlands also seek to meet the young. A panel for older people held this spring in the town of Hellevoetsluis indicated that older people feel that socio-cultural activities should not just be for older people but should be set up together with young people in a district-oriented manner. In fact, these elderly innovators, like the members of the Dutch Guilds and the participants in the Guide Program, are pioneers in intergenerational work in the Netherlands. These are all initiatives demonstrating that, more and more, adolescents and older people do not want to be treated as separate age groups or "target" groups and do want to widen their horizon and explore new values and behaviors.

Conflicts between the generations should not be denied, nor should they be exaggerated, as is often done in the media. Still, as there are forces on the micro-, meso- and macro-levels that undermine solidarity, there are also forces that promote solidarity. Intergenerational programs can help those younger and older people who want to achieve some form of mutual solidarity in everyday life. How can these programs be developed and implemented successfully? In the next section we will explore some characteristics of successful intergenerational programs in the Netherlands.

Characteristics of Successful Intergenerational Programs in the Netherlands

Intergenerational work is subject to the complex interplay of numerous forces that should be analyzed thoroughly first, if the work is to exceed the stage of good intentions and is to effectively prevent the social exclusion of younger and older people. The points of departure and expected results of any intergenerational program will have to be substantiated with a thorough social analysis and with empirical facts. A potential pitfall in this is to regard intergenerational work as a panacea for every social problem in this country. Clear choices will have to be made about settings, goals, and tools. In the Dutch context, intergenerational programs will have to be built on three pillars: a neighborhood approach (settings), empowerment (goals) and diversity management (tools).

Pillar 1: A neighborhood approach

In the Netherlands, there is no support for the idea that intergenerational work should be implemented by means of special intergenerational institutions and training centers. Yet, most people in the professional field agree that an intergenerational approach can be a promising new dimension in various areas, such as labor, education, training, day care for children, child care, care for older people, recreation, sports and culture. With so many potential parties, a Babel-like confusion could easily be created. In order to prevent that, it is necessary to be clear about the focus of specific programs, as well as about the co-ordination of various constituencies. In this article, we plead for a neighborhood-building approach, where all sectors mentioned above could contribute to intergenerational networks and programs that promote safe and viable living conditions for all generations.

The Netherlands has a decentralized policy with regard to living, welfare, safety and sharing care tasks, employment and income. In these areas local councils have an important coordination task. Therefore local social policy would seem to be a suitable policy framework for the further development of intergenerational programs. Within this policy framework, a neighborhood approach for the reduction of social problems offers important benefits.

Intergenerational support and exchange programs can be successful in the Netherlands if they focus on the improvement of living conditions and cooperation between the young and the old in local neighborhoods. Even in neighborhoods where everyday interests clash and there is conflict in abundance, the programmatic conditions exist for the creation of an effective, integrated, and consistent approach. These conflicts provide opportunities that can be used to encourage neighbors to meet with each other, to learn from each other, to work towards common goals, in short to practice living together.

Just how high intergenerational community building should aim depends on the specific circumstances in a given neighborhood and on the wishes of the residents themselves. In situations of animosity between young and old, the first task will be to establish a form of peaceful coexistence. Here an intervention such as the organizing of a neighborhood discussion between loitering youngsters and the residents of a senior citizens' flat who have made a complaint against them would be suitable, for example. This could be followed by an intergenerational future workshop as described above (Neighborhood Memories). Interventions like these would be more effective than trying to get rid of the conflict, for that will usually amount to getting rid of the young people. It would be more interesting and more challenging to use the conflict by identifying it as an interlude in a process in which one at least is still aware of the other's existence.

Providing opportunities for the exchange of standards and values is important here: in what type of neighborhood do we want to live? How do we want to deal with each other? What are my standards and values and what are other people's? Each person would ask: What am I willing to accept, and what will I most decidedly reject? How can we accept each other for what we are? What do we need in order to feel respected? Can we mean something to each other? And the main question: how can we deal respectfully with each other instead of neglecting each other? The common interest that is the basis of such questions is a livable and safe neighborhood in which all generations and cultural groups can live with pleasure and respect for each other.

Pillar 2: Empowerment

With its long tradition as a welfare state, the Netherlands has many activities aimed at dealing with "problem neighborhoods" and with taking care of "underprivileged groups." However, people can feel deeply insulted if they are told they live in a "problem neighborhood." A strategy with a better chance of success is the reinforcing of resources already present in the local community. Intergenerational neighborhood work fulfills this role by tracing, mobilizing, developing and connecting the social capital of the young and the old. This brings us to the principle of empowerment.

In a manual on community development work, *Building Communities from the Inside Out: a Path toward Finding and Mobilizing a Community's Assets* (Kretzmann and McKnight, 1993), we find special strategies by means of which the social capital of the young and the old in neighborhoods can be traced and used on behalf of a livable environment. Empowerment is the developing and reinforcing of skills that enable people to manage their own lives and to function adequately in society. Many Dutch projects concerned with neighborhood management, such as the "street cleaning campaign" in Rotterdam, show that residents themselves are willing and able to give the neighborhood the appearance that is important to them. Residents can decide for themselves what needs to be improved; they can do it their own way and attribute the results to their own efforts.

Solutions devised by residents themselves and carried out under their own steam are the most effective way towards a livable neighborhood, in the long term. The feeling of ownership, expressed in terms such as "our neighborhood," "my street," makes the residents feel involved and motivated to make something of their neighborhood cn their own. It appears from the practice of intergenerational work that under these conditions children, the young, and the old, the neighborhood users par excellence, are willing to take responsibility, to fulfil socially productive roles, and to contribute as well as they can to the quality of social life in the neighborhood. Therefore community workers should not impose intergenerational programs, but should, rather, initiate a communication process and create framework conditions by means of which neighborhood residents can discover for themselves what they can mean to each other, how they can explore their neighborhood, how they can make improvements and be heard.

Pillar 3: Diversity management

Diversity is a key word in an individualized society. People differ as to generation, stage of life, culture, sex, education, and experience of life, etc. Differences can hamper contacts but can also be used to stimulate new contacts. Exactly because people are different, they can learn from each other and add value to each other's lives on the basis of shared interests and goals. The fact that people grow up in different stages of history and are influenced by different socio-economical and cultural circumstances offers opportunities for contacts in which everyone's horizon is broadened and in which mutual support and exchange of information can lead to mutual advantage. Being able to put this diversity to use and providing effective support to innovative groups are some of the core skills of the intergenerational community worker. Combining different people with different ways of thinking can create synergy necessary for the solving of social problems.

Neighborhoods are no longer homogeneously composed communities, if they ever were. In recent years a livable neighborhood has often been defined as a neighborhood in which the residents manage to respect differences in standards and values, are able to communicate with each other about them, and, whenever possible, can co-operate and improve the physical and social environment. The recognition of differences, and learning to deal with those who hold different opinions, are important targets of local social policy. The goal is not that persons of different generations and cultures agree on all points, but that people can have dealings with each other without fear and suspicion, that they can accept each other as they are and that they can mean something to each other. Intergenerational community building can be a viable vehicle for realizing these goals, provided that there is a strategy for ongoing program support and quality improvement.

Strategies for Ongoing Intergenerational Community Building

The examples in this article demonstrate that in the Netherlands there is no lack of interesting intergenerational initiatives. But in spite of enthusiastic reactions of participants and project managers, there are still too many one time, ad hoc projects, at both the local and regional levels (and even the national level), organized by numerous organizations that have hardly any contact with each other. Among all these, few of the intergenerational projects advertise themselves as such. The result is that intergenerational programs are not part of a strong financial structure and often depend on accidental factors such as the presence of an enthusiastic project manager or once-only subsidy funds. In order to fully realize, in this country, the potential of the intergenerational approach to community building, strategies are needed, both on the community and on the national level, that connect initiatives and organizations into collaborative networks.

A local community strategy

In my book *The Neighborhood for All Ages* (Penninx, 1999) I explained the possible significance of a neighborhood-oriented strategy for improving intergenerational communication and connections. In a joint program—preferably as part of a more broad-ranged district safety or livability plan, a neighborhood management plan, or a social structure outline—residents, institutions and local councils decide together which are the actual intergenerational communication goals, what activities are to be carried out and in what way evaluation should take place. This strategy requires a process that can start on a very small-scale with a few activities but that in the course of a few years time can develop into a widely supported neighborhood-oriented set of programs for change.

A successful strategy for intergenerational community-building has the following characteristics:

1. The strategy is an answer to concrete needs of the young and the old and is suited to actual and urgent social problems in the neighborhood.
2. It has clear and verifiable targets.
3. There is support and involvement of groups from the intermediate generations: parents, professionals, teachers, managers, financiers, etc.
4. The strategy is inclusive by nature, grafted on existing policy frameworks such as education, parenting support, child and youth care, and care for older people.
5. It is the result of cooperation between provisions, residents' and target groups' organizations and the local municipality.
6. It is monitored by an inspiring leader who looks beyond the separate institutions and target groups and is capable of handling the principles of community-building, empowerment and diversity management.
7. Intergenerational programs are the elements of the strategy and match its targets.

8. Younger and older people are involved as much as possible in the creation of the strategy and in the preparation, execution and evaluation of the various programs that it includes.

Using this strategy intergenerational activities and programs can create a platform for exchange and collaborative program development, funding, and evaluation. Intergenerational programs with this joint frame of reference can more easily be incorporated into the frameworks of already existing structures. In a district with a community school, for example, an intergenerational program can add a new dimension to existing practices by allowing older residents to enter into the pedagogic community. The scene of action can be the school, or it could also be the recreation room of a nearby senior citizens' center, or both. Thus the young and the old literally enter into each other's living environment. Intergenerational working and thinking is thus seen not as a new domain only for intergenerational specialists, but as the property of broadly trained community workers who can promote the intergenerational approach in their own programs and fields of work.

A National Strategy to Foster Intergenerational Awareness and Effective Programs

Research shows that local intergenerational programs have to meet certain requirements if the results are to last. For example, the interaction between the young and the old must be functional; i.e., it must serve a purpose recognizable to both parties. It must also be equal, personal and ongoing instead of incidental. In the Netherlands, intergenerational thinking and working is not yet a part of the community worker's standard equipment. However, the time is ripe for a national stimulation program by means of which intergenerational community building can grow to achieve its full potential. The Netherlands Institute of Care and Welfare is the coordinator of a national strategy called "For all ages: a national program to promote intergenerational neighborhood development 1999 - 2003." It is anticipated that in three years the following goals will be achieved:

- Each municipality in the Netherlands will have at its disposal a method by means of which it can, together with institutions and citizens within one or more appointed districts, draw up a neighborhood strategy for intergenerational community building.
- Local councils, institutions and citizens will be able to carry out and evaluate the programs needed to execute this strategy, programs that focus on intergenerational conflict reduction, community action, service learning or mentoring.

- An infrastructure, including a national newsletter, a video, training modules, a database and a website, will be developed at the national level to provide the necessary support and improve skills.

Intergenerational workers in the Netherlands will be happy to share these results with interested parties within and outside the country. In doing so, local and national networks can be connected in a global community of intergenerational initiatives that make a difference in the improvement of living conditions for all generations.

References

Central Bureau of Statistics (1998). *Statistisch jaarboek 1999* [Statistics yearbook 1999]. Voorburg: 1998.

Diepstraten, I., Ester, P., & Vinken, H. (1998). *Mijn generatie* [My generation]. Tilburg: Syntax Publishers.

Granville, G. (1999). *Evaluation of intergenerational community action. An intergenerational program of young and older people serving together.* Stoke-On-Trent: Beth Johnson Foundation.

Kaplan, M. (1994). *Side by side. Exploring your neighborhood through intergenerational activities.* Berkeley: MIG Communications.

Kretzmann, J. & Mcknight, J. (1993). *Building communities from the inside out: A path toward finding and mobilizing a community's assets.* Chicago: ACTA Publications.

Kuhne, V.S. (1999). Building intergenerational communities through research and evaluation. In: *Generations*, Vol. XXII, No. 4, Winter 1998-1999, 82-87.

Mercken, C. (1997). *Gedeelde werelden. Peuters op bezoek in verzorgings en verpleeghuizen. Projecthandleiding* [Shared worlds. Toddler visits in nursing homes and sheltered homes for the elderly. Project manual]. Utrecht: NIZW.

Mercken, C. (1998). *Karweiteam evaluatieverslag 1998* [Choreteam evaluation report 1998]. Utrecht: NIZW.

Penninx, K. (1998). *De buurt voor alle leeftijden. Intergenerationele buurtontwikkeling in het kader van lokaal sociaal beleid* [The neighborhood for all ages: Intergenerational neighborhood development as a tool for social policy]. Utrecht: NIZW.

Walker, A. (1993). *Age and attitudes, main results from a Eurobarometer survey.* Brussels: Europese Commissie.

Notes

1 Netherlands Institute of Care and Welfare / NIZW was given the opportunity of developing and implementing such a strategy, with financial support from the government. This national expertise centre will, together with a number of local, national and international collaboration partners, make an effort on behalf of the realization of the National Stimulation Program *For All Ages 1999-2003*.

2 The facts and figures in this section are taken from the Netherlands' social welfare system fact sheet on the European Social Welfare Information Network, a web-site that enables professionals to obtain information on social welfare topics in various countries of the UN-European Region. See: http://www.eswin.net/

Intergenerational Engagement in the United Kingdom: A Framework for Creating Inclusive Communities

By Gillian Granville and Alan Hatton-Yeo

Introduction

In contemporary Britain, the concept of social exclusion, based on a recognition that social structures can exclude sections of society from mainstream social activities, defines a class of social relationships and underlies a number of social policy issues. The UK government has sought to put this concept at the center of its political reforms, and in 1997 created a special department to co-ordinate government action that would eliminate exclusion and bring disadvantaged groups back into mainstream society. This chapter looks more closely at the concept of social exclusion and the difficulties and implications of adopting it as a paradigm for policy formation and implementation. We argue that social exclusion can be applied to age groups, and that intergenerational programs represent a powerful, effective approach for bringing diverse people together and addressing many of the issues raised by social exclusion. An example of a community-based intergenerational initiative is given to illustrate how exclusion due to age can be overcome, and a discussion follows on how this approach to social welfare can influence policy, practice and research.

Understanding Social Exclusion

A useful way of understanding social exclusion is in the context of communities and the development of social cohesiveness or social integration. A community is commonly perceived as the neighborhood where people live, and to function well for all its members, those members need to be skilled at mobilizing its resources. In a community, individuals are interdependent on each other, and everyone has a meaningful role to play. Kleinmann tells us that "social inclusion has something to do with community, with networks, with belonging" (1998, p. 10). He is concerned that the term "social exclusion" is rapidly becoming a cliché for covering almost any kind of social ill.

Atkinson and Hill (1998) argue that social exclusion is a relative concept and that it is manifest in social relations and not individual circumstances. It is caused by the action of those who exclude others, as well as people's own ability to reciprocate, and moves away from the idea of "victim blaming" where the individual is held responsible for his or her own circumstances. The concept recognizes how social structures can exclude sections of society and suggests that disadvantage should not be seen solely in material terms, such as poverty. Importantly, social exclusion is seen as a dynamic experience that occurs over a period of time and is transmitted across generations, thus perpetuating the exclusion of individuals and groups from the mainstream activities of society (Hobcraft 1998).

The distinction between poverty and social exclusion has attracted considerable discussion, and social commentators are insistent that the concepts are not seen as synonymous. Room explains (1995, in Alcock 1998):

> The concept of social exclusion is taking over from poverty which is more static than dynamic and seen more often as exclusively monetary poverty. Social exclusion does not mean insufficient income, and it even goes beyond participation in working life. More generally, in stressing the rupture of the social link, it suggests something more than social inequality and therefore carries with it the risk of a two-tier society, or the relegation to the status of a welfare dependent (19).

This definition stresses the importance of social relations, a theme taken up by Atkinson and Hill (1998) who maintain that the disruptive consequences of social exclusion affect the whole of society and not just the excluded. Alcock (1998) suggests that it can be seen as expanding our understanding of the social context of need, and that social exclusion is concerned with what others do to us as well as what we are, or are not, able to do for them.

If social exclusion is described in relation to social structures, then a number of networks that create social cohesiveness and a sense of belonging can be identified within a community. These include the political and civil structures that enable people to participate and campaign for change as well as employment opportunities that link people to a number of activities through the labor market. Convenient access to major public services allows individuals to pursue their entitlements to support and welfare, while private services assist people in their daily activities. The voluntary and community sectors provide individuals with a range of meaningful opportunities to actively participate in their local neighborhoods, and the services offered by the voluntary sector can supplement mainstream services.

The ability to be part of community and family networks is essential for creating close links of friendship and support, and in the development of health and well-being (Coleman, 1996). Kleinmann (1998) however, has suggested that 'socially excluded' implies that there is a majority population that is included:

> The key social cleavage is not between social groups or economic classes, but between a comfortable majority and an excluded minority. One effect of this analysis is to minimize differences and conflicts of interests in the majority population (p. 10).

Kleinmann believes this seriously weakens the potential of the concept of social exclusion to improve understanding and assist policy development. In spite of this, it has formed a significance discourse in UK social policy development.

The Social Exclusion Unit

In 1997, the UK government created the Social Exclusion Unit as the cornerstone of its political agenda to address social inequalities. The Unit, whose remit is restricted to England but which maintains close contact with the Welsh, Scottish and Northern Ireland offices, is based in the Cabinet Office with a "champion" Minister reporting directly to the Prime Minister. Its main aims (Social Exclusion Unit, 1998) are to help break the vicious circle of social exclusion and co-ordinate government action by:

- Improving understanding of the key characteristics of social exclusion and its impact on government policies; and
- promoting solutions, encouraging co-operation, disseminating best practice and, where necessary, making recommendations for changes in policies, machinery or delivery mechanisms.

An intensive program of policy development is now in place, with 18 Policy Action Teams based around five themes that include getting people back to work, increasing access to services and making government work more efficiently. These themes have recently been brought together into a consultation document (2000), which focuses on deprivation and neighborhood decay.

The Government is moving forward with its policy changes, and it recently has asked that the approach being adopted by the Social Exclusion Unit be used more widely across the whole of its departments. One of the departments at the heart of the Government's reform agenda is the Active Community Unit (1999), based in the Home Office, which is charged with mobilizing communities through volunteering opportunities. It is developing initiatives for younger and older members in communities to become involved but as yet has been slow to recognize the potential of intergenerational programs to meet its policy plans.

Social exclusion and the generations

The concept of people being socially excluded because of their age is underdeveloped in the discourse that is taking place in this policy debate, but it could be a helpful framework for explaining the circumstances in which old and young people find themselves. We are suggesting that chronological age is a crucial factor in social exclusion, as people can be excluded from mainstream activities because of the characteristics of the age group to which they belong. Ageism allows social structures to be created that discriminate against people because of their age, and this in turn further perpetuates prejudice and stereotypical thinking. An example of this in the United Kingdom is the absence of age discrimination within equal opportunities legislation. The young are thought to be irresponsible and uncaring by other age groups, with a recent focus on school exclusion policies and juvenile crime. The old are considered lonely, unhappy and a burden on others, which has been reinforced by the current debates on healthcare, pensions and welfare benefits in old age. These stereotypes, which are often perpetuated through social networks and relationships, artificially separate the generations from each other.

The paradigm of social exclusion also allows for a multi-dimensional approach to be included. It is often the case that people who have been excluded from society for other reasons, for example through unemployment or poor health, or race and gender divisions, are further disadvantaged by age. A woman who has had part-time employment with a low income is more likely to experience poverty in old age (Bernard and Meade, 1993). A young black person who is subjected to racism, and exposed to discriminatory practice from a young age is likely to become more excluded from the dominant groups as he or she passes through life.

The United Kingdom is not alone in experiencing social changes over the last two to three decades that have caused the generations to become progressively disconnected from each other at an individual, family and community level. These changes include smaller families, greater geographical distance between family members, an increased number of divorced and single-parent households, and the conflicting expectations of working women (Arber and Evandrou, 1993). This fragmentation can obstruct the natural connections between young and old and reduce opportunities for mutual support that normal generational exchange offers.

The disconnections have been exaggerated by the lack of value society places on its older and younger members. This has affected the natural relationship between age groups and generated suspicion and uncertainty. Thus both generations are being excluded from mainstream activities and, as divided groups, are marginalized from many political and decision making processes.

Moving from exclusion to inclusion

It has been argued (Alcock, 1998) that the reasons for social exclusion can also indicate the way to find the solutions. Intergenerational activities that are carefully facilitated can bring the old and young together in ways that include them in the social fabric of society and benefit all its members. The old can be a resource for the young, through giving their time and experience to guide and support them. The young can offer practical support to the old, who, through the frailty of age, are often less able to engage independently in existing social networks. The old and young together can work on behalf of their community, and in doing so, can break down barriers that may have previously caused them to be disregarded, marginalized, and otherwise excluded from mainstream activities. Intergenerational exchanges can rebuild social networks, develop community capacity and create an inclusive society for all age groups.

In the United Kingdom, there has been increased recognition of the importance of community development approaches to resolving social issues. At the Beth Johnson Foundation, we are developing intergenerational approaches that engage people in the communities where they live. In this way, communities can be rebuilt to be more sensitive to the needs of all members, which promotes social inclusion.

Programs that enable an older person to go into a local school and work alongside a young person who is having difficulties getting the most from education, demonstrate a commitment from the community to young people's futures. An older person offering support in a constructive way to a young person who has committed a criminal offence means that the community has not given up and is willing to help that young person to be reintegrated into society. This is a particularly powerful message in a contemporary society where old people are perceived as being afraid of young people, for reasons of personal safety. Similarly, an older person offering friendship to a young person who is caring for a sick or disabled family member, shows all members of that family that others recognize the isolation of the young caregiver.

Young people and children can demonstrate care and responsibility to those members of their community who, due to frailty in old age, may be prevented from engaging with others. Young children from a local primary school may join in structured activities with a local nursing home with residents who have dementia. This approach can enhance the lives of residents by including them in the activities of the community. At the same time, the children receive unconditional attention from an older adult. Similarly, young people may also be involved with befriending schemes that support older people who are unable to leave their homes unaided. And the confidence that the younger generation displays towards technology can be harnessed to promote these skills in generations that did not have the same opportunities. Both generations can be accepted for themselves and make a contribution to creating a healthy community.

Such community action enables two marginalized sections of the population to be active in shaping their community for the benefit of all. Properly developed programs of this nature ensure that different groups within a neighborhood recognize the importance of taking responsibility for each other's wellbeing. They also give a positive message to all of society by showing that individuals of two age groups that are considered to have opposing and diverse viewpoints can come together on issues of common concern.

This model of addressing the social exclusion of two groups at different ends of the lifecourse through the development of a range of community-initiated intergenerational programs is particularly powerful because it is so visible and because it is integrated into the everyday life and fabric of a community. Recently, a mentor working with a student in a junior school explained it in this way: "It's like a pebble going in the water, and [the ripple] goes out bigger and bigger, and you get contact with more people. And that's, as I say, from one child" (volunteer mentor).

A Community Action Project

The rest of this chapter will now look in more detail at the outcome of a UK intergenerational program at the Beth Johnson Foundation that sought to engage people in their local community. Following this will be some other examples of successful intergenerational initiatives, before we conclude with a re-examination of the usefulness of social exclusion as a concept for social policy formation.

Based in the North West of England, the Beth Johnson Foundation is a charitable trust that has an international reputation, primarily in the field of gerontology, for its action research projects. During its 27-year history, it has sought to be at the forefront of ageing issues and is particularly known for its work on healthy ageing (Bernard, 2000) and advocacy (Ivers, 1994). Its history of innovation and responsible risk-taking has been documented elsewhere (Granville, 1998), and as the new millenium begins, the Foundation is seeking new ways to improve the quality of life for people as they age. One way it is looking to do that is through developing a theoretical and practical understanding of intergenerational exchange and its implications as a model for social change (Granville and Ellis, 1999a,b).

The community action intergenerational program evolved from a prior piece of work at the Foundation between 1993-1996, [SCIPSHA: Senior Citizens involved in Public Services, Health and Advocacy, Final Report, Beth Johnson Foundation, 1998] which sought to demonstrate a model for involving older people in decisions which they considered important to their lives. It was a process model concerned with the way older people may be able to influence decision-makers about changes in their neighborhoods, and it used a community development approach.

The model for engagement was the formation of small groups, facilitated by a paid worker at the Foundation, who met in their neighborhoods and decided on their concerns. The groups often met in the local school or at Senior Citizens clubs and community centers. It became apparent at an early stage of discussions that the issues that concerned older people were similar to those which worried the younger members of the community, and that they could perhaps work together to influence change. In 1997, an intergenerational coordinator was appointed to test out the potential of an intergenerational approach to community action.

Old and young people were recruited from the locality where they lived and came together to decide what they wanted to change in their neighborhoods in order to improve the day to day life of their community. The generations were initially surprised to find that they both shared similar concerns, and this immediately broke down stereotypical barriers and strengthened the resolve of the groups to make changes. The young people felt particularly encouraged by the older people's support for their difficulties. In turn, they also recognized that older members of the community may have worries about the behavior of the younger generation. Examples of improvements they wanted to see included local, low-priced leisure and cultural facilities, a youth-friendly café, and measures — such as efficient lighting — to enhance community safety. Other issues were litter in the town and the high cost of public transport for both age groups.

The groups concentrated on learning the process of influencing change through careful preparation and working together. The two intergenerational groups consisted of eight to ten young people and a similar number of older members. They met approximately monthly over a period of a year. Other meetings were convened between the regular monthly ones when it was necessary to find information on the topic or meet with other people, such as local authority officers. The group meetings, which were facilitated by the project coordinator, used a range of group activities such as brainstorming, role-playing and small group discussions to help members decide on their priorities and rehearse their approach. This enabled the groups to grow in confidence and present a well-organized and thoughtful view to the decision makers. The groups sought to avoid confrontation and sensationalism by a well-planned media strategy and instead illustrated positive cooperation and successful outcomes.

The groups achieved a range of positive outcomes such as litter reduction and increased publicity for cheap bus fares. They were influential in setting up a user committee at the local leisure centers that included members from all generations, and they lobbied for a youth café in the town center. The evaluation (Granville, 1999) drew out four conceptual themes that demonstrated the links to social inclusion: learning about democracy, developing responsibility as a citizen, establishing supportive networks, and overcoming discrimination.

Learning about democracy

The groups learned together about the democratic system and how they could use that knowledge to influence change. One of the indicators of social exclusion is being outside political and civic networks, and this model demonstrated how both generations came to learn more about the processes of power. Many of the individual group members had never been to Council meetings; nor had they talked to Council members and officers, or understood the committee structures. Some of the young people expressed it this way:

> Yes, we have learnt how to work it now. Like, you have to get in touch with someone who is in charge of something, you can't just go up. We know where to go now.

The structure of the groups allowed them to plan their strategies and to support each other when the gains were small. There was an acceptance, particularly from the young people, that progress was slow if change was to be made, but a general sense that, through learning the democratic processes, they were beginning to make a difference and influence issues that were important to the community. One older person said: "We have started stuff."

It was also clear from discussions with policy makers, community workers and school staff, that they recognized the strength of a group of people who had previously been perceived as at odds with each other now agreeing on similar issues. There was surprise at the similarities and the mutual drive for change that the groups demonstrated, and this intergenerational voice was difficult to ignore. It was possible to see that with sufficient time and persistence, this collective voice could create significant change in its local community.

Developing responsibility as a citizen

A second emerging theme was a sense of responsibility that developed among the group members at an individual, group and community level. As individuals, there was a commitment to be part of a group and to give up time to work together on collective issues. This was not about personal gain, but about working alongside others to promote change for the greater good. It required that the young people talk to their peers, gather information, and organize their time to meet together. The older people felt a responsibility to the young people as much as to themselves. As one woman said: "I want to make it a better place for our children," meaning the young people of the community.

The other area of responsibility was towards each other as members of different generations. By working alongside older people, the young people in the project recognized that age could bring physical frailty, and that practical support was sometimes required to facilitate their involvement in the community. There were many examples of non-patronizing and sensitive ways that the young people assisted the older members, such as escorting them to the bus through the school corridors, or crouching down to speak on the same physical level as a chair, rather than talking above the seated person. In return, the older people developed a greater understanding of the pressures on the current generation to succeed in examinations, and the stress that this created. They offered a listening ear and showed understanding and tolerance if young people could not be available at times because of school work commitments. They also expressed concerns regarding the future for young people in the employment market.

Establishing supportive networks

A very clear outcome from this model of intergenerational community action was the development of a supportive network. The old and young made strong friendships with each other that they all recognized and highly valued. The group members had fun together, shared disappointments and triumphs, and became friends. There was a distinction made between the relationship of grandparents and grandchildren and the friendships in the groups. One older man explained:

> With your grandchildren, you think they are little angels and you let them get away with things. The children we are working with are **equal** to us; we are not overpowering them. That is the secret of this.

There was evidence of friendships outside the groups, in the way the old and young greeted each other in the streets and arranged visits to the local pensioner clubs and bowls club. They demonstrated their relationship to others and allowed a sharing of activities, as one young woman explained:

> We're more like friends. We've got quite close to them all now, haven't we, and they are all really nice to us in that they took us to Bingo and things. That was really nice. We didn't even know the rest of the elderly people around the place, and they were so nice to us and everyone just appreciated us being there.

Friendships develop between people who share similar interests, and the generations realized that they did indeed like similar things, even if the contexts were different. They spoke of enjoying meeting their friends on a regular basis, and having activities and outings to join in.

Overcoming discrimination

The links between developing responsibility and establishing friendships demonstrates how bringing the older and younger generations together in a structured and sustained way, enabled the breaking down of ageist stereotypes. Over time, the older people realized that the young people were not atypical of their generation, that, in fact, they were the majority, and that it was a small number who caused problems and perpetuated the stereotypes. They also understood more about the pressures on young people and recognized how society excluded them from main stream activities.

Conversely, the younger people were surprised and delighted in the way the older people worked alongside them without dominating or disregarding their views. They learned that their stereotypical ideas were also unfounded, and that older people were individuals as much as anyone else, with their own preferences and choices. They also learned more about the discrimination that occurs in the workforce, and how older people, too, are often disregarded by the authorities.

There was a strong sense that in the process of breaking down these negative views on an individual basis, the perceptions of the wider community were also changing to a more positive approach. Other young people in the schools wanted to join a group, and older people heard from their peers about the "courteous, thoughtful and kindly way" the young people behaved towards them. Professionals and policy makers expressed surprise at how well the two generations worked together, in contrast to the tensions that had been evident in the community.

Examples of other Intergenerational Initiatives

In the United Kingdom, there is a paucity of evidence on the impact of intergenerational initiatives, although there are examples of good models of practice. Hatton-Yeo (2000) gives a general overview of the status of intergenerational programs in the United Kingdom, with examples from the range of models that are currently being developed. Age Concern England has developed a network of Trans-Age Action projects, following an initial pilot phase in three sites (Ivers, 1999). The aim of the project is for older people to work as volunteers alongside children or young people who are in need of support. An intergenerational organization, "Magic Me," based in London, works with professional artists to facilitate interaction between school children and older people with dementia in residential or day care settings through arts activities. The same project adopts a similar approach with young people and Asian and Somali elders in order to promote cultural understanding and reduce social isolation. There are other examples which involve young offenders (aged 17-21 years) who, towards the end of their sentences, have taken up community placements in settings with frail elderly people, some of whom have dementia related illnesses.

Another range of intergenerational initiatives has sought to support young people's learning in schools and their development into employment through a mentoring approach. Government policy has been keen to develop mentoring, and two intergenerational mentoring schemes are part of the National Mentoring Network. One, "Generations in Action," is based within a Business Educational Partnership in North West England. In the other, at the Beth Johnson Foundation, older volunteers are paired in a one-to-one relationship with children in their first year at high school (aged 11-12 years). This does not include children who have special educational needs and are entitled to statutory educational support, but instead focuses on the social barriers that may prevent a child from learning, such as conflict at home or difficulties in integrating into school life (see Ellis, 1998, 1999b). This particular project has received a National Innovation Award from a government initiative that concentrates on addressing health inequalities in deprived communities (Granville, 2001).

These particular initiatives are pertinent to the current UK government's drive to promote volunteering in communities as a means of addressing social exclusion. Attention has recently focused on older people as resources in their community, and the Prime Minister (Blair, 2000), at an Active Community Convention in London, announced the government's intention to promote an "Experience Corp" of older volunteers.

The significance of intergenerational programs on social exclusion can be seen through their impact on the wider community. A recent study (Granville, 2000) examined the experience of older volunteers working in primary and high schools and highlighted the way such programs went beyond one-to-one relationship between young and old and led to the development of wider social networks. This was demonstrated in three ways: acting as "champions," being a good citizen, and challenging stereotypes of old age.

Acting as "champions"

One of the outcomes of older people going into schools was that they became "champions" for other groups in the community who are often misrepresented and suffer criticism from the wider society.

First and foremost, they became champions for young people. Repeatedly, the volunteers said that they now understood more clearly the pressures and difficulties experienced by young people today. They believed that it was more difficult for the younger generation than it had been for them, because of the changes that they observed in society's values. They spoke about the material deprivation and poverty of their own youth, but considered that the high expectations to succeed and the observable lack of support given to young people today were greater barriers to happiness and self-confidence. Many volunteers told of occasions with family, friends or acquaintances when they had spoken up and defended young people. They disliked hearing stereotypical images of young people being perpetuated and felt able to challenge these remarks because of their direct involvement. They were able to offer positive examples from young people's lives and to demonstrate their achievements, often against very difficult circumstances.

The second group that the volunteers "championed" was the teaching staff. The older people talked of their admiration for teachers, and of their hard work. The elders themselves had not realized how schools had changed and the challenges that teachers faced, and they now spoke up on teachers' behalf whenever they heard criticism of them outside the school environment.

The older volunteers were also more sympathetic to parents and less likely to blame them for the lack of support and direction they observed in some young people. They were more able, through their experiences in intergenerational work, to appreciate the wider pressures placed on parents, and the way changing family structures and societal values had contributed to a lack of support for many of them.

Being a good citizen

In spite of the modesty with which they carried out their work, and the benefits they gained for themselves, it was clear that the volunteers felt a responsibility to be an active participant in their local community. They wanted to make a contribution which would impact on the lives of others, and many of them referred to their wish to *"give something back,"* or spoke such phrases as *"it's pay back time"* or *"having a responsibility as a human being to give back."*

Most elders carried out their volunteering activity at their local school. The reasons they gave were that either they or their children had attended the school, or they were aware that the school served some large estates with poor reputations, and they felt that it was where their support was most needed. They recognized the importance of obtaining a good start in life through education, and they were committed to helping the younger generation to obtain it. Furthermore, they demonstrated how citizenship is promoted through taking responsibility, developing networks with other groups in the community, and pursuing opportunities for lifelong learning and active aging.

Challenging the stereotypes

As part of their citizenship role, intergenerational volunteers also helped to break down the stereotypes of old age. They made connections with groups outside their traditional spheres, through being actively involved in schools. They became known by the young people's friends and were well-regarded figures around the school in their role of supporting young people. They had contact with the teaching and other school staff, as well as the parents of the young people. The volunteers told many stories of being greeted in the neighborhood by pupils from the school, and of hearing the parents wanting to know *"who was that?"*

In those areas where the volunteers either chose, for issues of privacy, to work outside their direct neighborhood, or where there was no school near them, they still found they made contact with the school children in community venues such as the shopping center, petrol stations, supermarkets, libraries or local restaurants.

They became more visible as active members of the community, and this challenged the image of old age as being lonely and selfish. It also demonstrated that two sections of the community who had been portrayed as at odds with each other were now able to engage with each other and enjoy a relationship. There were indications that the older people were less fearful of crime and vandalism, which they had previously associated with young people. One volunteer told a story that demonstrated this change in attitude very vividly:

> Doris lived opposite the local High School and had had her car frequently vandalized by some young people who went past her home. She had been anxious about approaching the young people, and was unhappy about going out in her community at night. However, due to a change in

her life and in the search to find something worthwhile to do, she volunteered for the mentoring program at the school. One year later, she was greeting young people around the neighborhood on a regular basis and one day, three boys were sliding down the grassy bank by her house and narrowly missed her car. Doris went outside and politely pointed out to the boys that they may damage her car, and would they mind moving along a little. The boys cheerfully agreed, for which Doris thanked them and offered them some ice cream.

This small case study shows how through a greater understanding and respect for each other, it was possible to begin to change negative stereotypes and lead to safer communities.

Conclusion

At the beginning of this chapter, we aimed to address whether the concept of social exclusion was useful for the formation and implementation of social policy. Alcock (1998) rightly points out that social exclusion is not a new term; it has its roots in ideas promoted in the United States in the 1960s, and in Europe in the 1980s, when it was closely linked to poverty. The new Labour government has reopened that debate and is looking at solutions that also have an historical context. The Community Action Programs of the 1960s were based on targeting resources for people in deprived areas to develop community capacity, which was an element of U.S. War on Poverty initiatives. Studies in the United Kingdom and the United States (Clark and Hopkins 1968) concluded that government policies had not contributed to changing the lives of poor people, and community capacity building went out of fashion.

Three decades later, social exclusion is embracing a wider concept than social inequalities. It is concerned with reconnecting social links that enable people to be full members of society. The emphasis is on reciprocity and the acknowledgement that exclusion occurs when people are unable, for a number of reasons, to be engaged with others in exchanging support.

We argue therefore, that social exclusion is a useful framework for understanding what has occurred in fragmenting the generations, and that so defining the problem does lead to the solution. These examples of intergenerational programs in the United Kingdom illustrate how reconnecting the generations at each end of the life span can foster inclusion in the main fabric of society. Planned interventions that bring the old and young together in the communities where they live enable those people to fully participate in a range of social relationships and networks. These programs demonstrate connections with political and civic life, the employment environment, and the public, private and voluntary sectors.

The success of such work has also been dependent upon adopting a mechanism that is seen as relevant to all participants. Currently in the United Kingdom, there are a number of government-led initiatives where re-engaging and empowering the young and old could be considered an important long-term goal. By showing the mutual benefits that take place for all members of a community, this approach to policy implementation can be a way of making social inclusion a reality.

References

Active Community Unit. (1999). *Giving time, getting involved.* A strategy report by the Working Group on the Active Community.

Alcock, P. (1998). Bringing Britain together. *Community Care,* November 26 – December 2, pp. 18-24

Arber, S. & Evandrou, M. (1993). *Ageing, independence and the life course.* London: Jessica Kingsley Publications.

Atkinson, A. B. & Hills, J. (Eds.). (1998). *Exclusion, employment and opportunity.* CASE paper 4: London: The London School of Economics.

Bernard, M. (2000). *Promoting health in old age: Critical issues in self-health care.* Buckingham: Open University Press.

Bernard, M. & Meade, K. (Eds.). (1993*) Women come of age.* London: Edward Arnold.

Blair, T. (2000, March 2). Text of a speech by The Prime Minister at The Active Community Convention, Wembley. London: Author.

Clark, K. & Hopkins, J. (1968). *A relevant war against poverty: A study of community action programs and observable social change.* London: Harper and Row.

Coleman, P.G. (1996). Identity management in later life. In Woods, R. (Ed.), *Handbook of the clinical psychology of aging.* Chichester: John Wiley & Sons, Ltd.

Ellis S. W. (1998). *The intergenerational program mentoring project: Final research report.* Stoke-on-Trent: Beth Johnson Foundation/Manchester Metropolitan University.

Ellis S. W. (1999a). National curriculum testing across the interface at key stage 2/ key stage 3: a view from the bridge. *Curriculum, 20*(1), 38-52.

Ellis S. W. (1999b). *Developing whole-school approaches to intergenerational mentoring: Stage two evaluation final report.* Stoke-on-Trent: Beth Johnson Foundation/ Manchester Metropolitan University.

Granville, G. (1998). The foundation as a learning organization. *Education and Ageing 13*(2), 163-176.

Granville, G. (1999). *Evaluation of intergenerational community action.* Stoke-on-Trent: Beth Johnson Foundation.

Granville, G. (2000). *Understanding the experience of older volunteers in intergenerational school-based projects.* Stoke-on Trent: Beth Johnson Foundation.

Granville, G. (2001). Intergenerational health promotion and active citizenship. In Chiva, A. & Stears D. (Eds.), *Health promotion and older people: Rethinking Aging Series.* Milton Keynes: Open University Press.

Granville, G. & Ellis, S. W. (1999a*)*. Developing theory into practice: Researching the intergenerational exchange. *Education and Ageing, 14*(3), 231-248.

Granville, G. & Ellis, S. W. (1999b). Theory and practice in intergenerational work: A model for social change. *Generations Review: 9*(2), 14-16.

Hatton-Yeo, A. (2000). The United Kingdom. In Hatton-Yeo, A. & Ohsako, T. (Eds.), *Intergenerational programs: Public policy and research implications, an international perspective.* Stoke-on-Trent: The Beth Johnson Foundation and UNESCO Institute for Education.

Hobcraft, J. (1998). *Intergenerational and life-course transmission of social exclusion: Influences of childhood poverty, family disruption, and contact with the police.* CASE paper 15. London: London School of Economics.

Ivers, V. (1994). *Citizen advocacy in action: Working with older people.* Stoke-on Trent: Beth Johnson Foundation in association with the European Commission.

Ivers, V. (1999). *The evaluation of the three year pilot phase (1995-1998).* London: Age Concerns England.

Kleinmann, M. (1998). *Include me out? The new politics of place and poverty.* CASE paper 11. London: London School of Economics.

Newman, S., Gregory, A. M., & Streetman, H. (1999). *Elder-child interaction analysis project (ECIA).* Pittsburgh: University of Pittsburgh: Generations Together. Unpublished.

Room, G. (Ed.). (1995). *Beyond the threshold: The measurement and analysis of social exclusion.* London: Polity Press.

Social Exclusion Unit. (1998). *Bringing Britain together: A national strategy for neighbourhood renewal.* London: The Stationary Office.

Social Exclusion Unit. (2000). *National strategy for neighbourhood renewal: A framework for consultation.* The Stationary Office.

German Pupils and Jewish Seniors: Intergenerational Dialogue as a Framework for Healing History

Toshio Ohsako

Introduction

In the International Year of Older Persons (1999), the UNESCO Institute for Education undertook an analysis of innovative intergenerational projects (Ohsako & Cramer, 1999). One of these, the program of encounters between German pupils and Jewish seniors, organized and hosted by the Free and Hanseatic City of Hamburg since 1994, is an example of an intergenerational learning project in which both groups—the younger and the older generations—engage in a dialogue designed to promote mutual understanding. The continued intensive debate about the Holocaust, even almost 60 years later, bears witness to the fact that it is an event still deeply affecting people's thinking, feeling and conscience. In this intergenerational program one can see Hamburg residents, young Germans and older Jewish Holocaust survivors, discuss together, in a friendly and open manner, one of the most inhuman moments of contemporary history. In the dialogue between the victims of a major historical incident and the "innocent" generations—the offspring of perpetrators— one can also see how the process of sharing and understanding history enables the healing of wounds that history has inflicted.

The importance of experiential learning about the history of one's country cannot be overemphasized. The theoretical understanding of an event is not a sufficient condition for history learning if the learners are to "experience" and "feel" a fresh view both of their own personal history and of humanity's whole record of cruelty, misunderstanding, and joy (Zeldin, 1994). Such experiential understanding is possible through intergenerational exchange. The generations who lived through a period of history can directly verify, through dialogue, the impact of the past on the reality of the present society and can thus establish desirable future relationships between generations. History teaching can be substantially enhanced and history itself can become an enjoyable subject if it is conducted through a learning-by-experience approach.

Healing history is not simply a challenge but a necessary prerequisite for a lasting peace for present and future generations. After examining in detail the Hamburg project, this essay will indicate some potential applications of its history-healing framework in other parts of the world.

Healing History in Hamburg

The former German President, Roman Herzog, speaking in Parliament in 1988, said that then recently renewed debate in Germany about the Nazi past showed "that we have not yet found [a] lasting form of memory" (Herald *Tribune*, 28 January 1999). Before the Nazi-regime, about 24,000 Jews lived in Hamburg. Today, the city counts approximately 1,300 Jews and another 700 in the surrounding area (Bar-On, 1996). Many of these were born in Eastern Europe and survived the concentration camps. In all, about 85,000 Jews live in Germany today.

In 1965 the mayor of Hamburg initiated announcements in German-language Jewish newspapers in Israel and the United States asking Jewish former citizens of Hamburg to make contact with the Senate of Hamburg for information about the political, cultural and economic development of their native city. Some 2,685 former citizens of Hamburg have made contact, people who were born in the city who fled from Germany during the Nazi-regime, and who now live throughout the world.

A one-week visit program was organized for these Jewish seniors. Initially the program included only visits to their former living quarters, the present Jewish community living in Hamburg, and a luncheon in the city hall. One afternoon in 1994, an elderly group of Jewish former citizens chanced upon a German student who was copying down the words written on a stone memorial in the Grindel area, Hamburg's former Jewish community. The stone commemorated the Hamburg Synagogue, dynamited and burned on the night of broken glass (Kristallnacht), November 9-10, 1938. One of the Jewish seniors, an elderly lady, cautioned her: "You should stand up, otherwise you will catch a cold!"

The young girl looked up and answered back "But, are you aware of what was here before?"

"Of course I am," answered the elderly lady. "I used to pray in this synagogue when I was your age."

The encounter, an eye-opener to the organizers of the visit program, became the beginning of a regular and useful intergenerational program. With the cooperation and support of local school authorities, this chance encounter grew into a regular encounter program between young German students and visiting Jewish seniors.[1]

How the intergenerational program was conducted

Intergenerational encounters between German students and Jewish seniors—former Hamburg residents now living outside Germany—take place five to six times a year in the Grindel area of the city. On these occasions, a three-hour dialogue session is organized as part of the program for the Jewish seniors' busy week-long visit to Hamburg. Usually 15-20 students participate in the encounter.

The Jewish senior group and their historical tour guide meet with the pupils and their teachers in the old Jewish community quarter at the ancient Jewish girls' school in Caroline Street. At this point, no systematic structures for organizing the two groups are attempted. Together they listen to the explanations of the guide and then proceed to the Talmud-Tora Schüle (a former Jewish boy' school). Everyone concerned—the guide, the teachers, the pupils and the seniors—makes a short speech.

The teachers play an important role here as informal mediators and facilitators who make the two encounter groups at ease with each other by initiating conversation and discussion. Teachers ask the seniors to talk about their significant childhood experiences when they used to live in Hamburg. When the seniors have all had a chance to speak, the teachers ask the students to comment on the experiences of seniors, raise questions on the points made by seniors, and share their own perceptions about historical events.

The students are not asked to prepare questions in advance of the encounter because, as the organizers of the program have learned after many years of experience with it, an informal and natural flow of communication is the most conducive way to establish comfortable relations among the participants.

For the UNESCO study, in-depth interviews were conducted with the German pupils, the Jewish visitors, the teachers and the guide of the historical tour, using a guided interview approach. To gain a sense of how the participants in the encounter sessions perceived their experience of the dialogue, each was asked three open-ended questions:

1. What did you talk about with the each other?
2. What did you learn from each other during your encounter?
3. What do you think about the program?

Reactions to the dialogue sessions

Jewish seniors:

Jewish seniors, first of all, reported having ambivalent feelings about the week that they spent in Hamburg. They noted a resurfacing of bad and painful childhood memories of discrimination and deportation. At the same time, however, they had a nostalgic feeling about visiting the town in which they spent their childhood with their parents and friends. One Jewish senior wrote: "Ambivalence is no doubt the most important content of the week we spent in Hamburg."

They unanimously found it easier to speak to the younger German generation due to the noninvolvement of the young in the Nazi regime and the Holocaust. One Jewish native of Hamburg said that if someone was older than 80 years, he preferred not to meet that person.

An important concern for Jewish seniors was whether, in German schools, the subject of the Third Reich was being taught, and how it was being approached. Several of the seniors focused on the sense of shock that the young Germans clearly experienced when they listened to the horrors of discrimination and humiliation that the elderly had experienced in their native town. One Jewish senior wrote: "My wife and I were very touched to feel how sensitive these young people were. They could not seize the fact that a country like Germany, cultivated as it is, could suffer such an era."

The Jewish seniors witnessed the fact that German society has changed and is not homogeneous. In nearly all the classes that participated in the encounters, there were a number of pupils who were not of German origin. The visitors were glad to observe the fact that German and non-German pupils are studying together.

German students:

German pupils admitted that when they first encountered the Jewish senior visitors, they were anxious and felt a little bit awkward because they felt that they should not ask wrong questions about what happened during the childhood years of Jewish seniors in Hamburg. Nonetheless, the German pupils were amazed that, despite their painful experiences, the Jewish seniors remained open-minded and friendly towards the young Germans. The pupils also realized that the visitors were not struck only by negative memories of Hamburg and the Grindel area. One girl said:

> I was so surprised that they were not angry or sad. Most of them seemed to be happy and excited. I had expected the contrary; I thought

that all their [bad] memories would resurface.... These certainly did come up, but at the same time, they were happy to see the scenes of their childhood again. At that moment, maybe their interest to get to know us was greater than their bad memories, too.

The encounter significantly improved the level of empathy of the German pupils toward the Jewish seniors and their experiences. The young people felt that the Jewish seniors must have worked very hard to come to terms with their past experiences, because they had succeeded in differentiating the past from the present and good memories from bad. Even though they had many terrible experiences with the German youth of the Third Reich in Hamburg, they were still willing to get to know the German youth of today, and they were still able to talk about positive memories from Hamburg.

Some pupils spoke about the Jewish seniors with much respect and admiration:

I believe that the way of thinking of the Jewish visitors is a little bit advanced in comparison to others. I have never seen old people being so open-minded and tolerant. Maybe this is because they have experienced so many things, [and] they have seen so many different places.

While feeling embarrassed listening to what had happened to Jewish people during the Nazi-regime, German pupils felt relieved when many Jewish seniors reassured them that German pupils were not directly responsible for the horrors of the Holocaust. In the beginning of the encounter, however, they could not be sure that the seniors thought that way. One girl said:

I'm glad that they clarified that we are not guilty. We know that it is not our fault, but sometimes we still feel bad about it. They showed us that we should not stick to this sense of guilt forever, but that we should slowly start to get loose of it a little.

The German students also realized that they have the chance to learn from history and their ancestors' mistakes. They can contribute to a better future, for instance by voting for democratic forces or engaging in peace or interfaith activities.

Students and teachers agreed that the meeting could easily replace three months of in-class history teaching. One pupil declared:

History books cannot teach what we learned during this encounter. It is certainly horrible to read that in that year and that place 35,000 people died, but it will not touch you as much as if somebody in front of you says "my sister was murdered by them." We are supposed to learn that it was horrible and that it should never happen again, so I think that encounters like these should be made part of the school curriculum!

Planning and Implementation Considerations

Kaplan et al. (1998) assert that if the goal of an intergenerational initiative is to create opportunities for meaningful interaction and to improve the quality of life of the participants, the program planning must go beyond merely promoting intergenerational contact. It must ensure an exploration of deeper levels of interaction between the participants. The German pupils, Jewish seniors intergenerational program, focusing on educational intergenerational exchanges between the victims of a historically negative event and the innocent descendants of the original aggressors, is specifically designed to develop such a deeper level of understanding and mutual learning experiences. To generate the desired dynamic of open dialogue and mutual learning in this type of intergenerational exchange, the planners of the process must:

1. Clearly identify the goal of the dialogue.
2. Identify a priority issue to which an intergenerational dialogue approach can be applied. The selected issue must be a relevant subject for both groups, and it must be important to the past, present and future of all the participants. The Holocaust—for Jewish seniors and German pupils—is an example of such an issue.
3. Provide background materials, if necessary, in order to insure that all participants understand the historical events being discussed.
4. Use a moderator or facilitator who has strong group process skills and an understanding of the historical events to be discussed.

Interaction objectives

So that history can indeed be "healed," it is important to use the following interaction objectives to help focus and orchestrate the intergenerational dialogue so that all the participants perceive the sessions as mutually beneficial, positive and meaningful experiences.

1. The victims participating in the intergenerational dialogue must be convinced intellectually and emotionally of the innocence of the young generations through positive, natural, frank, pleasant and meaningful dialogue and discussion between the two groups.
2. The innocent young participants must communicate to the victims' generation that they are well informed of and understand the facts of the past, and they must express, face-to-face, their genuine empathy with the victims' hard and painful experiences, both at the time and as these have affected their entire lives up to the present.
3. The innocent young participants must communicate as well their determination never to repeat the mistakes of the past and their wish

to contribute to a peaceful and democratic society.

4. For the sake of the future of young generations, the victims must genuinely feel and express their forgiveness of what former generations have done to them.

Applying the Framework

The intergenerational learning model described here makes it possible for different generations of former enemies to engage in a constructive dialogue that can heal the past and hopefully pave the way to a peaceful future. There are a substantial number of conflict-ridden international situations to which the framework of this intergenerational learning program can be applied. The basis for selecting the following cases is somewhat arbitrary and subjective, relying primarily on the author's perception of what important recent historical events seem to call for history healing. The intergenerational program aspects of these historical issues need to be contextualized and structured by professional intergenerational program organizers in the countries concerned.

The United States of America and Vietnam
American Vietnam War veterans and young Vietnamese students

American Vietnam War veterans, including former prisoners of war held in North Vietnam the 1960s and 70s, could be brought into a dialogue with the young Vietnamese generation now in schools. In such an intergenerational program, they could together discuss the beginnings of the war, the suffering of innocent citizens in both countries, and the way in which intense feelings of hate mounted among some of these civilian populations during the War. The dialogue could be extended to consideration of the actions needed by both sides not only for a continued healing process but also for cooperation between the two countries. This intergenerational program might have a healing effect on the minds of former American soldiers who fought in Vietnam, and who still suffer from the post-Vietnam War symptoms—guilt feelings, nightmares, haunting gunshots sounds, intense death fear, etc. These symptoms of guilt as well as the feelings themselves, arising from participation in the destruction of Vietnamese cities and villages, may be reduced if the veterans directly witness the new, peaceful, developing Vietnam.

The program would also be a reassuring experience for Vietnamese young people who would encounter Americans who were friendly and who therefore differed from the hateful images held by their parents and grandparents, images based on wartime experiences and transmitted to the young generations.

Vietnamese war victims/survivors and American youth

Another opportunity for an intergenerational learning program such as Hamburg's would be the arrangement of visits of young American students to Vietnamese villages or to hospitals and rehabilitation centers that serve Vietnamese veterans or civilians who were wounded or disabled during the War. Discussion could focus on how the Vietnam War created misery and unhappiness to these older generations in Vietnam, what young American students think about the Vietnam War, and finally how Vietnamese senior citizens today see American youth and their role for a peaceful future.

Feelings of forgiveness for the destruction of Vietnam and its citizens will emerge among older Vietnamese warriors and survivors through a direct communication with the young, peace-loving new generation of Americans. Similarly, as American youth come to understand the effects of the war, they will develop a greater level of empathy about the painful and cruel wartime experiences, loss of lives and loss of limbs suffered by the former combatants. These new feelings are expected to influence the attitudes of young Americans as they are called on to exercise their civic and political obligations and participate in democratic and peaceful processes.

China/Korea and Japan
Chinese/Korean senior citizens and Japanese youth

In this situation, an intergenerational learning program would arrange visits to Japanese schools by seniors from China or Korea who were victims of World War II. In history classes in Japanese schools, these senior visitors and young Japanese students could frankly discuss the beginnings of the war and the ways in which it affected the lives of ordinary people, including the Koreans who were brought to Japan as forced labor. The Japanese students would learn how much Chinese/Korean people suffered during the Japanese occupation of their countries and how the Chinese and Korean citizens viewed their Japanese counterparts at the time of the war. This would help Japanese youths to develop a deeper understanding of what actually happened to innocent civilians in China and Korea during the war. It would also lead to a heightened level of empathy about the hardships and sufferings these people had to endure at the hands of the Japanese occupation. Inevitably, the Japanese students would express their expectations and wishes for peaceful, cooperative relationships between Japan and China/Korea.

Such an exchange would also provide an opportunity for Korean and Chinese seniors to come to terms with the reality of the changing Japanese society and to grasp the need for an understanding of the life of the young, postwar Japanese generation. Both groups would realize that new and constructive relationships between the young Japanese generation and their counterparts in the seniors' countries could provide a partial answer to past problems and contribute to an avoidance of future ones.

Conclusion

It is easy to invent an intergenerational program for "healing history" when the significant historical events are already completely terminated (e.g., the Holocaust, the Vietnam War, World War II). The record of these events are well documented, the aggressors and victims involved are clearly identified, and the social consequences recognized. A day may come when the different generations in both South Korea and North Korea will engage in an intergenerational dialogue and in the exchange of experiences for mutual understanding and cooperation. A similar day may come for senior citizens and young people from Israeli and Palestine. An intergenerational learning program similar to Hamburg's could bring the older generations in these countries into contact with their young counterparts or vice-versa. Such a program could become a dialogue for eliminating hostility and building a lasting peace in the Middle-East.

A history-healing intergenerational program might also be applied to other, more contemporary situations. In post-apartheid South Africa, the older, black generation who lived under apartheid could meet with the young, white South African post-apartheid generation. Or perhaps, in some hopefully not-so-remote future, young and old Serbians and Albanians or vice-versa can be brought into contact with each other for a dialogue that could lead to peaceful coexistence.

The history-healing intergenerational learning program holds enormous potential for application to education for peace and conflict resolution around the world. The success or failure of this approach largely depends on multiple factors:

- Successful identification of priority historical issues that the intergenerational program can address.
- Identification and use of effective persuasion techniques in the process of "putting together" relevant encounter groups.
- Creation of a variety of contexts in which an intergenerational program can take place.
- Availability of well-trained intergenerational program specialists who can moderate and conduct such a program.
- Successful specification of useful goals and projection of expected results.
- Social and political support which can influence substantially the effective dissemination of useful results and clarify the implications of the intergenerational program.

If we are to create effective history-healing intergenerational programs, we must collaborate with specialists and teachers able to convey a "living" history. It is desirable for these specialists and teachers to collaborate with a multidisciplinary team of specialists. For example, clinical or counseling psychologists can provide procedures for empathy building in the minds of students. These would serve as a basis for developing effective techniques of working out and healing the wounds inflicted by negative historical events. Human development specialists can offer techniques on how to help the individual learner to continue to self-actualize and to develop a larger framework for understanding the nature of human development from a historical perspective. The cooperation of teacher trainers and curriculum developers becomes essential if the proposed intergenerational program is to be integrated into a regular school curriculum. If the intergenerational program is to be implemented outside the formal school system, for example, in community centers or non-formal adult education programs, there must be a close cooperation between intergenerational program specialists, adult education specialists, community leaders and resource persons.

The history-healing intergenerational program is not a value-free attempt. It is, on the contrary, a value commitment. The message of "never forget our past" encompasses our concern and care about the younger generations of all nations. It is also based upon our perhaps optimistic belief that participants in the history-healing intergenerational program—whether they are victims or aggressors—will benefit from the facts and lessons of history, both constructive and destructive, as long as such facts and lessons provide a meaningful frame of reference for their lifelong efforts to develop positive attitudes and personality orientations towards people and events. War starts in the minds of individuals; it must end and be healed there.

References

Bar-On, D. (1996). *Die last des schweigens. Gespräche mit kindern von Nazi-Tätern* [The legacy of silence. Encounters with children of the Third Reich]. Rowohlt: Hamburg.

Herzig, A. (1991). *Die Juden in Hamburg 1590 bis 1990* [The Jews in Hamburg from 1590 to 1990]. Hamburg: Dölling und Galitz Verlag.

International Herald Tribune (1999). "Germany pays tribute to gay Holocaust victims." 28 January.

Kaplan, M., Kusano, A., Tsuji, I., & Hisanichi, S. (1998). *Intergenerational programs: support for children, youth, and elders in Japan*. Albany: State University of New York Press.

Newman, S., Ward, C.R., Smith, T.B., Wilson, J.O., & McCrea, J.M. (1997). *Intergenerational programs: Past, present and future*. Taylor & Francis, Bristol, PA.

Ohsako, T. & Cramer, M. (1999). Intergenerational dialogue and mutual learning between German pupils and Jewish seniors. *Education and Aging*, 14 (3), Triangle Journals Ltd., Oxford.

Simon Wiesenthal Centre (1999). Resources and Library: Timeline.
Zeldon, T. (1994). *An intimate history of humanity.* London: Sinclair-Stevenson.

Notes

1 Hamburg authorities, as far as the author is aware, have been very modest and discrete about this encounter program, and they have not attempted to persuade school authorities to generalize this approach to other schools in Germany. The German people are so sensitive and anguished about the Holocaust that hesitancy even about such a positive approach to post-Holocaust education activity, is understandable. UNESCO initially had difficulty even undertaking its inquiry into the German students, Jewish seniors intergenerational program but finally persuaded the authorities to allow a purely research-oriented investigation. It is in this sense that UNESCO, as an international organization dealing with educational and cultural issues, was able to study the program and to publicize this intergenerational approach to the rest of the world.

Intergenerational Relationships in Latin America and the Caribbean

By Martha Peláez, Ph.D.

Introduction

This chapter will discuss the importance of intergenerational relationships in Latin America and present a few experiences illustrating the development of intergenerational programming in the region.

Latin America is, in demographic terms, a youthful region in transition. The transition to population aging is occurring in the context of poverty with low rates of increases in GDP per capita, high levels of unemployment, rural to urban migration, and an overall decrease in the capacity of traditional families to deal with the care of the young and the old.

Among the most important changes occurring in the region are the transformation of the extended family into nuclear families and the increasing number of older persons living alone. Therefore, innovative approaches to the strengthening of intergenerational relationships are needed to ensure the health and well being of both young and old.

This chapter will examine the role of intergenerational relationships in:

- Enhancing the quality of life of the young and the old.
- Strengthening community participation by building stronger social networks.

The Social Demographic Context

The policies and programs that focus on strengthening intergenerational relationships at the family and community level can constitute a timely response to questions derived from considerations of the following contexts.

Rapid demographic growth

In Latin America, as is the case with the majority of the countries in the world, a trend can be observed in the reduction of fertility and the prolongation of life expectancy at birth, both of which indicate that the region is involved in an active aging process. In the 1950s, life expectancy at birth in most countries of the region was 51 years, but currently it is more than 68, and it has reached more than 75 in some countries.

Another way to appreciate the rapidity of population aging in Latin America is to examine the aging index in certain countries. This index measures the ratio of people aged 60 or more for every 100 under the age of 15. In the last decade of the 20th century, this ratio had a maximum of 71 in Uruguay and a minimum of 9 in Nicaragua. In almost all countries, the aging index is expected to double or triple over the next two decades, which will represent an unprecedented population change as illustrated by the projections for Venezuela. Today Venezuela has 19 persons 60 and over for every 100 persons under the age of 15; in 25 years this number will change to 62 older persons for every 100 children (Pan American Health Organization/World Health Organization[PAHO/WHO], 1998).

A growing urbanization process

Over the last few decades, the population in Latin America has experienced intensified migration from rural areas to urban ones. The reasons for these shifts have been frequently identified as the search for better employment opportunities and access to education and other services. One important aspect of this process is that large urban conglomerates are the areas of choice for this migration, and the resulting overpopulation of these areas has generated many changes in familial relationships while rural areas are often left with large numbers of elders and children (PAHO/WHO, 1998, 23-25).

Transformations in the institution of family

As a consequence of living, learning and working in a global village, cultural identity and tradition are being substantially affected, particularly family structure and relationships. In Latin America we find important transformations in the family as exemplified by:

- A shift from an extended family to a nuclear family.
- The emergence of incomplete nuclear families made up predominantly of mothers and children.
- A growing predominance of common law marriages and the resulting shift in the duties and rights of couples and children (PAHO/WHO, 1998, 10-12).

The Concept of "Intergeneration"

The intergenerational focus is based on the assumption that the answers to a number of family and social problems lie in strengthening the ties among old and young and promoting solidarity among the generations. The examples presented in this chapter illustrate how the concept of "intergeneration" is used to encourage the encounter between generations of grandparents and grandchildren for the promotion of health, the teaching of cultural values, and the promotion of peace and development.

- The older adult can become a new social actor and a human resource in the area of health, as demonstrated by the experience in Guatemala, where older adults are part of the vaccination campaigns.
- Adolescents require acceptance, support, and accompaniment during the processes of creating an identity and making the transition to adult life. This need has been analyzed and addressed in an initiative developed in Uruguay, where older persons have become relevant in the emotional care and development of children and adolescents who have been abused or abandoned. Furthermore, the relationship between older adults and adolescents is possible and can become a positive experience for both.
- Older adults can also develop leadership by participating in projects that promote, through the public school system, healthy environments and peace. In this regard, coordinated efforts by the government, academic groups and international organizations in Costa Rica implemented a community program in the promotion of peace and the environment involving retired teachers and students.

Programs Fostering Intergenerational Relationships

Chile, Costa Rica, Guatemala, and Uruguay have used different strategies for intergenerational programming. What follows describes the ongoing initiatives in each of these countries.

Older adults as agents of socialization in Chile

In Chile, over the last decade there have been numerous experiences intended to promote a closer relationship between older persons and the younger generations. The majority of these programs are promoted by the "Older Adult Programs" executed by the municipalities, the decentralized administrative instance of the local government, and non-governmental organizations (Villaseca, 1997).

One example is the program developed by the "Hogar de Cristo," a not-for-profit organization that provides shelter and community services to abandoned or abused children and to older persons with no family or economic support. Two programs, "Cuenta-Cuentos" (Story Telling) and "Caminando Juntos" (Walking Together), were developed for the specific purpose of developing closer relationships between older persons and children served by the program. The programs were supported by the Pan American Health Organization/The World Health Organization.

The Story Telling program is conducted at the day care center for children up to five years old. On average, 25 children participate in the program with three older adults who have been through a training program that focuses on selecting stories and organizing developmentally appropriate follow-up activities. After each story the children are led by the older adults to draw pictures and sing or dance to music related to the story. Occasionally they are assisted in representing a skit with the message they learned from the story.

The evaluation of the program included interviews with the older persons who have participated, with the children, and with the staff of the day care center. The program has generated positive feedback from all participants. Both the elders as well as the day care staff repeatedly emphasized how wonderfully enriching the experience was. The program targeted the most difficult children, many of them suffering from hyperactivity. The staff had very low expectations of the results of the program, and at the end of the semester documented that the children participating in the special program with elders had demonstrated better self-control and discipline during the rest of the program.

Walking Together is a program that takes place at the Home for Abused Children. The program included 25 children ages two to five years old and seven older women. Initially 25 older women volunteered for the program. Of these 10 were selected and trained, and seven were actually included in the program. The main goal of the program was to enhance the growth and development of the children by providing them with a foster grandmother and tutor. The foster grandmothers visited the home one day a week on a rotating basis so everyday the children had a grandmother at home for five-hours a day. The grandmothers were given specific assignments with a few children at a time, and they blended into the daily routine in a supportive role for both children and staff.

The evaluation of the program included observation of the relationship between the children and the grandmothers as well as structured interviews with grandmothers, children and staff. The grandmothers felt "useful," "accepted," "needed," "responsible," and "grateful." The children considered the grandmothers' visits as "something to look forward to," "happy time," "having someone to trust." The staff evaluated the experience as very positive, especially since the presence of the grandmothers was able to bring "tenderness" to the lives of very needy children. The staff was often too busy teaching and disciplining to be able to give each child the loving tender care that the grandmothers were able to provide.

Both projects shared three basic objectives:

• Improve the respect and value of older adults for the young.
• Improve social integration for both age groups.
• Support the psychological processes that allow the participants to improve their self-esteem.

In summary, the dynamic that is generated by these programs seeks the emergence of stable affective relationships that allow for the better psychosocial development of each of the project's participants (Arteaga, 1999).

Retired persons for peace and the environment in Costa Rica

In Costa Rica, intergenerational relationships have undergone a process of promotion and strengthening through the implementation of social projects with diverse participants. One of these is a project started recently called "Older Persons for the Promotion of Peace and the Environment" (Brenes, 2000).

Why Peace and the Environment? Peace in the community and care for the environment are very important values for the people of Costa Rica, where there is a tradition of peaceful resolution of conflicts and of protecting the environment. However, with the growth of the population and the increased migration from neighboring countries, the need to sensitize and educate the community on issues related to peace with and for the environment has gained new significance for the community.

In the pilot phase of the study, the University for Peace trained 22 retired teachers on current problems related to peace and the environment. In addition, the retired teachers received training on how to develop and implement a community project. Part of the course requirement included the development of a community environmental project involving students from a local school in their neighborhood. The retired teachers, jointly with the students, implemented the selected projects over a period of six months. Some of these projects included: "Saving our planet in a climate of peace," "Beautifying my community," and "Recycling trash/ Avoiding Conflict."

The success of these projects led all involved parties to continue the experience by training a second class of 20 additional retired persons in peace and the environment. Costa Rica plans to expand the program in order to maintain a corps of peace and environment mentors for most community schools.

This initiative coordinates efforts by government, academic and international bodies, with the object of fostering the strengthening of networks and organizations of older persons as agents of change within a framework of creating a society for all ages. With this purpose in mind, the need to develop permanent training strategies to allow older persons to occupy important positions in community development was addressed. In this manner, older adults are provided opportunities for greater social integration and contribution to sustainable development in their communities.

"Grandparents for Health" in Guatemala

In 1998, the Public Health Ministry's National Program for Maternal and Infant Health shifted its focus from addressing only health problems of children and women of childbearing age to include a more comprehensive approach to the delivery of health care for the entire family, including older members of the family (Estrada, 1998). As part of this process of change, the National Plan of Health for Older Persons was created. The culmination of the planning and approval process by Ministry authorities coincided with National Health Week, the purpose of which was to vaccinate the maximum number of children. During that week, vaccinations were the first priority for all health care personnel. These events created an ideal scenario for the integration of children, adolescents, and older adults in a specific activity, thus launching the "Grandparents for Health" project.

The project began with the purpose of contributing to child welfare through health care services and health education and promotion. Notwithstanding, the following objectives were also considered:

- To develop shared links between the National Program for Maternal and Infant Health and plans for children, adolescents, and older persons.
- To develop and promote social leadership for older persons.
- To start a process within the health services that demonstrates the need for working jointly with common objectives among the various vulnerable groups seen within the ministry.
- To create a concrete space and organizational framework for participation by older persons who wish to serve their community.

Development and implementation began with a general invitation to people 50 years old and over to participate in community-based voluntary programs. These were distributed through recreational clubs and organizations especially those sponsored by the Ministry of Culture and Sports. Additionally, several reunions were held with the purpose of informing prospective participants about the objectives of the program. Approximately 500 persons participated in these informative reunions, and 332 elders agreed to participate in the program. Their participation was fostered by the perceived opportunity to work for the community and the children and also by the opportunity to be socially engaged with other people.

In order to implement the program, a team was created that integrated personnel of the Ministry of Health and the Ministry of Culture and Sports with the purpose of coordinating the different aspects of the program. The older adults were distributed based on their area of residence in order to facilitate their participation within their own communities. Nine groups of elders were created, and a coordinator for each group was selected. The coordinators worked with the coordinating inter-ministerial team.

Although 332 older adults had initially agreed to participate in this program, only 125 persons remained at the end of the program. Some persons just didn't show up. Others cited household duties and grandchildren caregiving responsibilities. The majority of the participants were retired with an age range of 52 to 84 years and predominantly female (70 percent); most lived in or near the capital city. A small number of participants were retired health care workers, predominantly nurses.

The participants in the program attended a training session, sponsored by PAHO/WHO, that included theoretical and practical information related to the importance of vaccinations for the prevention of communicable diseases, the general characteristics of these diseases, communication skills, motivation and community work. The group of retired nurses received specific training by the Ministry of Health in vaccination techniques.

The program was finally implemented in two sites, the capital, Guatemala City, and small towns surrounding it. In the small towns located near the capital city, promotional activities were conducted by both the local municipal and health authorities through home visits, informal meetings with parents and teachers, and recreational activities for the children. The retired nurses participated as health care personnel for the administration of the vaccines. In Guatemala City, a health festival was conducted for children who live and/or work in the streets. Several groups participated, including Casa Alianza, Physicians Without Borders, the National Commission against Child Abuse, the Red Cross, the municipality of Guatemala and private businesses. During this activity, in addition to the recreational and sports events, volunteer retired health workers vaccinated 902 children.

As result of the program the coverage of the vaccination programs was increased, especially in those locations in which the older adults participated. The activity made it possible to provide preventive health services to an otherwise elusive population. Additionally, by working as a team, health care personnel and older adults realized the benefits of pooling resources and cooperative problem solving. The initiative illustrated the value of older persons as potential social change agents and contributors to public health.

"Grandparents by Choice" in Uruguay

In Uruguay the population aged 60 years and over constitutes more than 17 percent of the total population; life expectancy is 72 years for men and 79 years for women (Bezrukov de Villalba, 1997). Uruguay is among the oldest countries in the Americas. Older persons in Uruguay are highly educated, largely independent and to a large degree live alone or with a spouse. Over the last two decades, out migration has changed the nature of intergenerational family dynamics, leaving many older persons without nearby grandchildren and saddened by the lack of their grandparenting role. In addition, there is an increase in interfamily violence and in child abuse and neglect. Abused children are often removed from the home and placed in foster group homes managed by the National Children's Institute in the Ministry of Children and Families.

In the group homes, the children receive protection, food, shelter and education. But, they often lack the emotional and psychological support that is usually provided by the relationship with parents and grandparents.

Considering these two realities and the problems and opportunities presented, a program was begun several years ago by the Catholic University of Uruguay. The program started with a course offered by the University for older persons on "Grandparenting." The course focused on adolescent psychology, the needs of teenagers in today's society, communication skills for dealing with teens, etc. A module of the course dealt with the problem of abuse and maltreatment, and as part of the course the group visited the State Group Home for abused children. Out of this experience, "Grandparents by Choice" was born.

The psychologist teaching the course interviewed each person wanting to volunteer and prepared the first orientation program. An agreement with the National Children Institute ensured coordination among the University, the older persons and the group homes. The Institute assigned a psychologist to provide on-going support to the older persons participating in the program. A key element of this experience was the creation of the support group for Grandparents by Choice. Grandparents in the program are committed to weekly visits with the grandchildren and telephone contact as often as possible during the week.

The success of the program is evidenced by the fact that since the program started eight years ago, each new group that joins the program remains faithful to the commitment made to the children. The only attrition from the program to date has been due to the illness and then death of a grandparent.

For the grandchildren participating in the program, the grandparents have become a "significant" person in psychological terms. The process has contributed to their recovering trust and security, thereby providing significant support for their social integration. An evaluation of the program has shown that the children participating in it do better at school, have fewer disciplinary problems, and are able to deal better with stress.

Those who have now graduated from the group home program and are on their own continue the relationship with the grandparents and say that more than anything else they were able to mature and become independent because of the stimulus and mentoring provided by the grandparents.

Conclusion

Lessons learned

The program reports and interviews with program coordinators reveal that in general each of these intergenerational programs helped to broaden social networks and diversify the sources for psychosocial support for young and older adults. Social support is defined by the program in Uruguay as "the information that leads someone to believe that she matters and is loved and esteemed as a member of a network of communication and mutual obligation." Social support also refers to the set of interpersonal transactions that include one or more of the following key elements: affect, affirmation, and assistance.

Furthermore, intergenerational relationships have become experiences in love, friendship, and care by a "significant other," as well as a factor of social protection that can mitigate the stress factors resulting from the biological, psychological, and social changes that occur simultaneously, albeit in different ways, in both adolescents and older adults.

Additionally, intergenerational relationships have provided the possibility and opportunity for:

- Social integration: Young persons and older adults can share common concerns and experiences while addressing a social need.
- Meaning and significance: Older persons who freely assume the responsibility for a child's well-being regain the feeling of being needed and a reason for living, as can be observed in the "Grandparents by Choice" program in Uruguay.

- The development of social capital: This dimension has particular relevance since it enhances the ability of public and private initiatives to meet community needs with the contributions of older persons, as was observed in "Grandparents for Health" and the Costa Rican projects on peace and the environment. Older persons also gain an intergenerational social network that enables them to compensate for the loss of peers their own age.

In addition, intergenerational programs have:

- Contributed to modify the negative images associated with aging as a passive and dependent stage.
- Created a new role and space for the social participation of older persons.
- Shown promise as effective and low-cost responses to addressing social problems.

We also have learned, that intergenerational programs can be replicated and adapted to the context of developing countries. The main requirements for the development and implementation of these programs are the following:

- A committed project leader who inspires and motivates others and is able to mobilize needed resources without much support.
- An institutional environment of respect, where older persons are given responsibility and support for the work to be done.
- Appropriate training programs addressing the needs of both the old and the young.

Thus taking into consideration the context of population aging in Latin America, we consider that intergenerational programs may well hold the key to maintaining strong intergenerational solidarity. However, more data, better evaluation, and more public debate on the value of promoting formal intergenerational programs are needed.

Lessons to be learned: Questions for future research

Some of the questions that still need to be explored are:

- How do intergenerational experiences contribute to the processes of developing life skills, positive attitudes, and self-esteem in younger persons?
- How do intergenerational experiences contribute to the promotion of health and improved functional capacity in older persons?

- What models of intergenerational programs are most successful in the promotion of peace in a community and peace with the environment? How can these programs become sustainable in developing countries?
- What models of intergenerational programs can be adapted to developing countries in order to promote the use of older persons in the education and training of at-risk children?
- What models of intergenerational policy contribute to the strengthening of the family in terms of support for parents and children while promoting autonomy and respect for older persons?
- How can an intergenerational policy contribute to the empowering of older persons and adolescents for political participation?

As we have been able to observe, the social spaces for the development of intergenerational experiences cannot be limited to the scope of family. Rather it is necessary to explore the spaces offered by school, work, and the community in order to foster new and improved ties among the generations. New data and research on successful intergenerational programs can provide policy makers and program developers with good cost–benefit analyses to justify the investment in these programs and stimulate ideas on how to finance and sustain them.

References

Arteaga, V. C. (1999). Intergenerational programs: Hogar de Cristo. Unpublished program report by the Coordinator of Children's Programs at Hogar de Cristo.

Bezrukov de Villalba, L. (1997). "Adultos mayores deciden ser abuelos de menores en situación de riesgo social: Una experiencia desarrollada en Uruguay (1992-1997)." Report from Envejecimiento Poblacional e Integración Social. Foro de las Américas. Pan American Health Organizatiion/World Health Organization. Washington, D.C.

Brenes, A. B. (2000). "Formación de personas mayores en la promoción de la paz y el ambiente." Pan American Health Organization and Caja Costarricense de Seguro Social. San José, Costa Rica.

Estrada, G., M.D., (1998). "Report from Grandparents for Health project". Pan American Health Organization, Guatemala.

Pan American Health Organization/World Health Organization (1998). *Aging in the Americas into the XXI century*. National Institute on Aging, and U.S. Department of Commerce, Bureau of the Census. Washington, D.C.

Pan American Health Organization/World Health Organization (1998). *Health in the Americas* (Vol. I). Scientific Publication No. 569. Washington, D.C.

Villaseca, P. S. (1997) "Intergeneración: Conceptualizaciones básicas y posibilidades" in *Envejecimiento poblacional e integración social foro de las Américas*. Pan American Health Organizatiion/World Health Organization. Washington, D.C.

Notes

1 This project was sponsored and implemented jointly by the Pan American Health Organization/World Health Organization, the Costa Rica Social Security office, the University for Peace, and the Office of the First Lady of Costa Rica with the active participation of Costa Rica Association of Retired Teachers and the Friends for Peace Foundation.

Cuba: Fertile Ground for Intergenerational Arts Movement

By Susan Perlstein

Introduction

I arrived in Havana during the Carnival in August 2000. That first evening, I sat in the bandstand along the Malecon and witnessed all generations dancing, drumming and making music. They came from every region in Cuba, from cities, villages and countryside, to celebrate their culture—from folk traditions rooted in an afro-Cuban heritage to lavish Copacabana-style club dancing. This extraordinary introduction framed my understanding of the promise and potential for an intergenerational arts exchange in Cuba. An article on intergenerational relations in Cuba by Raul Hernandez Castellon, Professor at the Center for Demographic Studies, Universidad De La Habana, anchors my impressions in some of the social realities and demographic trends of modern Cuba (Hernandez Castellon, 2000).

The Situation

In Cuba, the state provides free education and health services and subsidized housing to all its citizens. Every citizen has the right to work and to social security. Because the state provides support, the elderly in Cuba are well cared for and, in fact, they enjoy a better standard of living than in many other countries. However, the amount being paid for social security makes up a very high portion of the country's national budget. The result is a national campaign towards reduction of costs and better use of services (Hernandez Castellon, 2000).

Services for older people

Hernandez Castellon reports that while long term care facilities and day care centers have increased considerably, there are still not enough. The family is the main caregiver, since tradition and economic conditions in the country mean that older adults normally live with their sons. However, there are a wide range of informal services at the community level, where volunteers from different NGOs (non-government organizations) help meet the domestic needs of retired persons by doing such tasks as laundry, house cleaning, food preparation, washing, etc.

Creating homes for the elderly, day care centers, geriatric day care hospitals, and grandparent's clubs are some of the achievements of Cuban society for its elderly. Because of the neighborhood health clinics, the elderly can avail themselves of medical services near their homes.

I had the opportunity to visit homes, elderly institutions, schools and cultural centers and to speak to people about the relationships between generations. At the present time, most Cuban people seem culturally connected to the traditional extended family in which three generations live together under one roof. The role of the grandparents is to take care of the children when the parents are at work and to accomplish the household chores such as cleaning and shopping. This is especially important given the need for both parents to work. Grandparents act as caregivers, thus enabling hundred of thousands of mothers to work outside the home.

One of the grandmothers spoke with great love for her grandchildren, but felt unappreciated and simply expected to do chores. She loved going to the neighborhood "Casa de Abuelos" ["Casa de Abuelos" literally translates as grandparent's home, but its United States equivalent is a senior center] where she could share her history and interests with other older people, volunteer, and go on trips.

Casas de abuelos

In every neighborhood in Havana, there are Casas de abuelos. Every day older people come to them to participate in activities for the day. The centers offer an exciting range of activities — discussion groups, trips, cultural programs, and meals. I learned to play dominos. I learned to speak about other things as the game played on. I heard stories from the days under Bautista before the revolution. People were hungry, uneducated and without health care. One elderly women became a teacher after the revolution and took part in the education campaign to help farmers learn to read and write. She carried within her the pride of having transformed herself into an informed educated person and having helped Cuba to become an educated nation. Her warm, embracing, informed spirit impressed me.

An elderly gentleman described how important he felt as a youth who fought in the revolution and helped to set up local committees, like community boards, for neighborhoods. He spoke about all the changes that his eyes had witnessed. He lamented that no one seemed interested in his story.

Here was a great opportunity, I thought, for the older people to share their stories with the neighborhood school children. On speaking to the director of the center, I learned that the older people do go on trips with the school children to the zoo and botanic gardens, but there is no venue yet for them to pass on their experiences and insights about history and culture. The director expressed enthusiasm about the possibility of such a special intergenerational program.

Casas de cultura

In every neighborhood, there is also a cultural house that is a community arts center where people can learn music, dance, and the visual arts. Artists teach and perform at the casas de cultura as well as at the grandparent centers and at the schools in the neighborhood. Often the older musicians are mentoring the younger musicians. There are weekly community dances and musical presentations. Everyone is invited. Arts are integrated into community life.

While I was visiting, I spoke to the Director of Cultural Affairs for the City of Havana. She expressed great interest in learning about intergenerational cultural programs in the United States and quickly saw the possibilities for connections of young and older Cubans who share the rich Afro-Cuban music and dance heritage.

School interest in social studies curriculum

I also visited a high school in a Vedado neighborhood and had the opportunity to speak with several social studies teachers. The teachers were seeking ways to bring history to life. At present, there is a short supply of paper and books. Programs in which the students could do primary research by interviewing key elders seemed to be compatible with the educational needs of the curriculum. Oral history interviewing was not a part of the social studies, but could easily be incorporated. There had been specific projects, but not a concerted program aimed at integrating intergenerational learning into the curriculum.

Conclusion

Informal intergenerational experiences are common in Cuba and include informal mentoring programs such as job-related apprenticeships in both commercial areas — as in the sugar industry, where the older workers mentor the younger new technicians — and the arts, as older musicians mentor younger musicians. However, while there are few formal programs, the infrastructure is in place for a variety of beneficial intergenerational cultural programs.

The educational and cultural system is set up so that there is coordination between the national, provincial, municipal and neighborhood People's Council level. The country has experienced the coordination of projects through social and community mobilization projects and programs. Community education programs have been developed specifically to address the needs of people who live in rural settings and the countryside. A wide range of adult educational opportunities have been developed to enable a response to the increasing needs of the young and adult population.

From my observations, I agree with Hernandez Castellon: "Even though there are not currently formally developed intergenerational programs, opportunities can easily be identified" (2000, p. 25). The organizational structures are in place. The Ministry of Education and the Ministry of Culture together could carry out actions aimed at involving older people close to a school or by zones, in support programs for education. In senior centers and community-based cultural organizations, elders can be enlisted to teach various kinds of arts and crafts and conduct storytelling sessions to pass on the history and culture. In Cuba, there is clearly great promise and potential for a national policy to develop intergenerational cultural programs.

References

Hernandez Castellon, R. (2000). Report on Cuba. In A. Hatton-Yeo and T. Ohsako (Eds.). *Intergenerational programs: Public Policy and research implications, an international perspective*, pp. 22-25. Hamburg, Germany: UNESCO Institute for Education.

Intergenerational Initiatives in South Africa: Reflecting and Aiding a Society in Transition

By Cathy Gush

Introduction

Recent socio-demographic and economic trends show South Africa to be a developing country with a number of pressing social problems. It is also a society in transition, which contributes to the complexity of its situation.

Within this framework, intergenerational programs are reflective both of the problems of a society in transition and of the efforts to find solutions to some of these problems. These programs are needed in their own right to heal the intergenerational rifts caused by rapid urbanization and modernization, and they are needed as a mechanism for addressing the problems caused by social and demographic changes and factors such as AIDS. This chapter will describe some of the salient socio-economic, cultural and demographic factors in South Africa and examine intergenerational relations and initiatives against this background.

Socio-Demographic Background and Trends

Population statistics

South Africa has a population of approximately 40 million people, of whom some 75 percent are Black Africans, 13 percent are White, 9 percent are Colored (mixed heritage) and 3 percent are Indian (CSS, 1996). The

African National Congress (ANC) government has decided to retain this racial classification system, one of the reasons being that there is a correlation between population group membership and various indicators of socio-economic status and trends. It is indeed very difficult to discuss trends and dynamics of intergenerational relations and programs for South Africa as a whole, simply because of a wide divergence in population and culture, and the historical pattern of development. As is well known, South Africa had, in the period from 1948 to 1994, a policy of apartheid, an official policy of racial segregation where social services as well as most other aspects of society functioned on a basis which discriminated between people of different races. The coming to power of the ANC in 1994 brought an end to this system and the process of equalization was begun.

With respect to age, the composition of South Africa's black African and white population groups differs substantially. South Africa has a relatively young and expanding black African population and an aging and shrinking white population. Only some six percent of black Africans are more than 60 years of age, while about 14 percent of the white population are in this category. More than 50 percent of black Africans are under 25 years of age (Ziehl, 1999). However, indications are that for society as a whole this is changing, and that the percentage of black Africans under 25 years of age will decline significantly in the future, due to factors such as a greater-than-expected decline in fertility and the impact of AIDS. Projections are that the older population will increase from 6.9 percent in 1997 to 10.8 percent by the year 2025 (Kinsella and Ferreira, 1997).

Of the current population aged 60 and over, nearly two-thirds (61.1 percent) are women. Many of them are the heads of households and/or provide the main source of income by way of their pensions.

While the number of old people is increasing, there is also a large number of young children. It is estimated that in 1996, 35 percent of the population was under the age of 15 years (Institute for Futures Research, 1996 cited in SAIRR, 1998). This statistic, coupled with the one above regarding the number of women more than 60, begins to give an indication of the number of older women (grandmothers) interacting with young children, a process which is in the black African population significantly aided by cultural and economic factors. None of this, however, is static nor is it unproblematic, as further discussion will show.

Socio-economic indicators and trends

Although South Africa is categorized as a medium income country and as having a human development index that is in the middle range, there are a number of areas (especially rural) where there is still substantial poverty, particularly among the aged. Unemployment in some areas is as high as 30 percent and for many households the only source of income is the old-age pension contributed by an elderly member of the family. (South Africa is fairly unique in Africa in that it pays out a non-contributory state old-age pension to men more than 65 years and women more than 60 years.)

Urbanization has occurred quite rapidly over the past decade, and the majority of South Africans (55 percent) now live in urban areas. The primary sector activities (mining and agriculture) on which the South African economy was built now account for less than 15 percent of the GDP.

Key Social Issues

Within the Black African family

The urbanization process in particular has significantly affected the social fabric of black South African families. Coupled with major political changes and increased Westernization, there has been much pressure for change in family structures and intergenerational dynamics. At present, extended families and multi-generation households are still prevalent, but many of the current debates amongst sociologists and gerontologists center on just how much the pressure of a society (and its values) in transition will affect this practice and intergenerational relations in general.

Valerie Moller, head of the Institute for Social and Economic Research, argues that pension money serves to hold together the contemporary South African three-generation family and strengthens the position of respect and authority of the pensioner head of household, especially women, as they contribute to living as well as other family-related expenses (Moller, 1998). Most black African grandmothers are pensioners. In-depth research in KwaZulu-Natal by Cattell found that grandmothers see themselves as important in their families as family builders, peace-keepers, problem solvers, promoters of harmony and respect, and teachers of the young. The grandmothers expressed a strong sense of generational continuity, of passing knowledge down the generations, and of the value of their knowledge to the development of younger generations.

However, even though extended households are still the norm, the dynamics of the intergenerational relations within it are undoubtedly being affected. A disturbing number of cases of abuse of older people (physical, emotional and psychological) are being uncovered. This was highlighted on national television recently on a high-profile actuality program, and fieldwork research is currently being done amongst a wide range of old people in the Cape metropolitan area to obtain their stories first-hand. High unemployment rates, over-crowding in urban areas and widespread poverty create tensions that spill over into the abuse of older people, often by family members eager to obtain their money or property. At the same time, the extended family structure of the rural areas is weakening, as for the first time there is evidence of grandparents being unwilling or unable to take back grandchildren in times of hardship (Mail & Guardian, 2000).

Within the White African family

With regard to the white African population, a somewhat different dynamic pertains. Extended families are not the norm; the tendency is much more towards nuclear families or even single-parent families, as the divorce rate is high amongst white South Africans.

Many older white South Africans live independently or are housed in old age homes. Part of the reason for this is that white families on average are better off financially and are not as dependent on income from a pensioner in the household. Amongst white middle class South African families there is also less of a tradition and culture of extended households, and privacy /autonomy for the family unit of parents and children is more highly valued. This also means that there tends to be more separation between generations. The older people in these communities are financially more independent and able to pursue their own interests.

AIDS

The AIDS epidemic will significantly and increasingly affect the social, economic and demographic status of the country. At the end of 1996, it was estimated that approximately six percent of all South African men, women and children were infected with HIV (Myslik, Freeman and Slawski, 1997). Current projections indicate that by 2005, nearly 25 percent of the adult population will be infected (Southern Life AIDS model), and that number could be as devastatingly high as 45 percent by 2010. The majority of HIV infections occur in women between the ages of 15 and 20 and in men between 20 and 30 years. Since the burden of illness and dying falls mainly on people of working age, the burden of supporting sick adults and orphaned children will fall on the elderly, particularly the women.

As the AIDS epidemic progresses, there will be an increasing number of children who have lost one or both parents and fewer adults of normal parenting age to take care of them. Hand in hand with an increase in elderly-headed households is an increase in the number of female-headed households as a result of AIDS. This will exacerbate the existing trends towards the feminization and gerontification of poverty. Clearly the demographic changes created by AIDS will have a significant impact on the socio-economic position of many African families, on the age structure of society, and consequently on intergenerational relations.

Child care

For both black and white South Africans, the percentage of single parents is very high, although for different reasons. Teenage pregnancies are high amongst black South Africans, and are often a major source of friction between generations, especially grandmothers and granddaughters. This is largely due to the fact that these grandmothers see their role as being the moral teachers and guardians of their granddaughters and that a pregnancy seems to indicate a failure on their part. However, they are also very forgiving and often end up being the ones that care for the unplanned babies, as they did with their own daughters.

Among white South Africans, the high divorce rate means that for all groupings there is need for more guidance and care by an older person.

Economic factors also play a big role in determining the need for children to be taken care of by persons other than their own mother. A mother may be of an economically active age, for example, and may need to work for an income. Other young mothers may need someone to care for their child so they can return to school.

Among many South African families, much of the education and care of young children under the age of six falls therefore to older women. While many single white South African mothers will make use of professional day care services, the extended black South African households often result in the grandmothers taking care of their grandchildren at home. What often happens is that this expands to taking in other children in the community for daycare. Thus a great number of small, home care groups (usually caring for about 6 children) have developed, to the extent that in many black African communities the name for a caregiver is "*gogo*," the Xhosa word for grandmother, meaning that the two are almost synonymous. The sense of communal living will also cause many children in these areas to call a number of older women "*gogo*," even though these women are not their own familial grandmother. The home care groups also serve as a means of income for these older women.

Education

With regard to intergenerational support for education, indications are that, in particular, grandmothers in the black African community are eager to contribute money from their pensions to expenses relating to the education and careers of grandchildren. They attach great value to education, not only for the sake of advancement, but also possibly because so many of them were denied the opportunity. Many members of the older black South African generation dropped out of school at a very early age, due to a range of socio-economic factors coupled with the fact that until the '90s, schooling was not compulsory for black South Africans. This has also been the cause of a high rate of illiteracy (functional competence in reading and writing) among black South African adults.

Research findings also point to the fact that education and learning issues are sometimes the source of intergenerational tension within families. Some grandparents perceive the exposure to education and schooling as being responsible for what they see as irresponsible (usually sexual) behavior and a deviance from traditional cultural values by their grandchildren. In other instances, young people use education as a threat to get what they want from their parents and grandparents, because they know that schooling is important to them (i.e. they threaten to drop out of school if they don't get their way). These factors emerged in a particular study on intergenerational relations conducted in the urban and rural areas of KwaZulu-Natal in 1995 and 1996, entitled "They don't listen: Contemporary respect relations between Zulu grandmothers and granddaughters/ sons"(Moller and Sotshangaye, 1999).

Changes to the education system, and the implementation of outcomes-based education as a national policy in schools, have meant that there is a far greater emphasis on community involvement and participation in classroom teaching. This has meant that in all South African schools, whether predominantly black or white or mixed, people of the older generation are being encouraged to participate. They are given the opportunity to share their expertise, knowledge and experience, especially because "life skills" is one of the key learning areas. This practice also provides the opportunity for improved race relations and understanding, as older people share their culture and history through story telling, and pupils receive assignments for obtaining oral histories from older members of other races.

A prominent economic advisor to the president of South Africa has attributed skyrocketing unemployment to problems with the country's education system and said that it needs to be transformed by introducing skills-related schemes. If this change is implemented, it will mean a greater demand for skilled people from the community to participate in school curricula, and those most likely to have the time and means to do so will be the older generation.

Also playing an important role in drawing more older people into classrooms is the fact that class sizes are very big and teachers need assistance in order to function effectively. The older people play a useful role in working with one group — helping to listen to children's reading, for example — while the teacher is busy with another. This is a need in all schools, across the board. Fulfilling it this way can also contribute to improving race relations through providing positive role models of other races and banishing racial stereotypes.

Retirement and volunteerism

Although the official retirement age for men is 65 years and for women 60 years, many white South African men and women who are still of an economically active age have been given an early retirement. This practice developed because of the need (particularly in government and parastatal services) to create opportunities for previously disadvantaged population groups to be employed. This in effect means that a lot of spare capacity has been created in the 50 to 60 year age group, many of whom are highly skilled. This capacity and skills base could be harnessed to benefit children and the younger generation. Factors in favor of such a development are the reasonably strong culture of volunteerism and positive attitudes toward volunteer work in retirement which exists amongst white South Africans, as well as the fact that these persons have the means to get involved in intergenerational programs without needing to be financially compensated.

The picture is somewhat different among the black African population. First, most black African men and women who are economically active remain so for as long as possible, as this provides the financial support for what is in most cases an extended family. Also, they would not be the ones to be offered early retirement on the scale mentioned above. These family and cost-of-living commitments, coupled with often long years of hard physical labor, mitigate against a large-scale involvement in voluntary activities during retirement. Volunteering is in many ways a luxury for those who have the time and financial means that free them from constant concern with matters of survival. Initiatives are needed that can tap into this resource and create easy avenues for voluntary involvement with youth.

Trends in Intergenerational Relations

The effects of urbanization, modernization and Westernization on black African intergenerational relations have been considerable and multi-dimensional. A look at some of these effects highlights the following:

Declining importance of traditional knowledge

In urban areas, older people are not the source of authority they used to be, as there is less need for, and therefore less value attached to, traditional knowledge and skills. A different set of skills and knowledge is required for survival in an urban setting, and older people are not familiar with these, which means that their traditional roles as teachers and advisors are less appropriate and less valued. Many older women feel they are open to ridicule and abuse, and in extreme cases may even be branded as witches, if they convey knowledge that is not popular. The diminished sense of communal living in the urban context means there is less of an inclusive definition of elders to whom respect is due, which in turn means less helping behavior by youth and a wariness on the part of older people to offer advice to unknown youth.

Also, in urban areas it is more likely that at least one parent will be present and that it will be the parent's home, making the grandparent's role more superfluous. In rural areas, the parents are often absent, in cities or elsewhere in order to work, and the grandparent is the ruling head of household.

Television

The new generation of young South Africans is extensively exposed to television and has adopted many Western ideals through this medium.

South Africa has belatedly created a "me" generation that is more concerned with individualistic goals than were their parents' and grandparents' generations. Individualism contradicts many values of black African society which traditionally is collectivist and based on kinship support systems (Triandis, 1995). Television could be used to positive advantage if campaigns were created that covered intergenerational relations and awareness was raised regarding the contribution that older people can make to society.

Political values

To a certain extent South Africans' new-found political freedom after the 1994 elections also brought its own problems. There was a great emphasis on rights in the struggle for freedom, and less emphasis on responsibilities, which combined with the new individualistic culture to undermine intergenerational relations further. Ramphele argues that the role of children and youth in resisting apartheid in 1976 and after undermined traditional relations between children and parents/grandparents. Ramphele reflects a widely-held view that the political activist role of many young people led to a reversal of power relations between the generations in the late 1970s and 1980s, with the result that "children became used to power and control, and refused to yield to the authority of adults whom they despised for doing nothing — their parents and teachers" (Ramphele, 1992).

The end of apartheid created many expectations — economic prosperity, jobs, and housing for all — that have not been delivered, and this has led to a high degree of frustration. In many instances it is now this economic reality that is in conflict with the values of *ubuntu* and the African Renaissance.

Promoting *ubuntu*

President Thabo Mbeki has committed South Africa to the idea of an African renaissance, which, it is hoped, will inspire a sense of pride and confidence in the people of Africa. The supposition put forward here is that the African renaissance may strengthen the cultural values that promote strong families. In line with the sentiment of African renewal, the post-election era has generated a revival of *ubuntu*, the African concept of sharing and caring (i.e., "we are who we are because of others"). Mutual respect between the generations is a fundamental expression of *ubuntu*.

As *ubuntu* is the principal incentive to practice harmony in the multigenerational family, it is especially important for the younger generation to acknowledge the value of elders. A study of youth in the Gauteng Province indicated that both rural and urbanized youth accept *ubuntu* as an important value in their lives (Bureau of Market Research, 1995). Also, in a national study on intergenerational attitudes among South African youth undertaken in 1994, the conclusion was that young people value the family as an institution and, black Africans especially value the extended family (Everatt & Orkin, 1994). However, even though there has not been large-scale rejection of parental and family values by young people in South Africa, there have still been a number of pressures, some of which are described above, that have led to changes in the dynamics of family life and intergenerational living, especially in cities. It appears that work needs to be done on an intergenerational basis, within the desired framework of extended families, to help older people understand and adapt to modern trends, while encouraging young people to maintain respect for elders.

Specific Intergenerational Initiatives

Many of the aspects of intergenerational programs in South Africa are inextricably bound to the collectivist nature of African society, the adherence to extended family values, and the large number of multi-generation households. For this reason, a number of intergenerational programs in the country happen co-incidentally, as part of other training and support programs, rather than by particular design.

However, there are sectors where non-familial intergenerational programs are starting to happen and they are being promoted quite actively, especially through the well-developed NGO (non-governmental organization) sector and bodies such as the South African Council for the Aged and its regional affiliates. Since 1970 the official policy of the South African Council for the Aged has been to promote intergenerational contact for mutual benefit. The Council has encouraged young people in church youth groups, schools, community clubs, etc., to become involved with the old people in their communities. Similarly, where possible the Council has promoted the use of older people in initiatives that can benefit by their time, skills and input. By the same token, most youth projects, especially those on national scale, incorporate service to the elderly as part of their activities.

The South African government gave the International Year of the Older Person its full support and launched Operation Respect, an initiative designed to use schools and the media to encourage and restore respect for the older people in society and the role that they can play. This initiative has been enhanced by the role that ex-president Nelson Mandela has played and the respect that he commands as an octogenarian. However, it does not seem to have been a high-profile campaign, and evidence of its efficacy is lacking. It seems a mass media campaign and better use of television is still needed.

When examining the specific initiatives described below, links can easily be made to the socio-economic factors outlined earlier in the chapter.

246 Linking Lifetimes: A Global View of Intergenerational Exchange

Research initiatives

Issues around aging and intergenerational relations are being re-searched by several institutions, including the Community Agency for Social Enquiry. The Centre for Gerontology at the University of Cape Town is studying oral histories, accounts by older people about how they are being treated or abused in urban settings and squatter camps, and doing research and advocacy for the inclusion of age issues into teaching curricula, etc. The Institute for Social and Economic Research at Rhodes University is doing a comprehensive youth study and research-ing the practice of and attitudes toward extended families. The Human Sciences Research Council, which is the country's main government-funded research body in the Human Sciences, has a Cooperative Re-search Program on Aging. Issues and older persons are being looked at by sociologists, but gerontology is not a formal component of any tertiary training, which means there are opportunities for developing and promoting curricula that would focus on intergenerational pro-grams at this level.

The field of Geragogy, i.e., the theories of education for older people, is poorly defined and is not at this stage an active part of any tertiary curricula. However, the concept of lifelong learning is one that is being actively researched and promoted in South Africa by universi-ties, NGO's and the government's Directorate of Adult Education. This will in effect probably have a greater impact in terms of intergen-erational learning. Most South African universities have a center for adult and/or continuing education, or a division for lifelong learning that does research into the recognition of prior learning and issues of greater access for learners of all ages to tertiary institutions, etc. All of this points to the developing of institutions that cater to learners of all ages. Creating greater access to universities for older people will necessitate research into the dynamics of intergenerational relations on campus and in the teaching situation.

Family initiatives: Grandparents raising grandchildren

The first section of this chapter referred to some of the implications of the AIDS epidemic for South Africa. A number of initiatives, both from governmental and non-governmental sectors, have begun to address the issue. There are instances where women's organizations have made use of older women to communicate with young women about moral and family values, the implications of AIDS, etc. However, some research has shown that intergenerational contact is less successful than peer educa-tion on the latter issue.

The National Department of Welfare and Population Development re-cently funded a researcher from the University of Pietermaritzburg to con-duct an in-depth survey on intergenerational responses to AIDS and

AIDS-related responsibilities. The title of the report is a Zulu phrase that means, "It is destroying the children."

The South African Council for the Aged has launched a program that trains and prepares older people for the implications of AIDS and more specifically for their renewed role as surrogate parents. This involves, for instance, bringing them up to date on computers and information technology, making them literate, etc., so that they may be equipped to care for, guide and command respect from the young children who become their responsibility when their parents die of AIDS. However, indications are that a lot more work needs to be done in this area. Many communities are still in denial and will cover up a death from AIDS, as it brings shame to the family, rather than plan for its consequences.

Education initiatives

With regard to school-based projects, several intergenerational initiatives are latching on to the trend of valuing and utilizing the contribution that older people can make to the education process. (Mention was made earlier of how senior adults are utilized in classrooms to assist teachers.) An NGO called READ (Read, Educate and Develop) provides support services to disadvantaged schools in the area of book stock, library facilities, reading campaigns, teacher education, etc. This organization specifically advocates and encourages the use of grandparents and other older people in the community in visiting classrooms to talk about life in the past or to tell traditional stories.

The issue of family literacy, and how reading about cultures and cultural practices in families affects children's performances at school, is a study being undertaken by the Family Literacy Unit of the University of South Africa.

The developers of a new curriculum for a distance education teachers training course, based in the Eastern Cape, have built intergenerational work into the course. The training material incorporates ways in which teachers should get their pupils to obtain information from older people in their community or at home, on a specific topic, and bring it back to the classroom for discussion and further work.

A project on the East Rand has older people making educational toys and other items that help children learn. This is a church-based initiative, and in South Africa a number of progressive churches strive quite specifically to bring older and younger cohorts together.

Another of the READ projects encourages school children to read to elderly members of the community, something that not only strengthens intergenerational bonds, but is also very useful to the many black African adults who are still illiterate. The Minister of Education has launched a National Mass Literacy Campaign, and it is hoped that an intergenerational element will form part of this.

Seniors as childcare workers

In a number of instances, old people at service centers are in fact providing a service to young children; i.e., helping to look after them, supervising the homework of children of working parents after school. In other instances, the SA Council for the Aged has taken over the management of creches (child-minding centers) from the Child Welfare Society and often utilize the expertise of older members to assist in this process.

Mention was made earlier of the major role that many grandmothers and older women play in the "educare" (a word coined to indicate both education and care) of young children under the age of six. A number of NGO's are involved in training these women in the basic elements of good childcare and early education, and the level of training is usually geared to the capabilities of the women. Often they are also supported with home visits and donations of food, equipment, etc. Where possible, if they have successfully completed a certain level of training, the training organization will arrange for them to be accredited in accordance with one of the levels of the National Qualifications Framework.

While most of these educare programs have developed around familial responsibilities, there are instances where projects were structured more deliberately to create a role for seniors in educare. One such example, in the late 1980s, was the utilization of an old-age home in a township in KwaZulu-Natal as a vehicle for providing an educare service for the young children in their community. The committee overseeing the old age home launched a project whereby in-service training was given to grandmothers and other child minders in the surrounding community who care for a small number of preschool children at home. Where necessary, space in the old-age home was used for training purposes, and an eventual aim was to build a creche on the premises.

The feasibility study for the program covered broader issues of concern than reactions to educare. The educare concept was used as a vehicle to further explore topics relating to the social development of the very young and seniors. These included attitudes toward institutional care of the aged in general and perceptions of the role of the elderly in urban black society. A focal interest was the conflict situation arising from the need to care for different generations in a society in transition. The process is fully documented in "A role for black seniors in educare: a community assessment" and forms part of a publication series by the HSRC's Co-operative Research Program on Aging (Moller, 1990).

Age-integrated centers

The South African government is moving increasingly towards multipurpose centers, i.e. centers where old people can be serviced with health care, pension pay-outs, entertainment, etc. but also where they in turn can interact with and provide a service to children. Such centers are obviously important especially where older people are not living with children or where young people do not have the opportunity of daily contact with elders. For many older people, this is in fact quite a satisfactory arrangement as, having a desire for peace and quiet, they do not wish to live with families and young children, but at the same time would still like to make a contribution. In two of the country's provinces, models are being developed, through pilot projects, whereby a children's' home and an old age home are put together on the same site, and contact between the two groups takes place on a daily basis, for mutual benefit.

Resurgence of a sense of cultural identity and respect

The role of telling traditional stories and aiding the continuance of a culture is an important one for older people, and it is also seen as such by young people. In a study done in 1995-96, members of a granddaughter generation made specific mention of the role of grandmothers as storytellers. The reciters of myths, folk tales and legends play an important role in the transmission of values in a society that has a strong oral tradition. As one grandchild told the researchers, the stories are like history lessons in that they make a moral point that has relevance for contemporary times (Moller & Sotshangaye, 1999).

Obtaining oral histories and capturing them is an important focus for African intergenerational work, for a number of reasons. Not only does it promote cultural continuity, but also it ensures that important parts of people's history are not lost. It also promotes respect for older people, as the young people who are interviewing them come to realize what the older people have experienced and survived. This is particularly important in certain areas, especially urban settings, where respect for old people is waning and they are not the source of authority that they used to be when their skills and input were necessary for everyday living. Setting young people the task of obtaining oral histories across the race divide, as well as the age divide, will contribute to greater understanding and tolerance in both areas.

There are a few oral history projects in the country. The Centre for Gerontology in Cape Town is currently engaged in a project of this nature, where the focus is especially on the political histories of older people and their role during the apartheid years.

Youth projects

While many intergenerational initiatives seem to originate from those groups and organizations looking after the interests of older people, there is also evidence that youth projects are encouraging young people to serve the needs of older people on a voluntary basis. Some of this happens through schools and colleges, where visitation, garden upkeep, doing errands, etc., is arranged. In other instances they are community or church-based initiatives. Examples of this are the serving of lunches at Lunch Clubs for seniors and interaction with seniors at community service centers for older people.

The President's Award is a national youth project that involves more than 5000 young people around South Africa. Participating at various levels in the award program are many young offenders in correctional facilities around the country. There are four sections of the program, and one of these is community service. Included in this community service section is a strong element of service to the elderly.

Similarly, a large private company launched the "Youth for SA" awards in 1999 in order to encourage young people between four and 19 years to contribute to the uplifting of their communities through diligent and self-less volunteer work. Examples of programs eligible for these awards include anti drug-abuse programs, food aid, environmental programs, and holiday schemes for the elderly and disabled.

Conclusion

Many of the intergenerational initiatives in South Africa—for example the multi-purpose centers and the projects generated by concerns about AIDS, are still in the early stages and their effectiveness cannot yet be comprehensively or conclusively measured. There is a need for these and other examples of intergenerational initiatives to be evaluated and documented, so that more awareness is created and the field of intergenerational work can gain recognition and credibility as one that contributes positively to societal development.

Intergenerational programs can help South Africa deal with some of its most pressing needs such as the AIDS pandemic, teenage sexuality, etc., and can play a role in promoting racial understanding and harmony. The challenge lies in creating widespread awareness of intergenerational programs and approaches as a tool for social change. Intergenerational solutions need to become part of the mindset of policymakers (at the highest level), advisors, service providers, social scientists and non-governmental organizational leaders.

The challenge is also to create a framework and mechanisms that will facilitate the institutionalizing of intergenerational approaches within youth and aging networks: to formalize and provide an intellectual framework for what is already happening on the ground in a spontaneous way. Intergenerational approaches to problem solving need to be included in academic curricula of relevant courses at tertiary institutions.

In general, it can be said that while intergenerational programs still do not have a high profile in South Africa, there is ongoing research into intergenerational relations and an increasing move towards intergenerational programs and a learning society which includes all ages. As is clear from the description of the socio-economic and demographic situation, there are a number of areas that hold great potential for intergenerational programs.

References

Bureau of Market Research. (1995). *Aspirations, values and marketing issues among Black youth in Gauteng.* Research Report No. 223. University of South Africa, Pretoria.

Central Statistical Services. (1996). *Living in South Africa. Selected findings of the 1995 October Household Survey.* Pretoria.

Everatt, D. & Orkin, M. (1994). "Families should stay together: Intergenerational attitudes among South African youth." *Southern African Journal of Gerontology,* 3(2), 43-48.

Kinsella, K. & Ferreira, M. (1997). *Aging trends: South Africa* (International Brief (IB/97-2)). Washington, D.C.: U.S. Bureau of the Census.

Mail & Guardian. (2000). Urban Futures 2000 Supplement, July 7 – 13.

Moller, V. (1990). A role for black seniors in educare: a community assessment. Pretoria: Co-operative Research Program on Ageing, Human Sciences Research Council.

Moller, V. (1998). Innovations to promote an intergenerational society for South Africa to promote the well-being of the black African elderly. *Society in transition,* 29, 1-12.

Moller, V. & Sotshangaye, A. (1999). "They don't listen": contemporary respect relations between Zulu grandmothers and granddaughters/sons. *Southern African Journal of Gerontology,* 8(2), 18-27.

Myslik, W.D., Freeman, A. & Slawski, J. (1997). Implications of AIDS for the South African population age profile. *Southern African Journal of Gerontology,* 6(2), 3-8.

Ramphele, M. (1992). Social disintegration in the black community: implications for social transformation. In: Everatt, D. & Sisulu, E. (Eds.) *Black youth in crisis: facing the future.* Johannesburg: Ravan Press, 10-29.

South African Institute for Race Relations. (1998). *South African survey 1997/8.* Johannesburg.

Ziehl, S.(1999). *Families — A South African perspective.* Grahamstown: Rhodes University, Sociology Department.

Organizing at the National Level: Lessons from the U.S.A. and Japan

By Donna M. Butts and Atsuko T. Kusano

Introduction

To move the intergenerational agenda forward in any country requires more than great ideas and committed people. It also requires organization. At some point, individual intergenerational activists need to share information (about failures as well as successes), coordinate efforts to build visibility and market the intergenerational concept, and work together to influence funding policies and program development priorities. By examining some of the challenges and successes of organizers in the United States and Japan, this article will highlight several principles for effective organizing at the national level.

The United States: Generations United

Coalition: the early years

In the early 1980s, conservative forces in the United States sought to drive a wedge between age-based advocacy groups and stratify the generations. "Kids versus canes," "Greedy Geezers," and other sensational headlines were topped only by a journal that published a photograph of a young person and an old person standing back to back dressed in battle fatigues, holding guns ready to walk twenty paces, turn and shoot. The survivor would win which, in this case, translated to "winning" government benefits. Clearly, the photograph shouted, no other options existed. In 1986, tired of the rhetoric of growing intergenerational warfare, the leading children, youth and senior groups came together and established Generations United (GU), which to this day continues as the umbrella for the country's growing intergenerational interest and effort. GU's mission is to foster intergenerational collaboration on public policy and programs to improve the lives of children, youth and the elderly. A board of 20 national leaders from the non-governmental and corporate arenas governs and guides the work of GU. Its membership is comprised of hundreds of organizations and individuals, from the United States and other countries, who share a vision of a world that values all generations.

GU has been a catalyst to help to create or encourage state and local intergenerational networks and coalitions. Basically the **networks** began as conduits for groups to share information and explore the potential for collaborative programs. These groups would meet on a regular basis, generally quarterly or bimonthly, and some offered an annual statewide conference and newsletter. A few had special interest sub-committees or working groups to address particular areas such as legislative concerns.

The **coalitions** on the other hand, generally developed with the specific purpose of advocating in the public policy arena. They were created to monitor state legislative activity using an intergenerational lens. Their efforts were primarily reactive; however, some have sought to be proactive. For example, coalitions in two states have tried to get legislation passed that would provide tax breaks for seniors involved in intergenerational service. Recently groups in several states have been concentrating almost exclusively on the issue of grandparents and other relatives raising children. This growing issue is breathing new life into their work.

One of the important values of a national coalition or network is strength in numbers. It provides a working national mechanism to ensure civil relations and reciprocity between the generations. For example, as a national coalition GU will write letters to policy makers about specific legislation. In recent years, punitive juvenile justice legislation was introduced in Congress. The usual youth advocacy groups lobbied against many aspects including one provision that would have locked young people up with adults in adult correctional facilities. GU sent a letter signed by its national youth group members as well as by its national senior group members who normally would not have voiced an opinion about youth legislation. Through the coalition, the senior groups added strength to what some would have said was a single-age issue. Instead GU recommended additional funding for prevention programs that included intergenerational approaches and stated that locking kids and adults up together was not an appropriate idea.

Over the years, GU has found that to succeed, the members of the network or coalition need to see the value in the national organization and understand the relevance to their individual agendas and missions. Members must have a shared vision and be able to clearly articulate the purpose of the group. They must be involved in determining its direction, capable of compromising, and able to provide resources or generate capital to support the work. Key constituency groups must be identified and recruited early; however, reaching out to new groups is a continuous process to maintain membership numbers.

There are also times when GU does not function as an independent coalition, but rather as an informal mentor to other groups. At such times, GU is in the background offering key support and guidance, stimulating the thinking of other organizations to include intergenerational approaches. This is a "barnacle" approach: a barnacle attaches itself to something that already exists and makes its presence known. For example, in America teenage pregnancy is an issue. While overall numbers of teen pregnancies are declining, the United States still has the highest rate of any industrialized country. Some cities and states have established pregnancy prevention programs. Others have seen teen pregnancy as a broader issue and worked with existing groups that may be focused on economic development, school retention, youth employment, and so on. By working locally with such informal coalitions, GU has helped bring the issue of teen pregnancy prevention to the consciousness of whole communities and infuse in it all of the community's priorities.

Incorporation

The road has not always been smooth. GU has struggled over the years to mesh the priorities of individual organizations while seeking to keep a balance between the voices of different generations. Yet, in the last decade of the 20th century, after 10 years as an informal coalition, GU experienced a major break through in its development. Confronted with lagging interest and a sense that GU had grown as much as it could as a loose-knit coalition, the founders decided it was time to incorporate and begin a new phase as an independent not-for-profit organization. The transition has exceeded everyone's expectations. While there were several factors that converged, key elements to GU's success included:

- Expanding the board to include the executive directors or chief operating officers of the leading national children, youth and senior organizations and of corporations that have a critical stake in the well being of these age groups. The co-founders targeted the top decision-makers rather than simply recruiting an organizational representative. This signaled a strong endorsement and provided the new organization credibility.

With the popularization of concepts such as "productive aging" and "lifelong learning," the specter of "retirement" in Japan is not as dreadful as it used to be. Contributing to this re-conceptualization of retirement are the efforts of organizations like the Global Life Learning Center which aim to make people aware of aspects of life besides work, such as the joy of hobbies, opportunities to experience nature, the value of "life learning" skills, and the satisfaction of volunteering to help young people in schools and in other settings.

It is also noteworthy that in the early 1990s, funding to conduct a major survey of intergenerational programs and activities in Japan was provided through one of the agencies of the Prime Minister's Office, i.e., the Office for Senior Citizens ("Rojin Taisaku Shitsu") which is part of the Management and Coordination Agency ("Somucho") (Aging Integrated Research Center, 1994). However, such interest at the national level, and the excitement displayed in regard to intergenerational initiatives at the local level, have not translated into energetic leadership and commitment on the part of government agencies, non-profit organizations, or the private sector.

Despite the growing body of intergenerational program initiatives in Japan, those who are working in this area have difficulties connecting with each other. In the United States, one can speak of an intergenerational "field" which provides a unifying focus and overarching theoretical framework for linking all types of intergenerational initiatives — whether they are in educational, recreational, or human service settings — as long as they serve to promote sharing of skills, knowledge, or experience across ages. This is apparent, for example, in the multidisciplinary nature of national conference presentations and publications. In Japan, such an overarching theoretical framework seems to be absent. Intergenerational activities occurring in different types of settings and in response to different human service needs are typically viewed as being distinctly separate, conceptually unrelated initiatives.

Also, the interagency and cross-disciplinary collaborative arrangements that typify many American intergenerational initiatives and coalition-building efforts are not as readily found in Japan. In the words of one high-level national agency representative who, during an interview aimed at determining his views about intergenerational work, voiced skepticism about getting different agencies to cooperate: "Which agency would be responsible?" he asked. A similar spirit of hesitancy detectable in other national agency administrators suggests why there has been no support for the organizing-type of activity found in the United States, e.g., intergenerational conferences, forums, interagency meetings, research reports, coalition-building efforts, and other information and resource exchange mechanisms.[5]

Small beginnings

However, the seeds of a national intergenerational network in Japan do seem, now, to be taking root. Working under the umbrella title of "Japan Intergenerational Network," a group of academics, prefectural agency administrators, and activists in Nagano Prefecture in Japan have begun to organize an array of meetings for professionals and the public to establish networking mechanisms to connect intergenerational advocates in the region and develop educational resources. Shinshu University in Nagano City (home of the 1999 Winter Olympics) has been offering courses and organizing conferences and various intergenerational demonstration projects. The series of seminars and conferences organized locally, all of which are open to the public, include an ongoing weekly seminar held at Shinshu University, special symposia organized around talks given by visiting intergenerational specialists (e.g., Dr. Nancy Henkin from Temple University spoke twice), and special meetings held at other universities (e.g., Konan University Ashiya).

The strategy is one of working first at the local level, expanding to the regional level, and then expanding nation-wide. This clearly "bottom-up" approach[6] does seem to be working. At each level, circles of participating organizations are expanding as groups work together to promote inter-generational exchange.

Intercultural focus

One course at Shinshu University, "Integrated Seminar on Intergen-erational Exchange," conducted by author Kusano, emphasizes intercul-tural exchange as well as intergenerational exchange; foreigners living around Nagano City are actively encouraged to participate. The promo-tion of intercultural as well as intergenerational understanding repre-sents a distinctive characteristic of the organizing strategy.

For example, one of the events that has galvanized local interest and participation is the "International Intergenerational Potluck Party" orga-nized each spring and fall. About 100 people join in, each bringing a dish of American, British, Chinese, Philippine, Malaysian, Ecuadorian, and Japanese cuisine. The international participants include students, AETs (Assistant English Teachers in high schools), teachers in English schools, people who work for religious organizations, and business people. The spring 2001 event included 17 visiting students from University of Utah. Other intergenerational activities with an international thrust include having local Japanese older adults teach foreign students how to dress with Kimono, Obi and Hakama (Japanese culottes).[7] As part of this and other activities, students listen, record, and write about eld-erly persons' life histories.

National organization

One of the vital next steps in the evolution of a national Japan Intergenerational Network is to organize a national conference designed to meet several objectives:

- Publicize and provide recognition of successful intergenerational initiatives.
- Promote information exchange about program planning, implementation, and evaluation strategies and issues.
- Help to establish some of the conceptual and organizational platforms for bringing together a wide range of social scientists, educators, social policy analysts and administrators, and community activists.
- Provide intergenerational specialists with a needed sense of fellowship and unity.

Such a conference can lead to a variety of collaborative endeavors that might serve to further stimulate new demonstration projects, research studies, and efforts to replicate successful intergenerational program models. Furthermore, as Generations United's first conference in 1988 launched its entry into the public domain in the United States, a nation-wide conference would do the same for a Japan Intergenerational Network.

Other plans for the Japan Intergenerational Network include:

- Publishing a newsletter (in Japanese and English).
- Opening a main office with a professional staff.
- Establishing national and international ties to exchange information on successful intergenerational models.
- Maintaining a database on local and national programs.

Conclusion

This is a very exciting time for proponents of intergenerational approaches. Heightened awareness of changing demographics world wide, along with a deepening understanding of our youngest and oldest age groups as assets, is causing new sectors to consider intergenerational strategies. Business leaders and politicians are beginning to understand the importance of the growing resource found in our aging populations. At the same time young people are being viewed as a vibrant new resource. Together the combination is unstoppable. The role of a national intergenerational organization is to help make these combinations happen.

The details of organizing at the national level in the United States and in Japan represent contrasting approaches, yet in terms of vision and agenda, there are striking similarities.

A national coalition provides the forum and the infrastructure for national leaders to together identify priorities and then begin to develop partnerships among their local affiliates. When effective, we see how organizing nationally can play an important role in addressing social exclusion and helping to give a face to populations that have been ignored in the past.

References

Aging Integrated Research Center (Eijingu Sougou Kenkyu Senta) (1994). *Sedaikan koryu ni kansuru chosa kenkyu hokokusho* [Research report on intergenerational exchange], (Research sponsored by the Management and Coordination Agency). Tokyo: Aging Integrated Research Center.

Kaplan, M., Kusano, A., Tsuji, I., & Hisamichi, S. (1998). *Intergenerational programs: Support for children, youth and elders in Japan.* N.Y.: State University of New York Press.

Ministry of Health and Welfare (2000). Annual Report on Health and Welfare 1998-1999: Social Security and National Life. Tokyo: Japan International Corporation of Welfare Services.

Notes

1 The number of elderly people has continued to increase while that of children born has been on a declining trend in Japan since 1950. The total fertility rate (sum of the live birth rates by age for women aged 15 to 49) in 1997 was 1.39, which is far below the level necessary for maintaining the present population (Ministry of Health and Welfare,2000, p.229).

2 The average number of household members decreased from 4.97 in 1955 to 3.06 in 1990.

3 The number of consultation cases accepted at child guidance centers, which stood at 1,101 in fiscal 1990, increased to 5,352 in fiscal 1997.

4 It is not clear, however, the extent to which decisions to develop joint youth-elder service facilities are made on the basis of considerations of the benefits of enhanced intergenerational exposure. There are some examples of such decisions being made solely on the basis of economic considerations and shortage of space in urban areas.

5 The Somuchou (Administrative Affairs in the Prime Minister's Office), which belongs to the Naikakufu (Seat of Cabinet) from the beginning of this year, talked about the importance of intergenerational exchange in connection with references to the U.N. International Year of Older persons, but not so much has been mentioned after that.

6 This approach for working locally and growing to the national level is consistent with the approach taken in the Netherlands, as described by intergenerational specialists who participated in the first International Conference on Intergenerational Programs, held in Vaals, the Netherlands, October 1999. (This international conference will be described in detail in the next article.)

7 Hakama is a skirt-like formal piece of clothing usually worn at ceremonies. Female high school students used to wear hakama to go to school, and men and male students wore them as well, particularly to formal tea ceremonies.

Creating an "International Consortium for Intergenerational Programs"

By Sally Newman, Ph.D.

Introduction

Throughout the world, in countries with many differing economic and political infrastructures, there are common challenges: changing social structures, shifting roles within families, and the differing needs of generations represent some of these challenges. Of particular interest to the intergenerational field in this time of change is the dramatic and rapidly altering roles of older adults and children in many countries of the world. Examples of these changes include:

- In Japan, the historically revered role of elders in the family is changing as young families move to the cities leaving elders behind. Geographic separation is creating new and less favorable perceptions of the role of "the elders" in Japan's families.
- In China, the one-child-per-family law has shifted the balance of old and young in the families, a phenomenon that will result in increased responsibility of the young for their aging grandparents and a new role for the family's older members as China's "intelligence banks" that establish opportunities for the elderly to serve as a resource to the community.
- In South Africa, the high rate of teenage pregnancy among Black South Africans and high divorce rate among white South Africans

has resulted in an increase in single parenthood and a new role for elderly (black and white) as caregivers for the young.

- In the Netherlands, immigration of Turkish and Moroccan nuclear families without older adult role models has prompted the Dutch to systematically involve Dutch older adults as role models, tutors, and friends to immigrant youth who also provide companionship and home help to Dutch older adults.
- In the United Kingdom, the traditional practice of apprenticeship in which the young learned from the old has virtually disappeared. A growing number of U.K. elders are needed as role models and mentors for youth as part of a new social policy initiative to reintegrate communities whose social structures have been weakened through the erosion of traditional extended families.
- In the United States, the existence of large numbers of well, high-functioning, independent older adults, many separated from their biological families, has resulted in the creation of new roles for the elderly as non-biological caregivers for thousands of children and youth who lack adequate positive older adult role models. Similarly the existence of a growing number of low-functioning, dependent, and often isolated older adults has resulted in the creation of new roles for the young as support persons for this population of elders.

The social phenomenon of "intergenerational programs" that has emerged as a result of these changing roles, addresses the needs of the young and old and supports the creation of new and positive roles for children, youth and older adults in their families and within their communities. Though there are significant differences throughout the world in the structure of families and communities, and in the place of the young and old in these structures, it appears that social conditions associated with being old and young contribute to a global readiness for this new social phenomenon.

Many within these age cohorts experience conditions of isolation, disconnection, unemployment, violence, illiteracy, stigmatization, and ostracism. From the streets of New York City to the shanty towns of South Africa, many young children and older adults must endure social conditions that have a negative impact on their lives. A global social malaise seems evident in countries both developed and underdeveloped, nations both industrial and agricultural, that particularly affects the young and old.

In April 1999, in response to perceptions of this malaise, a group of human service leaders representing UNESCO, Europe, Asia, Africa, and North America gathered at Haus Bommerholz, of the University of Dortmund, Germany, to discuss intergenerational solutions to some of the universal issues and problems affecting the two generations at the opposite end of the human continuum. Their discussion led to the organization, in Vaals, of the First International Conference on Intergenerational Programs to Promote Social Change. Participants in both the Haus Bommerholz Working Meeting and the Vaals Conference acknowledged the importance of creating a formal organization that would give universal credibility to international intergenerational initiatives. Such an organization would provide both a framework for communication about diverse intergenerational initiatives and an impetus for the generation of such initiatives. This consensus was the genesis of the "International Consortium for Intergenerational Programs," an intergenerational organization designed to promote intergenerational programs and practices as agents for global social change.

Haus Bommerholz Working Meeting

From 10 countries, 25 persons came together at Haus Bommerholz, University of Dortmund, Germany for three days to address both philosophical and practical questions related to intergenerational programs as a concept and as a realistic solution to some issues confronting their young and old. The group faced two basic challenges: Could a group of strangers from different nations, cultures and political systems reach consensus on a process to promote social change? And if they could, what strategies were needed to form a partnership that could effectively use intergenerational concepts and programs to achieve the desired social change? In addressing these two basic challenges, the group considered the following questions:

- Could intergenerational programs become a universal vehicle to transcend cultural, economic, and political differences in an effort to improve the lives of young and old globally?
- Could a universal definition of intergenerational programs be developed?
- What social questions or conditions can intergenerational programs address?
- Was there a shared vision and common goals within this diverse group?
- Could members of an international group leave their national identities at the door and focus on universal needs of children, youth and older adults?
- What are some examples of current intergenerational programs, projects and experiences?
- What are characteristic measures of success of intergenerational programs?
- What are some strategies to enhance success?

- Could a strategy for international intergenerational cooperation be developed?

The host in Bommerholz, Ludger Veelken of Dortmund University, and planning team member Sally Newman of the University of Pittsburgh, led the group in a three-day process that helped the group reach consensus on these questions.

The first task was to discuss the theory and rationale for intergenerational programs and to develop a global definition that would reflect common values, extend beyond national boundaries, and function as the basis for further communication and exchange. From this discussion emerged a global mission statement able to accommodate nations with diverse needs, cultures, and social structures:

> *Intergenerational programs are social vehicles that create purposeful and ongoing exchange of resources and learning among older and younger generations.*

The discussion also generated consensus on common indicators of successful intergenerational programs:

- They demonstrate mutual benefits for participants.
- They establish new social roles and/or new perspectives for older and younger generations.
- They enhance the self-esteem and self-worth of both generations.
- They address social issues and policies relevant to the participating generations.
- They include the elements of good program planning and evaluation.

Universal social issues

In examining the elements common to the participating countries, the attendees observed several shared social issues that, irrespective of differences in language, culture or level of infrastructure, might be effectively addressed by intergenerational initiatives. The following issues—disconnection and isolation, adequate employment opportunities, literacy, and a livable environment—were common to several countries. Some of these issues are evident within the United States, Japan, and the UK, and relate to their nationals, while in Central Europe these same issues relate to immigrants who are becoming integrated into the culture of their new country.

Issues of disconnection and isolation of the young and old from mainstream society seem to be the result of several factors:

- Ageist structure inherent within services and housing patterns.
- Growing geographic separation of older and younger family members.

- Disruptions in families due to the loss of family members.
- Strained family life due to economic and political changes.
- Political upheavals.

Employment opportunities for both older adults and teens were reported as a significant problem in several countries. Though the need for job opportunities for teens is universal, the European countries reported adequate support for their older adults while representatives of other nations (South Africa, Japan, and the United States) identified a need for employment opportunities for their aging population, especially for those who may not have adequate retirement benefits.

A third issue of universal concern is literacy, including both basic literacy skills and literacy in new technologies. Skills in these areas are essential for citizens to function effectively within their countries. Though expectations related to basic literacy and technology may differ, the participants recognized that many of the young and the old in their countries lacked sufficient skills in these areas to become fully participating citizens. The European countries, the United States and Canada highlighted the need for literacy and technology skills both for nationals and for the growing number of immigrants who have fled their homelands and are seeking a new life and future in these countries. The nationals in these countries need expanded computer literacy for both young and old if these populations are to access workplace opportunities and to continue as members of mainstream society. For immigrant populations to survive and succeed in an adopted country, the ability to understand the written and spoken language and the ability to communicate in the new language are essential skills.

Representatives from South Africa, China and Cuba addressed the need in these countries for basic literacy skills among the peasant and working class populations as their nations move into expanded industrial enterprises, and the need for technology skills among a newly emerging class of industrial managers and professionals.

The final issue that resonated across countries was the environment as a social condition that often has negative impact on the young and old. In developing countries environmental concerns are related to overcrowding, air and water pollution as well as litter and garbage that is often present in the over-populated and impoverished communities in which numbers of old and young live. In the more industrialized nations, the environment is being threatened by over-development, and expanded recreation activities are usurping national resources (water, oil, forests, and gas) in rural areas that often house significant numbers of older adults and families with young children.

The discussions of these social issues validated and reinforced awareness that a number of social issues are common to all nations and emphasized the need for all nations to work together for global intergenerational solutions to these issues.

Intergenerational projects and experiences

As the representatives of participating nations presented examples of intergenerational programs that exist in each of their countries, it was evident that, although the models described differed in size, type, number of participants, activities, longevity and management, the basic design components and long-term goals were consistent. The models were represented by three basic program types:

- •Programs in which older adults were caring for or serving the young.
- •Programs in which the youth were caring for or serving older adults.
- •Programs in which both youth and older adults joined together in serving others in the community.

The program goals, universally implicit, though not always explicit, focused on improving the quality of life of both groups at the opposite ends of the life continuum. They specified opportunities for change in social, educational, economic, physical, and psychological conditions for both old and young participants, and they included overall measurable indicators of change in these conditions.

The rationale for cooperation

Integral to the Haus Bommerholz discussions was an awareness of the need for cooperation to achieve the goals of the working conference and to ensure the future of international intergenerational exchange. Indeed, a final and significant discussion revolved around the future of intergenerational programs on a global level. As consensus was reached on many questions, and group cohesiveness was achieved, the 25 participating representatives, from 12 countries, agreed it was essential to conclude the working meeting with a plan to develop a formal future for intergenerational programs that would have a global focus. These representatives articulated a common interest and a shared perception of need to move forward in intergenerational work. In a spirit of determination and cooperation, the group concluded this working meeting with an examination of three insightful questions:

- • Was it time to initiate a global intergenerational effort?
- • Were we ready to explore international partnerships?
- • Where and how might partnerships proceed?

The responses to these questions were positive and poignant. Several of the participants stated, "We came to Bommerholz because we were committed to a concept; we leave with a determination to make it work." Others stated their belief that intergenerational programs would be the key to "reuniting" their communities.

Specifically, the Bommerholz group accomplished the following:

- Identified shared needs and agreed upon common goals.
- Acknowledged similarities among their social issues.
- Recognized generic social issues common to many nations.
- Defined the underlying principles of intergenerational programs that offered possible solutions to a variety of social problems.
- Underscored the importance of encouraging and supporting intergenerational programs throughout the world, in isolated underdeveloped environments as well as in more connected and developed environments.

There was agreement, at Bommerholz, that the concept of an international organization informally reflected in the procedures of this working meeting, should be formalized. It was time to plan for an international intergenerational conference that would build on the work of Bommerholz and formally launch an international intergenerational organization.

The Vaals Conference

The First International Conference on Intergenerational Programs to Promote Social Change was convened in Vaals, The Netherlands, October 13-14, 1999. The conference was organized by Jumbo Klercq, Senior Trainer/ Consultant from Odyssee (Institute for Training, Education, Coaching and Consultancy), The Netherlands, in cooperation with UNESCO Institute for Education, Generations Together, the University of Pittsburgh (U.S.A.), the Beth Johnson Foundation (U.K.), the University of Dortmund, Germany, and the Dutch Institute for Care and Welfare (NIZW).

The objectives of the conference were:

- To share knowledge and information on intergenerational programs from all parts of the world.
- To identify projects as a forum for intergenerational education.
- To explore intergenerational project development, evaluation, research, and public policy as instruments to stimulate social inclusion and enhance social change.

More than 60 people attended the conference, representing UNESCO and 12 countries: Belgium, Canada, Cuba, France, Germany, Israel, Japan, the Netherlands, South Africa, Spain, the United Kingdom, and the United States. The attendees shared their countries' interest in and recognition of the need for intergenerational programs.

The conference consisted of interactive workshops and panel discussions on intergenerational issues related to social policy, community development, employment, childcare, education, multi-cultural issues, research and networking. Two days of deliberation reflected respect, openness and acceptance, and a consistent willingness to learn and share. In both Bommerholz and Vaals, the participants recognized the value in building international partnerships that work toward intergenerational solutions to global issues.

In the process of working together, the participants engaged in a variety of procedures that strengthened their mutual understanding, trust, and respect. The workshops and discussions were informative, enthusiastic and probing, with participants expressing a commitment to the value of the intergenerational approach to promote social change from a multinational perspective.

On the last day of the conference, organizers and participants launched an international organization that would become a catalyst for ongoing multi-national communication and collaboration.

The International Consortium

The "International Consortium for Intergenerational Programs" (ICIP) was launched in Vaals on October 14, 1999. Its objectives are:

> *To promote and develop the study and practice of intergenerational programs and to coordinate systematic development of intergenerational program theory and practice.*

The consortium is based in the Netherlands and will select as its governing body a management team of not more than 12 persons from different nations, with 4 elected officers (2 co-chairs, treasurer and secretary). The management committee will be responsible for deciding the overall direction of the consortium, its program initiatives, membership structure, benefits, and fiscal solvency. A rotation procedure for management committee members and elected officers will provide opportunities for new leadership and representation from different member countries.

The consortium membership will consist of individuals and organizations from nations across the world. Each member will pay a membership fee to support consortium activities, including: a bi-annual conference, to be held in the country of one of the members, and the publication of an annual newsletter. Additionally, members will have a special subscription rate to the *Intergenerational Programming Quarterly: An International*

Journal of Program Development, Research, and Public Policy to be published by Haworth Press beginning in 2002.

The consortium will hire a part-time secretary to be based in Maastricht, the Netherlands. This person will report to the consortium officers and will be responsible for communicating to consortium members about events, meetings, intergenerational highlights, and issues of concern. Funding for this position will be available through membership fees and support from UNESCO Institute for Education (UIE).

Outcomes

As a result of the consortium, an exciting new awareness of a potential global approach to social change has been promulgated and those working in the intergenerational field have begun to understand the universal potential for intergenerational programs to promote social change and the potential for adapting these programs to diverse cultures with diverse social, political and economic structures.

We have found a common ground and created new partnerships that will enable different nations throughout the world to find a way to promote social change. We have found a mechanism that supports diversity, promotes the concept of inclusion, and enables countries to move forward at their own rate with different degrees of structure in the implementation of appropriate nationally driven intergenerational programs. We have found a mechanism that provides opportunities for individual national programmatic choice while also offering support and communication from other nations.

We have learned that some issues transcend national borders, and that these can be resolved through cross-national partnerships that acknowledge their universality. The International Consortium for Intergenerational Programs reflects diverse cultural partnerships and is prepared to function as a forum to:

- promote information exchange,
- enhance the replication of best practices,
- generate research that adds to a deeper understanding of the importance of intergenerational solutions to social problems, and
- generate an international network that supports the growth of intergenerational exchange.

The "International Consortium for Intergenerational Programs" will be a catalyst to promote global social change through intergenerational programs.

Acknowledgements

The author prepared the U.S.A. Report and acknowledges Christina Mercken, who prepared the Bommerholz Working Meeting monograph that

272 *Linking Lifetimes: A Global View of Intergenerational Exchange*

was referenced in this chapter. She also acknowledges those who prepared the following Country Reports:

Raul Hernandez Castellon — Professor
Centro De Estudios Demographicos
Universidad De La Habana

Cathy Gush — Associate Researcher
Center for Adult and Continuing Education
University of the Western Cape

Alan Hatton-Yeo — Chief Executive
The Beth Johnson Foundation
United Kingdom

Jumbo Klerq — Senior Project Advisor
Odysee Institute for Training, Education, Coaching and Consultancy
Netherlands

Sun Maintao — Professor and Dean
College of Education Services
Central China Normal University]

Yukiko Sawano — Senior Reseracher
National Institute for Educational Research of Japan (NIER)

Ludger Veelken, Ph.D. — Professor of Sociology
University of Dortmund

Notes

The initial officers of the International Consortium for Intergenerational Programs are: co-chair, Dr. Ludger Veelken, Professor of Social Gerontology, University of Dortmund, Germany; Dr. Sally Newman, Executive Director of Generations Together, University of Pittsburgh, U.S.A.; Secretary Jumbo Klercq, Trainer/Consultant Odyssee, The Netherlands; and Treasurer Alan Hatton-Yeo, Executive Director, The Beth Johnson Foundation, U.K.

Index

AARP: 76
Across Ages (U.S.): 73
Adopt-A-Granny (Korea): 7
Advocacy: 79-80, 109-110, 111, 254
Age Concern England (U.K.): 203
Ageism: 22, 75, 122, 127-128, 196
AIDS: 237-238, 240, 247
Amsterdam Chore Team (Netherlands): 180-181
Apprenticeship: 36, 142-143, 235-236
Australia:
       Intergenerational communication dynamics: 19, 20
Ayer Rajah Center (Singapore):124-125, 129
Beth Johnson Foundation-Community Action Project (U.K.): 198-202
Bridges (U.S.): 73
Caminando Juntos (Walking Together) (Chile): 224-225
Canada:
Canadian aboriginal peoples: 85-86, 88
Early childhood education: 83-87, 97-98
      First Nations Partnership Programs: 8, 84-100
          Elders, role of: 87, 90, 96
          Generative Curriculum Model: 87-91
Center for Intergenerational Learning (U.S.): 79, 113
Chile
      Intergenerational Programs:
          Cuenta-Cuentos (Story Telling): 224-225
          Caminando Juntos (Walking Together): 224-225
      Older Adults Programs: 224

China:
      Confucian virtue of *xiao* (filial piety): 2-4, 11n1, 15-16
      Hong Kong: 3, 11n2, 16-17
      Social and demographic change: 2-3, 263
      Intergenerational communication patterns: 17, 20-21
      International dialogue: 216
Civic engagement: 76-77, 200-201, 204-205
Columbia:
      Volunteer work: 36
Costa Rica:
      Older Persons for Promotion of Peace and the Environment: 225-226
Cuba:
      Opportunities for intergenerational exchange: 234-236
      Services for older adults: 234
Cuenta-Cuentos (Story Telling) (Chile): 224-225
Culture:
      Cultural healing: 95-96, 244-245
      Cultural renaissance: 8, 92, 106, 249
      Culturally appropriate education: 85-86, 97-99, 135-136
      Cross-cultural understanding: 8-9, 84, 183-184, 189, 215-218, 250-251, 259-260
      Elders, role of: 5-6, 14-16, 20-21, 88-90, 140, 142-143, 148
      Proverbs (see "Language")
      Study of: 1, 40-41, 57-58
Demographic change:
      "AgeQuake": 29
      Global trends: ix-x, 29-30
      Japan: 152, 154, 261n1
      Latin America: 221-222
      Marshall Islands: 137-138
      Netherlands: 174-176
      Positive perspectives of aging trend: 31
      Singapore: 120-122
      South Africa: 237-238
      U.S.: 66-67, 76, 102-103
      Uruguay: 228
Dominican Republic
      Well-being of older adults: xi, 6
Dorot (U.S.): 73
Dutch Guilds (Netherlands): 181-182
Early childhood education: 83-87, 97-98, 179-180, 248
Elderhostel: 74
Elders Share the Arts (U.S.): 74
Experience Corps (U.S.): 71

Family:

> Awareness of ancestors: 53, 116n6
> Diverse conceptions of family: 2-5, 129-130, 160-161, 167
> Family ties and responsibilities: 52-53, 130, 140
> Legal mandates for family caregiving:
>> China: 3
>> Estonia: 31
>> Singapore: 3
> Mothers-In-Law: 54
> Primacy of: 2, 4, 57, 129, 140-141, 244-245
> Transformation: 222-223

FELLOWS (Fellowship and Lifelong Learning Opportunities at Waialae School) (U.S.): 107

Filial piety (*xiao*): 2-4, 11n1, 15-16, 103, 166

Foster Grandparents (U.S.): 70

Funding issues: 76, 107, 115

Generational memory: 7

Generations in Action (U.K.): 203

Generations of Hope (U.S.): 72

Generations Together: 79, 269

Generations United (U.S.): 70-72, 80, 253-257

Generative Curriculum Model: 87-91

Germany:

> Haus Bommerholz Working Meeting (on intergenerational programs): 265-269
> Healing History program in Hamburg: 7-9, 209-219
> Remnants of the Holocaust: 209-210

Grandfamilies (U.S.): 72

Grandma Please (U.S.): 73

Grandparents by Choice (Uruguay): 228-229

Grandparents for Health (Guatemala): 226-228

Guatemala:

> Grandparents for Health: 226-228

The Guide Program (Netherlands): 183

Hawaii:

> Economic factors: 113-114
> Hawaii Intergenerational Network (see "Networking and Coalition Building")
> Intergenerational festivals: 108-109
> Intergenerational programs (see under "United States")
> Native Hawaiian culture:
>> "Aloha", concept of: 114
>> Cultural renaissance: 8, 106
>> *Hokulea*: 106

Hula: 105
Language: 105-108, 116-117n7
Rainbow Connection: 108
Social, historical, and demographic forces: 101-103, 113
Healing history framework: 209-219
Help Age Korea (Korea): 6-7
Hokkaido Intergenerational Recreational Camp (Japan): 165, 167, 171n9
Indigenous peoples:
Canadian aboriginal peoples: 85-86, 88
Culturally grounded education: 85, 97-99
Maori (New Zealand): 116-117n7
Relationship between culture and self-identity: 7-8, 95-96, 104
Cultural survival: 7-8; 135-149
Intergenerational Communication:
Cultural distinctiveness: x-xi, 1-6, 9, 13-28, 56-57
Communication, as academic discipline: 13
Communication "climate": 15
Communication dynamics in Australia: 19-20
Difficulties: 31, 51, 67, 127, 184-186, 242-245
Elders' attitudes toward intergenerational communication: 18
Impact on older adults' sense of health, well-being: 16, 19-20, 225
Intragenerational communication, comparison with: 18-20
Social connectedness: 69-70, 76-77, 229-230
Social context: 22
Status of communicators: 6, 54-55, 128, 201-202, 243-244
Study of, 13, 16-22
Intergenerational Programming Quarterly: 270-271
Intergenerational Programs
Awards and recognition: 112
Childcare: 72-73, 179-180, 241, 248
Citizenship/Civic engagement: 200-201, 204-205
Communication dynamics: 22-23, 37, 211-214
Community building/community service: 36-37, 74, 110-111, 128, 178, 186-192, 198-200, 250
Conflict resolution/peace: 217, 225-226
Cross-cultural understanding: xiv, 8-9, 183, 217-218, 250-251, 259-260
Cultural regeneration, significance for: xii, 7-8, 90-93, 95-96, 235-236, 249-250
Definition: xi, 33, 265-266
Diversity management: 188-189
Eldercare: 75, 155
Empowerment: 188, 197-198, 206-207
Environmental improvement: 223
Facilitation strategies: 92-94, 189-190, 200, 211, 214, 230

Factors contributing to program success: 76-77, 91-94, 230
Family, considerations of: 2, 4, 72, 96-97
Festival traditions: 108-109, 126
Health, promotion of: 74, 223, 226-228, 247
International dimension: xii, 263-264
Literacy issues: 71, 122, 132n8
Mentoring: 107-108, 182-183
National sentiment, role of: 6-7, 9, 131, 167, 191, 209-210, 215-216, 218-219n1
National strategies: 80, 191, 253-262
Obstacles: 75-76, 115, 129, 147, 197, 258
Program replication, considerations of: xiv, 9-10
Publications: xv-xvin1
Regional initiatives:
       1:4 project (Western Europe): 31
Research:
       Considerations: 77, 246
       Need for additional research: 115, 230-231, 250
Social change:
       Social inclusiveness: 190, 193-198, 206-207, 229-230
       Transforming social institutions: 78, 250
Staff training: 230
Utilizing information from studies of intergenerational communication: 20, 23, 251
Youth development: 73-74, 197-198, 223
Intergenerational relationships:
       Conflict: 185, 253-254
       Equity: 35-36
       Interdependence: xii, 51-52, 57, 79, 131, 244-245
       Intergenerational solidarity: 184-186, 201, 230
       Multigenerational relationships: 33
       Reciprocity: 35-37, 141
       Relationship building: 201-202, 225, 229
       Social compact: xi, 67
       Study of, 41-42, 246
International Consortium of Intergenerational Programs: xi, 265, 270-271
International Intergenerational Potluck Party (Japan): 259
International Year of Older Persons: 30, 35-36, 113, 126, 246
Intragenerational communication: 19-20
Japan:
       Collective grandparenting: 161
       Demographic and social factors: 151-156, 166, 261n1, 261n2, 263
       Eldercare: 154-155, 170n4
       Event grandparenthood: 161-162

Filial piety: 4, 155, 170n5
Ikigai [purpose in life]: 159-160
Integrated Seminar on Intergenerational Exchange: 259
International dialogue: 216
Intergenerational Programs:
Hokkaido Intergenerational Recreational Camp: 165, 167, 171n9
International Intergenerational Potluck Party: 259
Kotoen: 161-162, 167
Rent-A-Family: 4, 159, 163-165, 167
Overview: 157-160
Japan Intergenerational Network, prospects for: 257-260
Views about aging and the aged: 5, 16, 153-154, 258
Kin Net (U.S.): 72
Korea:
Adopt-A-Granny: 7
Help Age Korea: 6-7
International dialogue: 216
World War II: 216
Attitudes toward the elderly: 17-18
Kotoen (Japan): 161-162, 167
Kupuna program (U.S.): 107
Language
Hawaiian: (See "Indigenous peoples")
Proverbs and phrases about aging and intergenerational relations: 39-64
African: 53
Arabic: 45
Chinese: 44-45, 47-52, 54
Chuuk: 53
French: 45
German: 45
Hawaiian: 44, 49, 52-53, 105
Hebrew: 44
Hungarian: 49
Icelandic: 55
Indian: 50, 52, 54
Indonesian: 47, 51
Irish: 48
Italian: 44-45
Japanese: 44, 50-51, 53-55
Korean: 45-46, 49, 53
Lebanese: 48, 54
Phillipino: 53

            Portuguese: 47-48, 50
            Romanian: 44
            Spanish: 44-45, 47, 48-50, 53-54
            Swedish: 44-45, 47, 54
            Tongan: 47, 52, 54
      Research considerations: 39-43, 57-58
Let's Talk Together (Netherlands): 183
Lithuania: 30-31
Magic Me: 203
Marshall Islands:
      Cultural preservation: 141, 143, 145, 147-149
      Demographic and social factors: 137-141
      Education:
            Apprenticeship: 36, 142-143
            Informal: 136, 142
            Peer education: 146
            Western influence: 141
      Intergenerational Programs:
            Conceptual framework: 135-137
            School-based initiatives: 146-147
            Waan Aelon in Majol [Canoes of the Marshall Islands]:
            144-145
      Volunteerism: 33, 141
Mentoring: 74, 107-108, 182-183, 203, 264
Mentor Link (U.S.): 74
Mexico:
      Concept of *confianza* (mutual aid): 35
Na Pua No'eau (Center for Gifted and Talented Native Hawaiian Children)
      (U.S.): 8
Neighborhood Memories (Netherlands): 184
Neighborhoods-2000 (U.S.): 74
Netherlands: 173-192
      Caregiving: 176
      Demographic and social factors: 174-176, 180, 192n2, 264
      First International Conference on Intergenerational Programs (in
      Vaals): 265, 269-270
      Intergenerational programs:
            Amsterdam Chore Team: 180-181
            Community building: 178-180, 186-188
            Dutch Guilds: 181-182
            The Guide Program: 183
            Let's Talk Together: 183
            Neighborhood Memories: 184
            Significance of: 173-174

National strategy: 261n6
Mentoring: 182
Netherlands Institute of Care and Welfare (NIZW): 191, 192n1
Toddler programs: 179-180
Social policy/social services: 176-178, 181-183
Networking and Coalition Building:
Advocacy focus: 109, 254
Generations United (U.S.): 70-72, 80, 253-257
Hawaii Intergenerational Network: 107-108, 111-112
International: xiv, 265-271
Japan: 257-260
Need for: 75
Netherlands, 191
Organizational issues: 79, 251, 255-257, 260
Singapore: 124-125
New Zealand: 3-5
Older Persons for the Promotion of Peace and the Environment (Costa Rica): 225-226
Project Dana (U.S.): 110-111
Project SHARE (Sharing Helps All Resources Expand) (U.S.): 73
Project SHINE (Students Helping in Naturalization of Elders) (U.S.): 8, 113
Rainbow Connection (Hawaii): 108
READ (Read, Educate and Develop) (South Africa): 247
Rent-A-Family (Japan): 4, 159, 163-165, 167
SASSIE (Seniors and Students Sharing Intergenerational Experiences) (U.S.): 107
SAVE (Senior Adults Volunteering in Education) (U.S.): 107
Shared sites (Age-integrated sites): 4, 73, 123-124, 158, 248-249, 261n4
Singapore:
Community building: 129
Demographic and social factors: 119-123
Elderly, lifecourse: 128
Festival traditions: 126
Intergenerational communication: 122-123
Intergenerational programs:
Ayer Rajah Center:124-125, 129
Multigenerational camps: 130
Tampines 3-in-1 Family Center: 124-130, 132n12
RSVP (Retired Senior Volunteer Programs): 123, 128
Language: 122, 132n8
People's Action Party: 119, 132n5
Shared sites: 4-5
Singapore 21: 120
Views about older adults: 122

Slovenia:
       National Network of Intergenerational Groups for Older People: 31
Social capital: 69-70, 230
South Africa: 34
       Age-integrated centers (see "Shared Sites")
       Aging and retirement: 242-243
       Childcare issues: 241
       Demographic and social factors:237-240, 243-244, 263-264
       Educare: 248
       Education: 241-242
       Grandparents raising grandchildren: 240-241, 246-247
       Intergenerational programs:
              READ (Read, Educate and Develop): 247
              Societal significance: 250-251
       Senior adults as childcare workers: 248
       Ubuntu: intergenerational concept: 244-245
       Youth volunteerism: 249-250
  Stereotypes
       Ageism (see "Views about Aging and the Aged")
       Collectivism versus individualism: 14
       Combating stereotypes: 8, 32, 55, 77-78, 202, 205-206, 230
Tampines 3-in-1 Family Center (Singapore): 124-130, 132n12
Time Out (U.S.): 73
United Kingdom:
       Elders as mentors: 264
       Intergenerational Programs:
              Age Concern England: 203
              Beth Johnson Foundation-Community Action Project:
              198-202
              Generations in Action: 203
              Magic Me (London): 203
              Social change implications: 199
       Social exclusion/social inclusion: 193-198, 206-207
       Social policy/social services: 193-196
United Nations: x, 29-31,
       Principles for Older Persons (1991): 35-36
       International Year of Older Persons (1999): 30, 35-36, 113, 126, 246
       UNESCO Institute for Education: 209, 218-219n1, 264, 271
United States: 65-82
       Children and youth: 67-68, 72-74
       Community issues and intervention: 69-70, 74
       Corporation for National Service: 76
       Eldercare: 73
       Elderhostel: 72

Family-related issues and interventions: 69, 72
Generations United (see "Networking and Coalition Building")
Intergenerational agenda/advocacy: 65, 77-80, 109-110, 253-255
Intergenerational programs:
    Across Ages: 73
    Bridges: 73
    Dorot: 73
    Elders Share the Arts: 74
    Experience Corps: 71
    FELLOWS (Fellowship and Lifelong Learning Opportunities at Waialae School): 107
    Foster Grandparents: 70
    Generations of Hope: 72
    Grandfamilies: 72
    Grandma Please: 73
    History of: 70
    Kin Net: 72
    Kupuna Program: 107
    Mentor Link: 74
    Na Pua No'eau (Center for Gifted and Talented Native Hawaiian Children): 8
    Neighborhoods-2000: 74
    Project Dana: 110-111
    Project SHARE (Sharing Helps All Resources Expand): 73
    Project SHINE (Students Helping in the Naturalization of Elders): 8, 113
    SASSIE (Seniors and Students Sharing Intergenerational Experiences): 107
    SAVE (Senior Adults Volunteering in Education): 107
    Time Out: 73
International dialogue: 215-216
Older Adults: 68, 71
Older Americans Act: 79
Public policy: 79-80
Social disconnectedness: 69-70
Social connectedness: 77
Uruguay:
    Demographic and social factors: 228
    Grandparents by Choice: 228-229
Views about aging and the aged:
    Cross-cultural comparison: 5, 453-48
    Eastern versus Western notions of aging and intergenerational exchange: 5, 13-29, 155
    Gender, role of: 56

Negative views:
        Ageism: 22, 75, 122, 127-128, 196
        Elders as burden to society: 152-154
Positive views about aging:
        Elders as champions: 204
        Productive aging: x, 258
        Respect for elders: 52, 85, 90, 105, 246
        Social capital: 230
        Successful aging: 77
        Other: 223
Views about young people: 49-52, 223
Volunteerism:
        Formal versus informal: 33-35, 141
        Role of culture: 6, 30-37
        Socio-economic factors: 31-32
        Typology of intergenerational volunteerism: 36-37
        Youth volunteerism: 36, 249-250
        Senior adult volunteerism: 36, 107, 123, 128
Waan Aelon in Majol [Canoes of the Marshall Islands] (Marshall Islands):
    144-145